Laugh About It:

Cartoons 2–The Weird Years

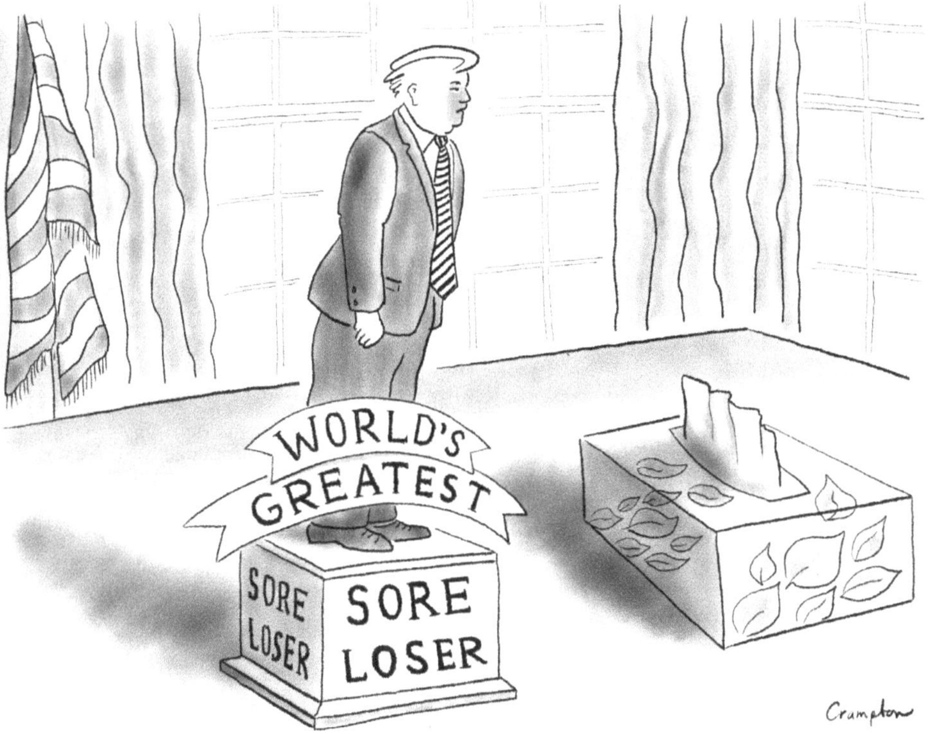

by Carolyn Crampton

Howell Park Press

Laugh About It:
Cartoons 2—The Weird Years
by Carolyn Crampton

Published by Howell Park Press
howellparkpress.wordpress.com

ISBN 978-0-9793088-6-4

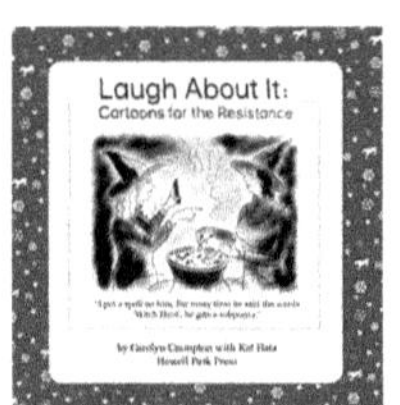

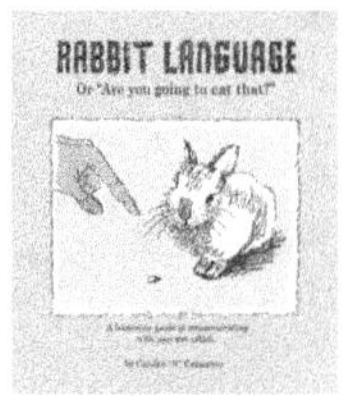

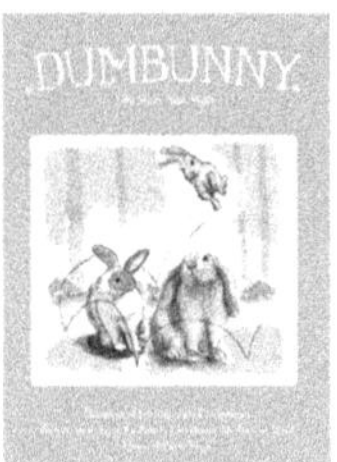

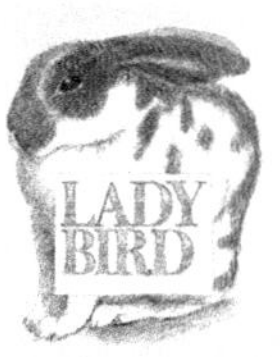

Follow

LinkTree *https://linktr.ee/CarolynCrampton*
X/Twitter: *@Laugh_About_It_*
Facebook: *facebook.com/laughaboutit/*
Instagram: *@laugh_about_it_cartoons*
Web: *laughaboutitcartoons.wordpress.com*

Acknowledgements

Thanks to all my friends and family who helped me more than you'll ever know. Thanks to my Twitter peeps for getting me through the pandemic. I tried to credit everyone. Thanks to "Always with Her". Shout out to fearless journalists who take risks to expose the truth.

Also by Carolyn Crampton

Laugh About It: Cartoons for the Resistance, by Carolyn Crampton with **Kat Hatz.** Don't miss how it all started with Trump descending the escalator in 2016, through his administration, and up to September of 2019. ISBN 978-0-9793088-5-7

Rabbit Language or 'Are you going to eat that?' by Carolyn Crampton. The original, humorous guide to pet rabbit behavior. ISBN 978-0-9793088-0-2

Dumbunny by **Mary Ann Wolf,** illustrations by Carolyn Crampton. An enchanting children's Easter bunny storybook for the child for feels different. ISBN 978-0-9793088-2-6

Ladybird: My Eight Lives, by Carolyn Crampton. A rabbit finally finds a forever home. May help teens develop empathy. ISBN 978-0-9793088-4-0

Introduction

These cartoons reflect my impressions of the daily new cycle absorbed through “X” (hereafter called Twitter), Facebook, TV news, and by reading online news. What I absorbed and portrayed is just my synthesis.

I’m a fine artist living in San Francisco. I paint and draw pictures of my pet rabbits. I’m not a comic. I can’t tell if other people will find my cartoons funny, but if an idea makes me chuckle, I go ahead with it.

I was so filled with horror when Trump descended that fateful escalator and spoke about “Mexican rapists”, that I began making and posting cartoons as an antidote. When there was a large quantity of drawings, I published the first book: “Laugh About It: Cartoons for the Resistance”.

This second collection picks up in September 2019, for the Impeachment, and the second Impeachment, and then continues through the Covid-19 pandemic, the subsequent election, and up to July 2024, when President Biden endorsed Vice President Kamala Harris for President. If there are fewer Biden-era cartoons, it’s because I felt less angst for our Nation’s future.

Each drawing has a date when I posted the cartoon (they can take a few days to draw) and a note about the inspiration. They were made to catch a moment. But if you look up the date and keywords, you will find the relevant, actual news stories.

I attempted to credit every person who suggested something I used. Twitter peeps asked me to include only their “handles”.

If it seems like I don’t know what’s going to happen…it is because I designed the book as I went along and wrote the comments concurrently. A few notes were added later. Enjoy!

—Carolyn Crampton

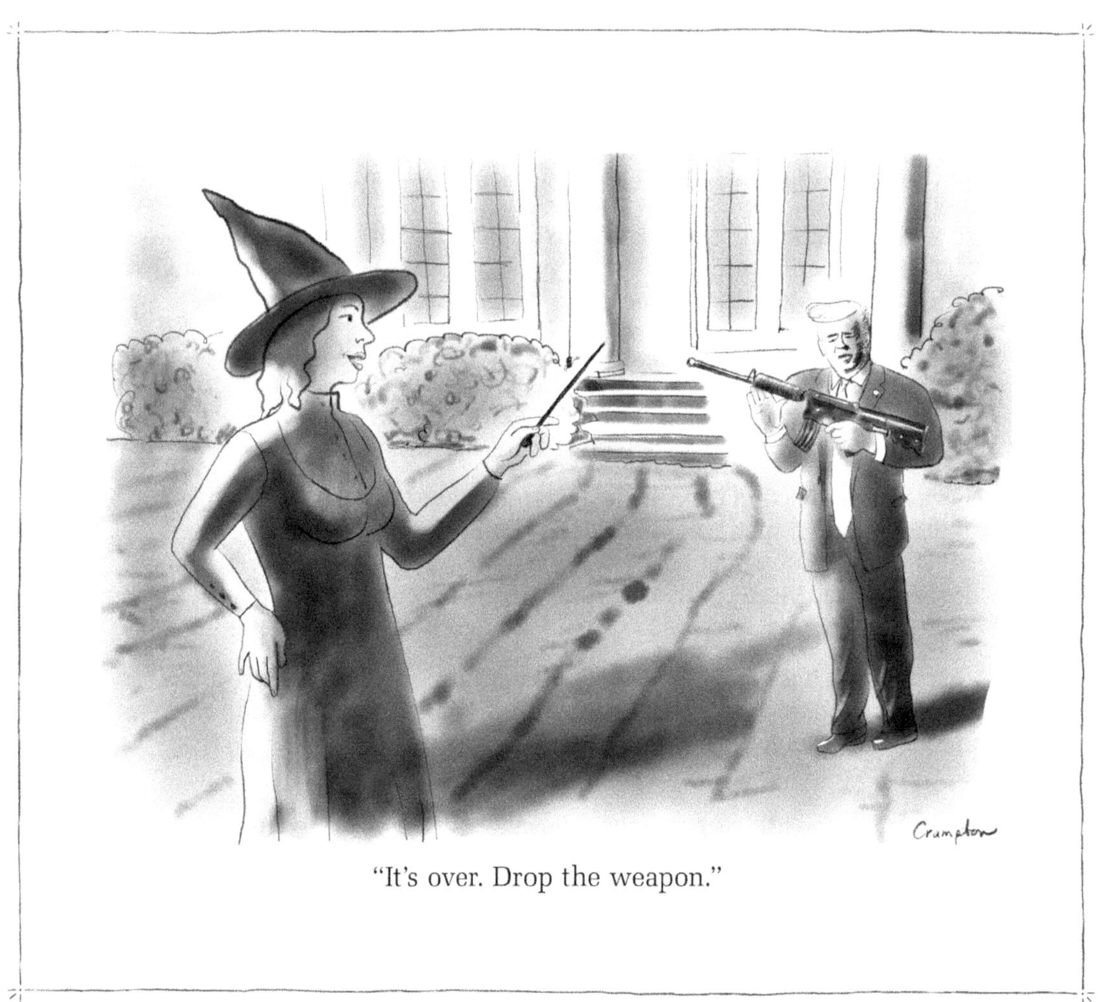

"It's over. Drop the weapon."

September 26, 2019
Whistleblower reports state that President Trump attempted to extort Ukraine for political gain, but he claims it's another "witch hunt".

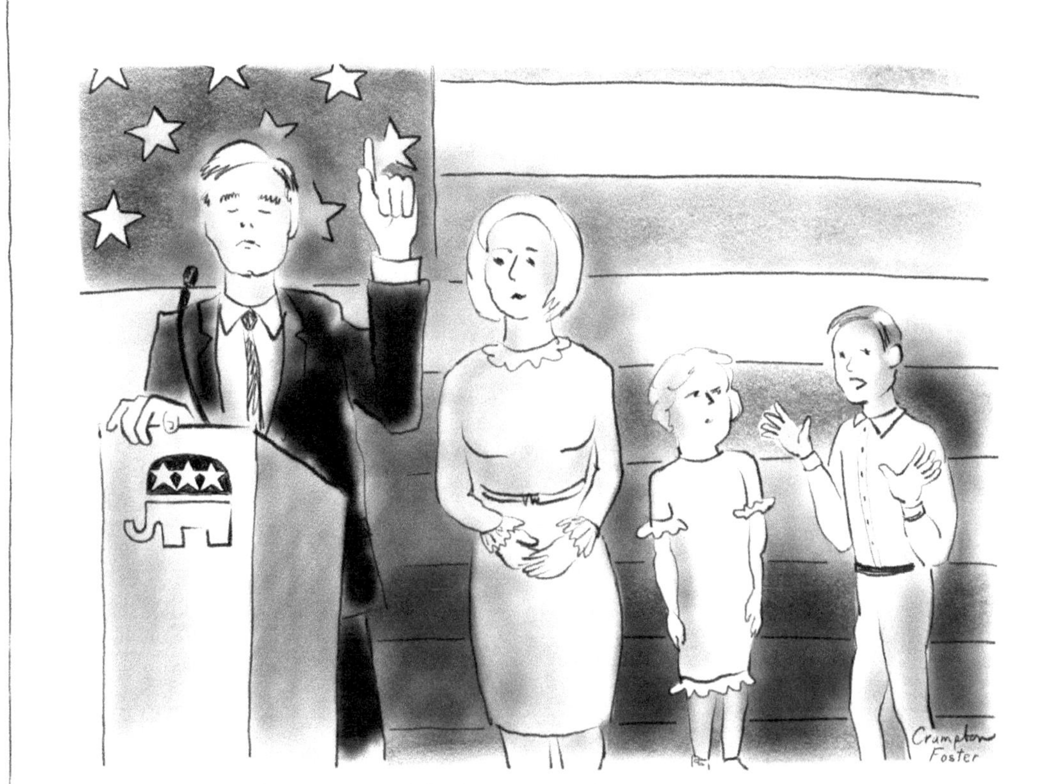

"If Dad says *global warming hoax* one more time,
we'll never get to meet Greta backstage!"

October 3, 2019
Greta Thunberg, star Climate activist, speaks at the United Nations. Many conservatives deny the science behind climate change. *Thanks to Michael Foster for this idea and for many more in the following pages.*

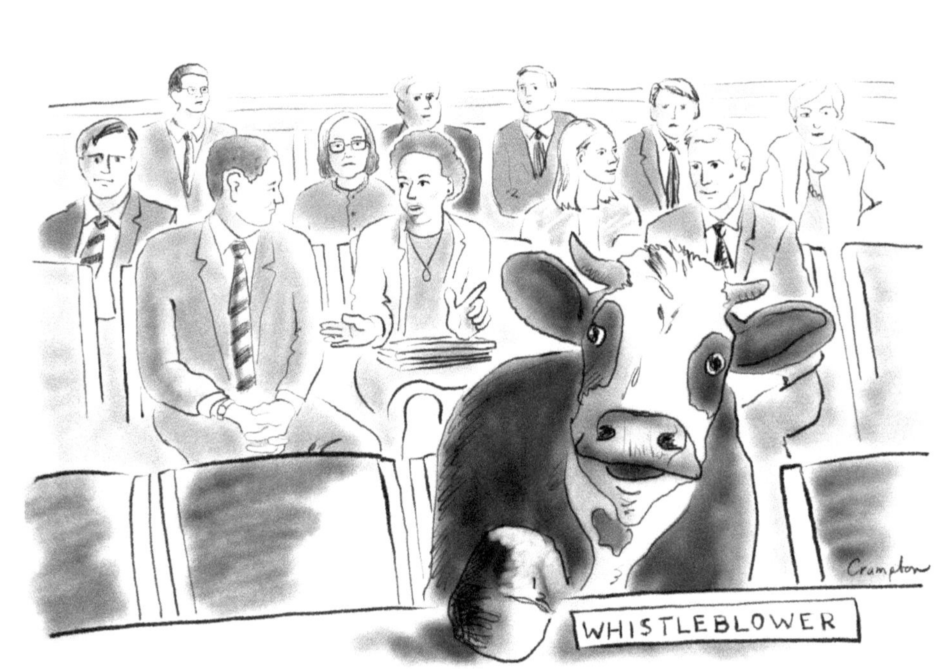

"Adam Schiff took extreme measures to disguise the identity of the whistleblower—and to give Devin Nunes a cow."

October 10, 2019
Representative Adam Schiff wants the Ukraine-call Whistleblower to testify for an Impeachment inquiry but remain anonymous in order to avoid retaliation. Former Congressional Intelligence Committee head, Devin Nunes, is suing "Devin Nunes' Cow", an udderly-silly Twitter profile.

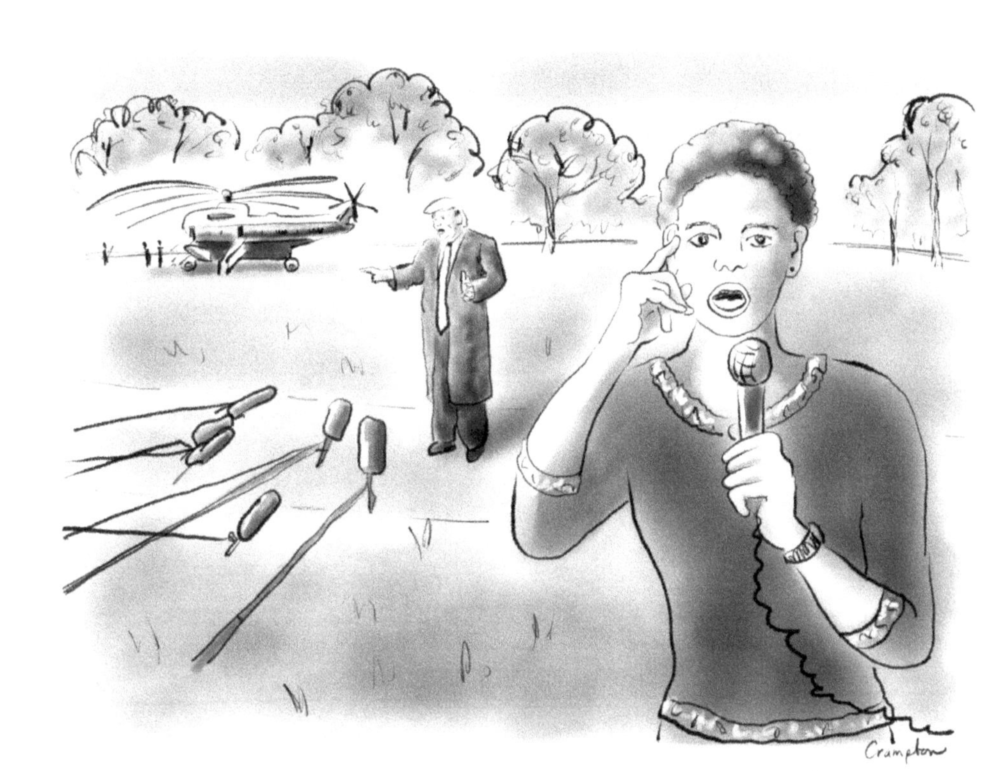

"If I heard correctly, he said we're now harvesting DNA from immigrants, and that he doesn't know anyone named Rudy."

October 22, 2019
America's mayor, Rudy Giuliani, seems to be in the middle of the Ukraine scandal. The White House announces that they added mandatory harvesting of DNA from immigrants as part of the Fingerprint Act (*28 CFR § 28.12.ed*).

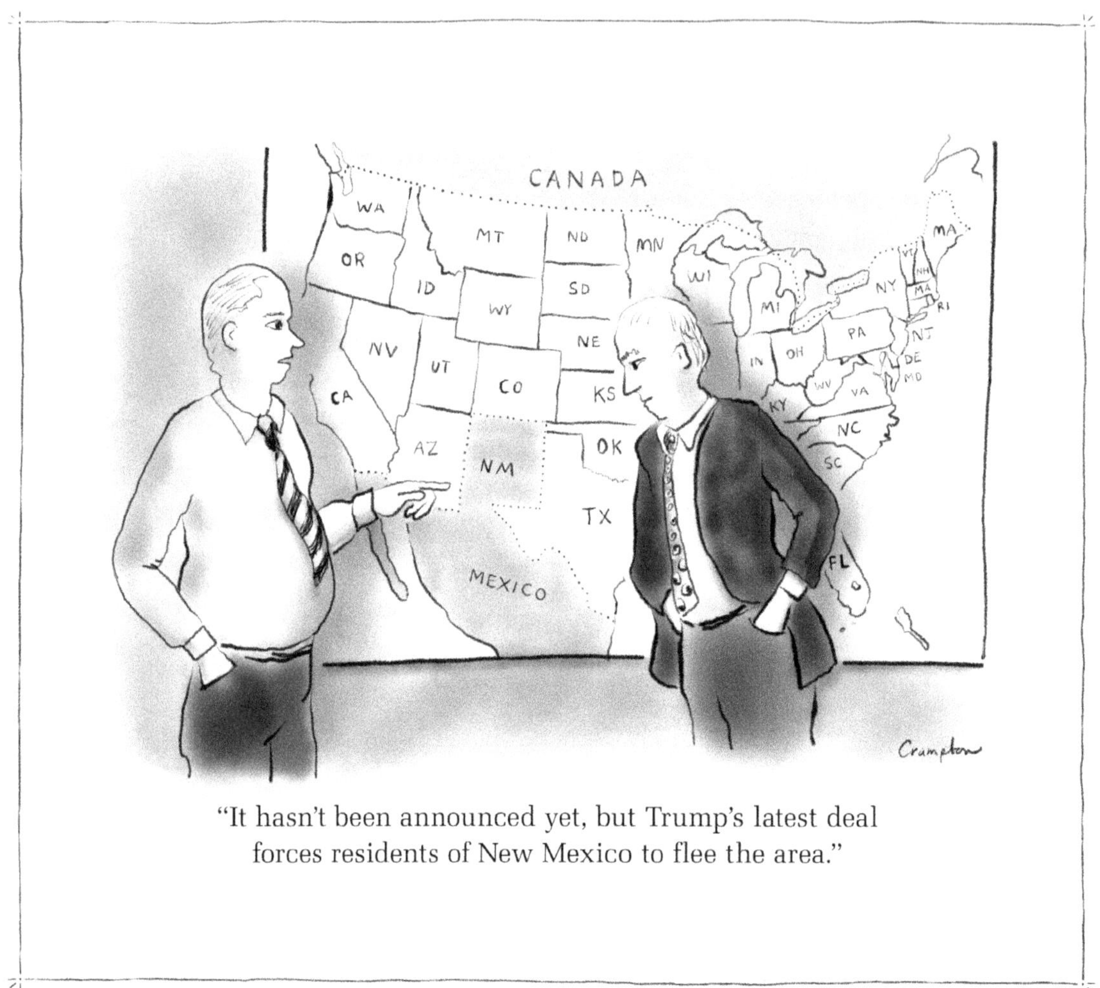

"It hasn't been announced yet, but Trump's latest deal forces residents of New Mexico to flee the area."

October 25, 2019
Trump made a statement about building a border wall around Colorado. Turkey and Russia invaded Syria. Trump said that our Kurdish-partners would have to leave their areas; maybe should move to protect the oil fields.

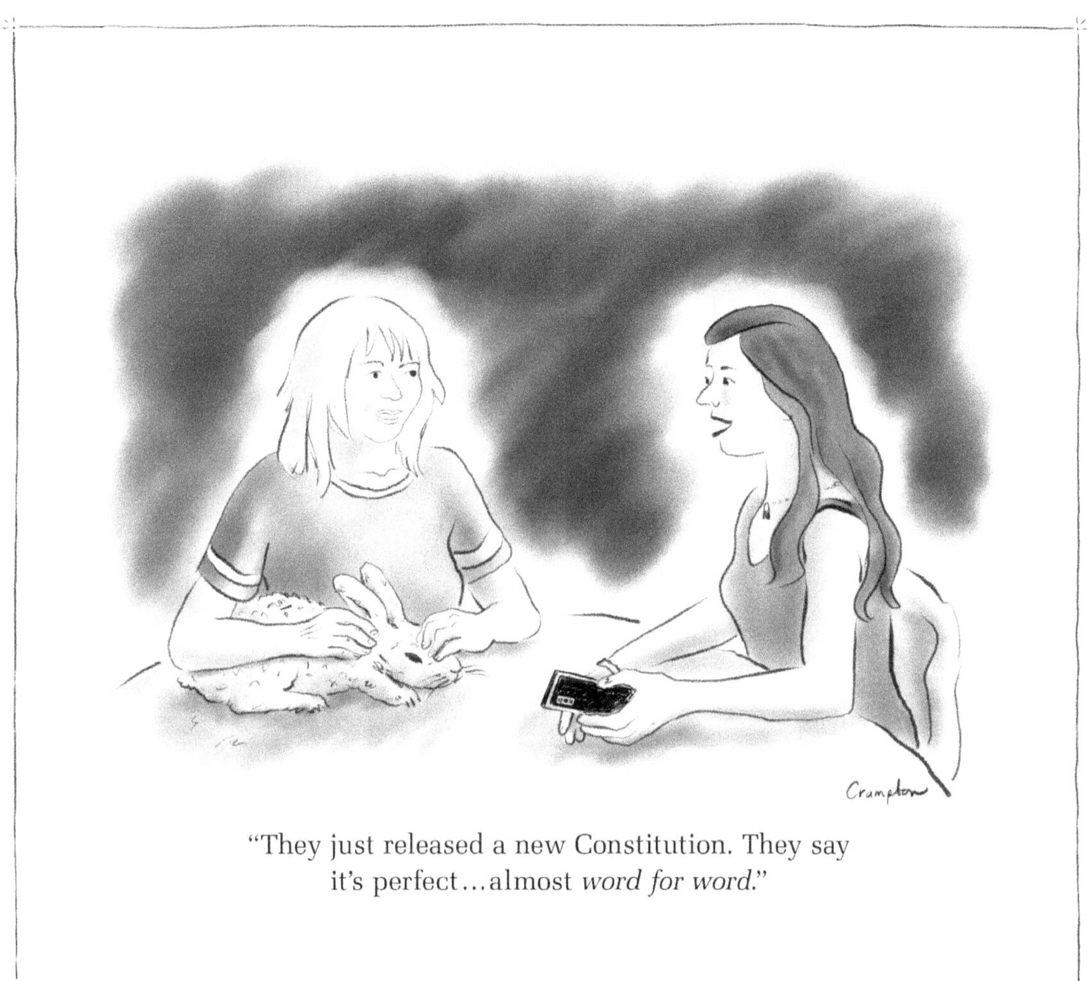

"They just released a new Constitution. They say it's perfect... almost *word for word.*"

November 5, 2019
The White House's word-for-word press summary of the phone call with Ukrainian President Zelensky, wherein Trump asks for dirt on Joe Biden (while illegally withholding $391 million of mandated military aid) does not match the official transcript prepared by witness Lt. Col. Alexander Vindman.

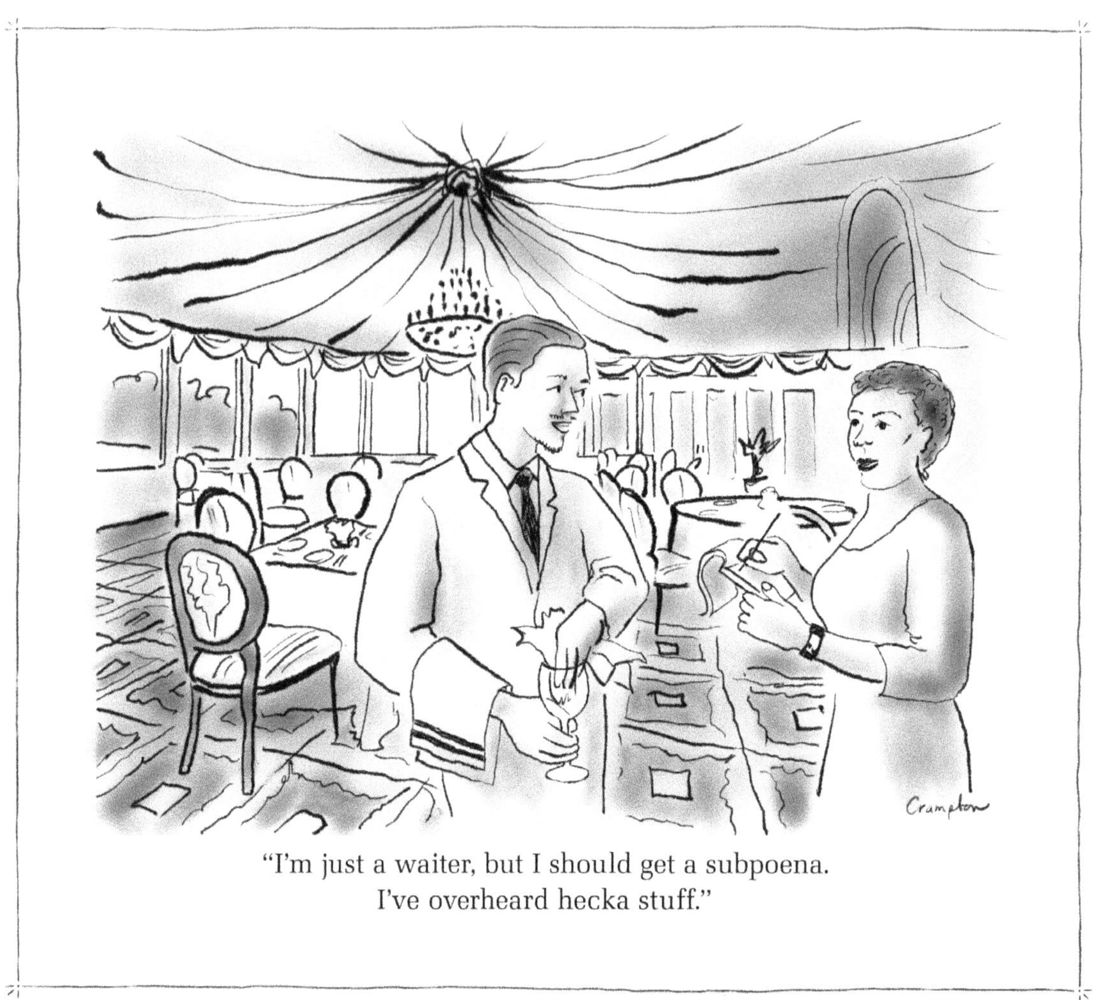

"I'm just a waiter, but I should get a subpoena.
I've overheard hecka stuff."

November 15, 2019
Trump's associates get subpoenas. Former Ambassador to Ukraine, William Taylor Jr., testifies that a staffer overheard Ambassador Gordan Sondland and Trump talking on a phone about "investigations" in an open air restaurant in Kyiv.

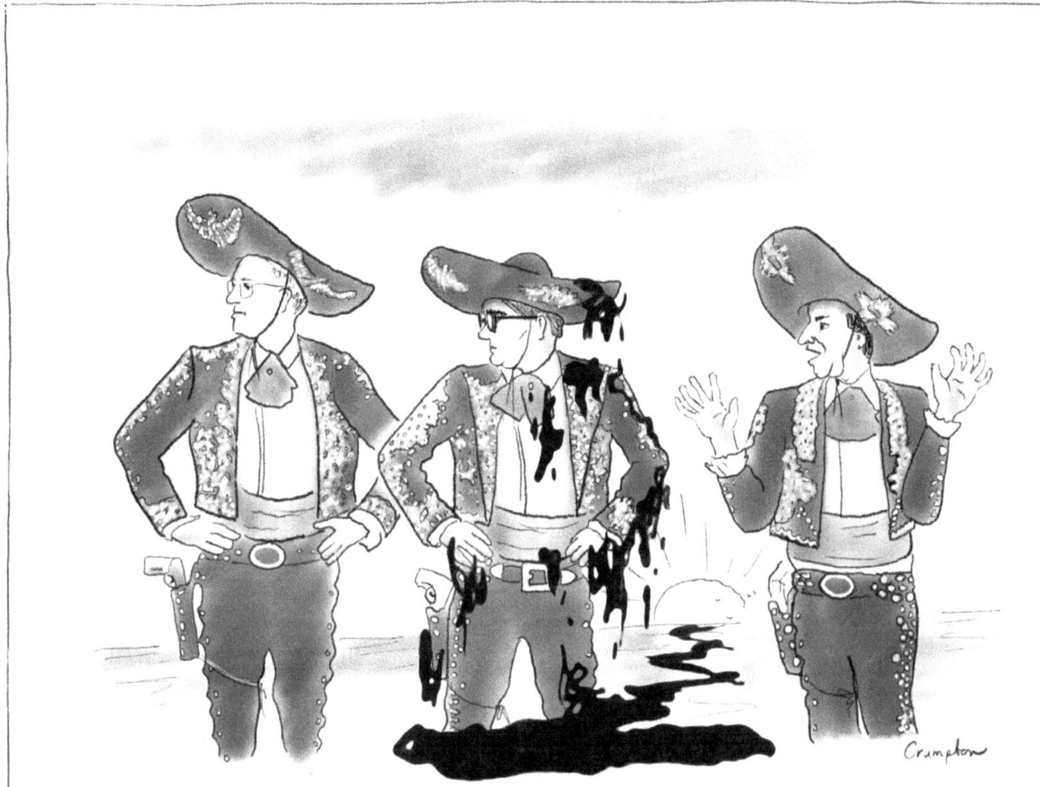

"Me, the fall guy? All I did was give a million bucks and go to some meetings. Why not Mister oil and gas smarty-pants?"

December 1, 2019
Former Ambassador Kurt Volker, Energy Secretary Rick Perry, and Ambassador Gordon Sondland, called themselves the "Three Amigos" in their Ukraine-deals. Rick Perry may have negotiated a corrupt deal for his donors in Ukraine. The so-called "infallible" Keystone pipeline just spilled oil again, fouling a wetland area in North Dakota.

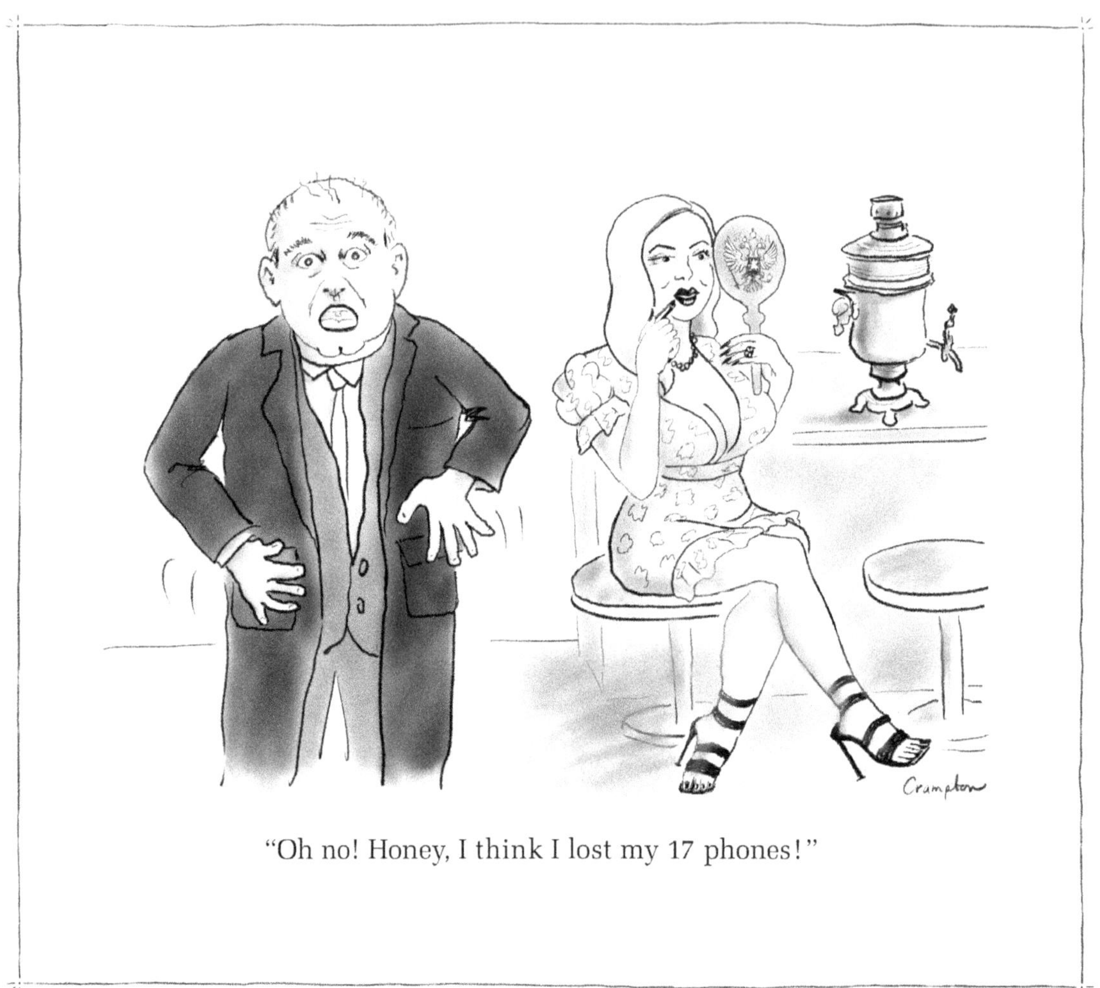

"Oh no! Honey, I think I lost my 17 phones!"

December 3, 2019
Associates of Trump's lawyer and allegedly part of the Ukrainian-pressure campaign, Lev Parnas and Igor Fruhman are arrested with one-way tickets on a flight to Vienna. Feds confiscated 17 phones from Parnas.

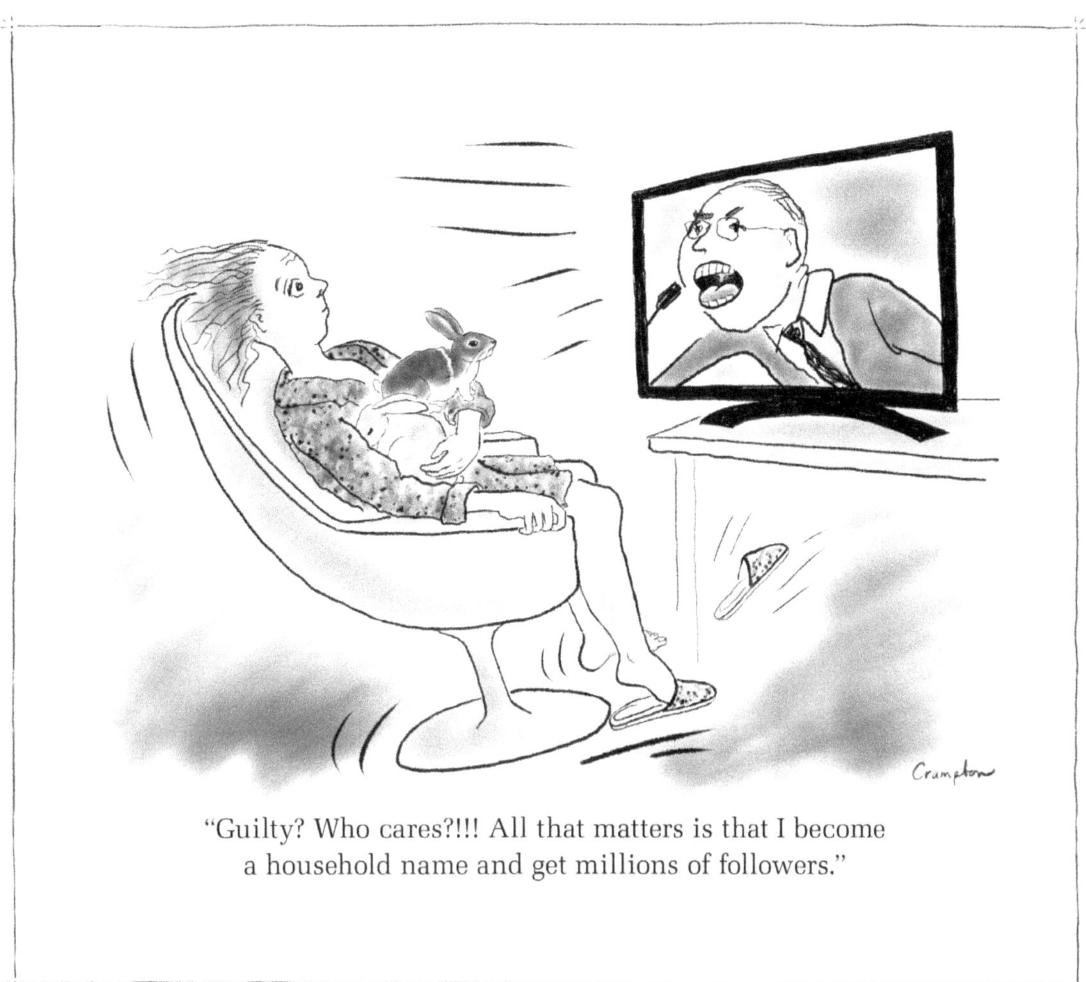

"Guilty? Who cares?!!! All that matters is that I become a household name and get millions of followers."

December 18, 2019
Republican members of the Judicial Committee yelled a lot during the House Impeachment Trial.
Doug Collins asks about the rush to convict: "Would you buy the first Christmas present you see?"
Ruth Geos suggested adding more selfies with rabbits to the drawings.

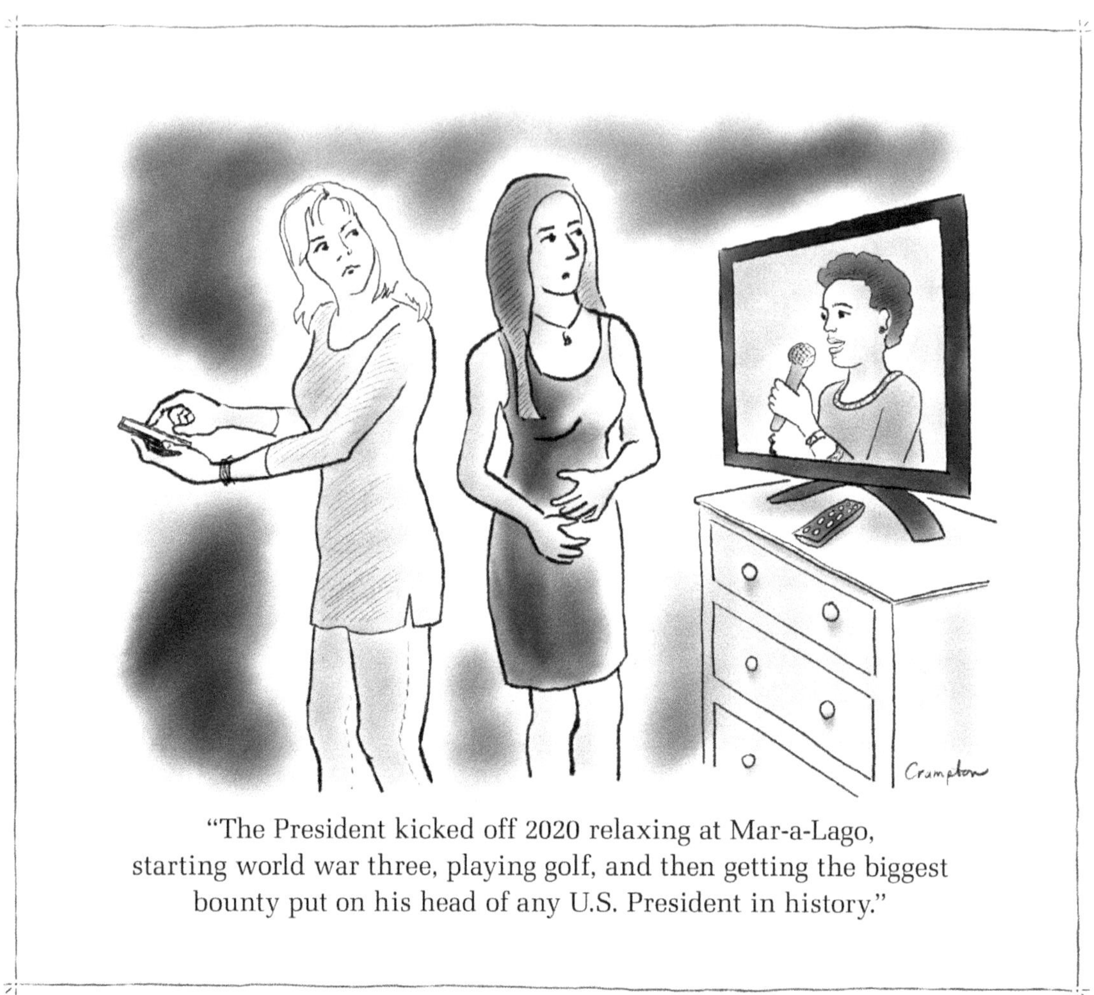

"The President kicked off 2020 relaxing at Mar-a-Lago, starting world war three, playing golf, and then getting the biggest bounty put on his head of any U.S. President in history."

January 5, 2020
Trump starts the new decade off with a bang: assassinating Qasem Soleimani, Iran's second-in command leader. Iran then announced a bounty on Trump's head.

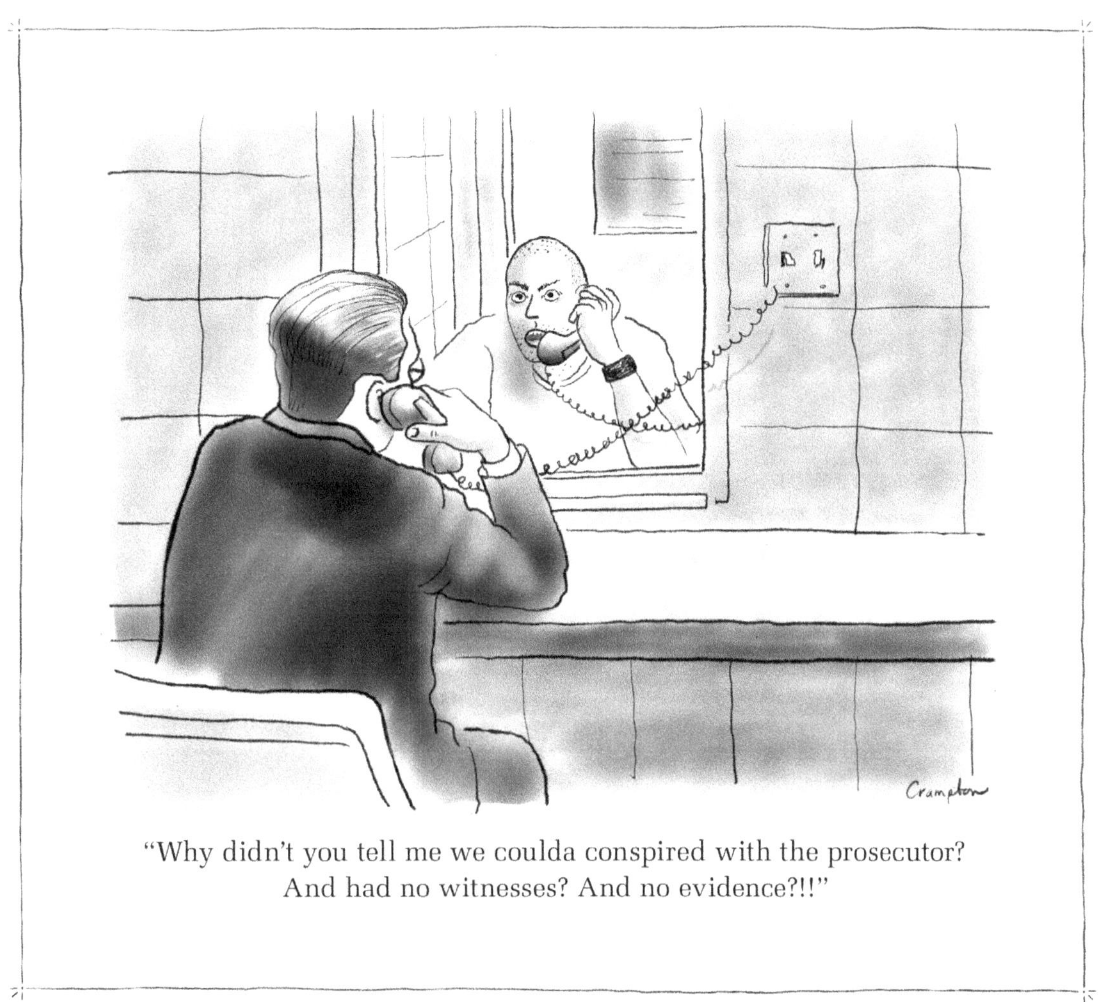

"Why didn't you tell me we coulda conspired with the prosecutor? And had no witnesses? And no evidence?!!"

January 17, 2020
Majority leader Mitch McConnell said he's working with the White House on the Impeachment Trial. He will allow no witnesses, nor evidence.

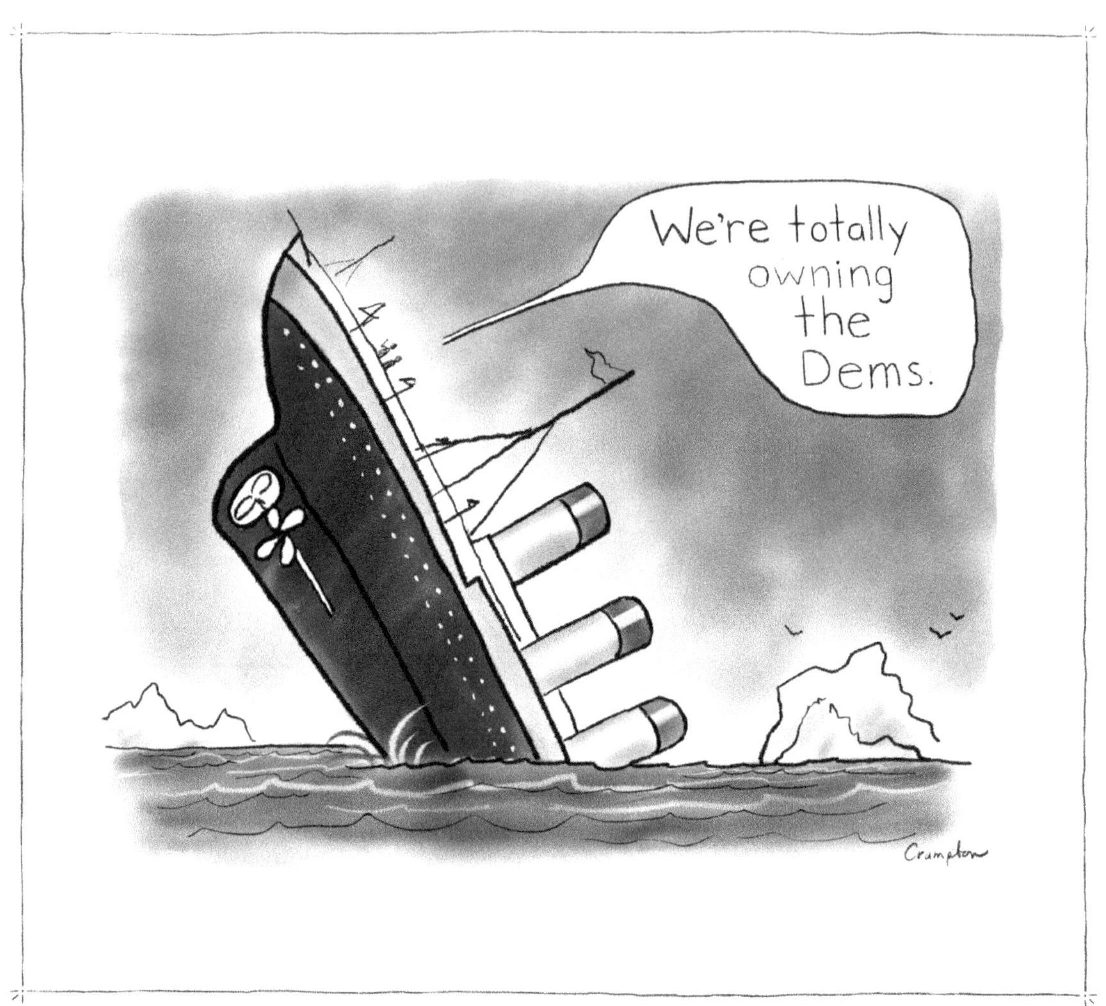

January 21, 2020
Impeachment Trial underway...

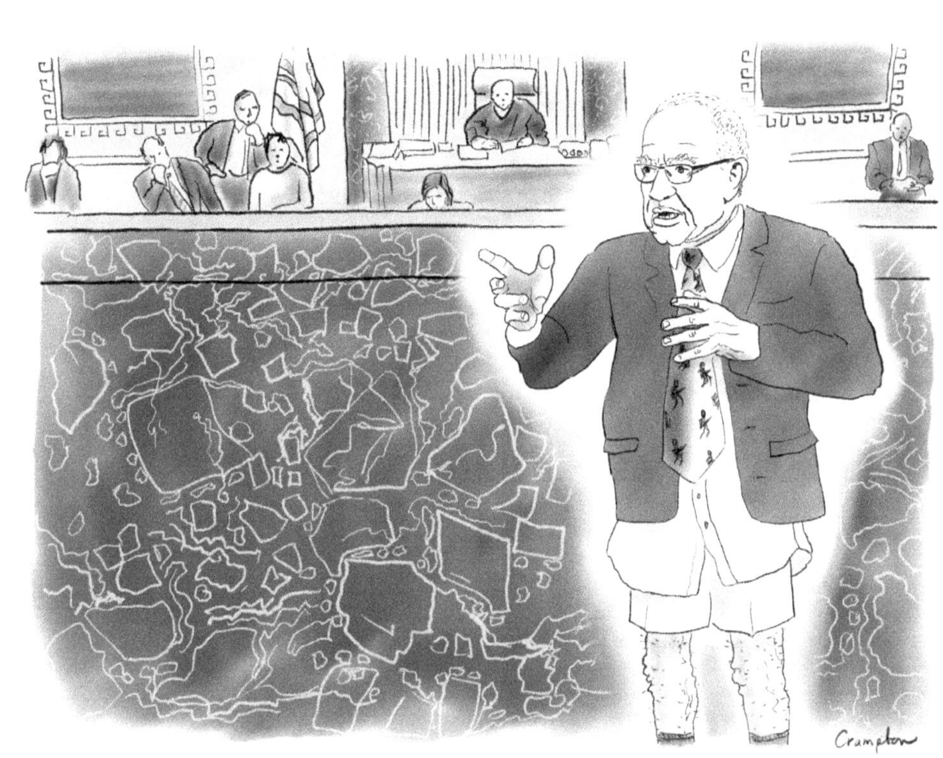

"If it's in the best interest of the candidate, it's perfectly legal to accept a massage from an underage sex slave on a private island."

January 31, 2020
One of the arguments by Alan Dershowitz, a defense attorney in the Senate Impeachment Trial, was essentially that 'if something was done in the candidate's best interest to get re-elected, then it couldn't be illegal'. Dershowitz is rumored to be a pal of sex trafficker Jeffrey Epstein—and this is all I could think of while watching him.

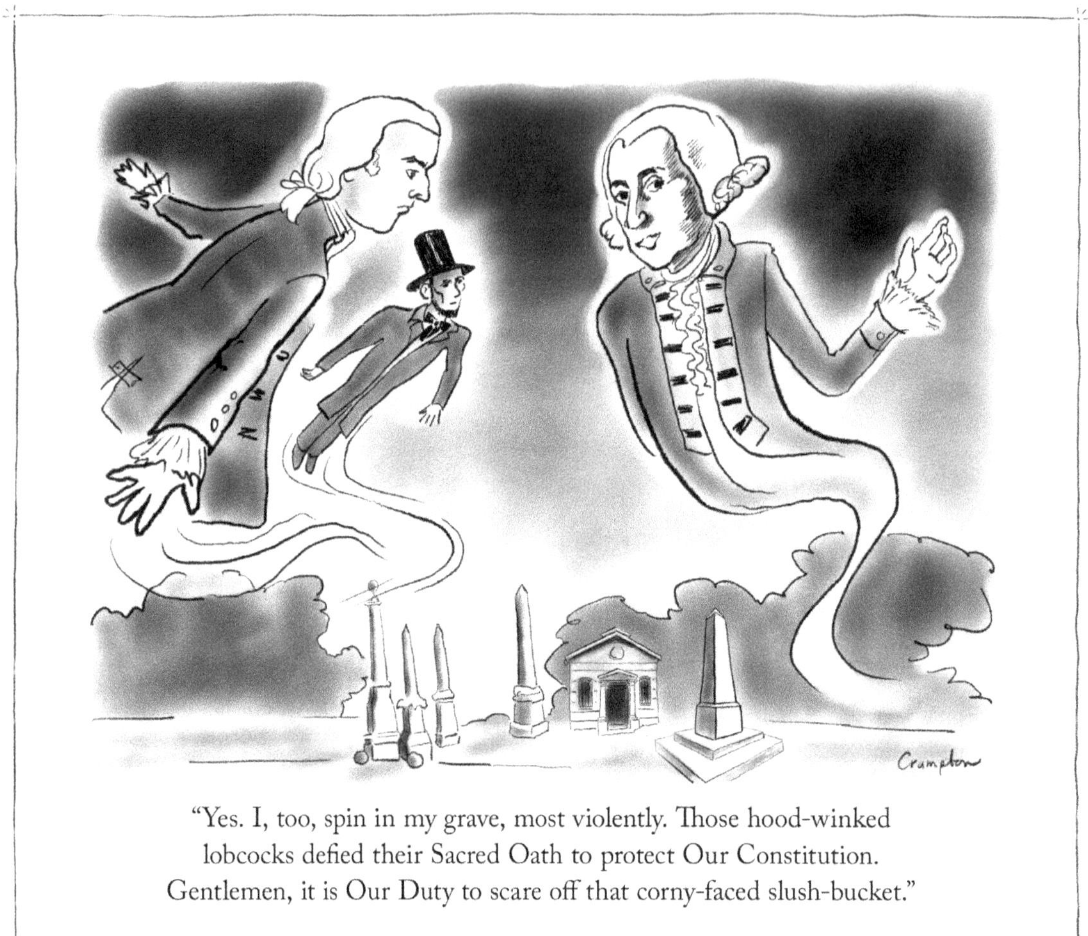

"Yes. I, too, spin in my grave, most violently. Those hood-winked lobcocks defied their Sacred Oath to protect Our Constitution. Gentlemen, it is Our Duty to scare off that corny-faced slush-bucket."

February 10, 2020
The Senate acquits Trump. Immediately afterwards, Trump sends Defense Secretary Pompeo to Ukraine, officially to calm their fears, but possibly to fabricate evidence against President Biden and his son, Hunter Biden.

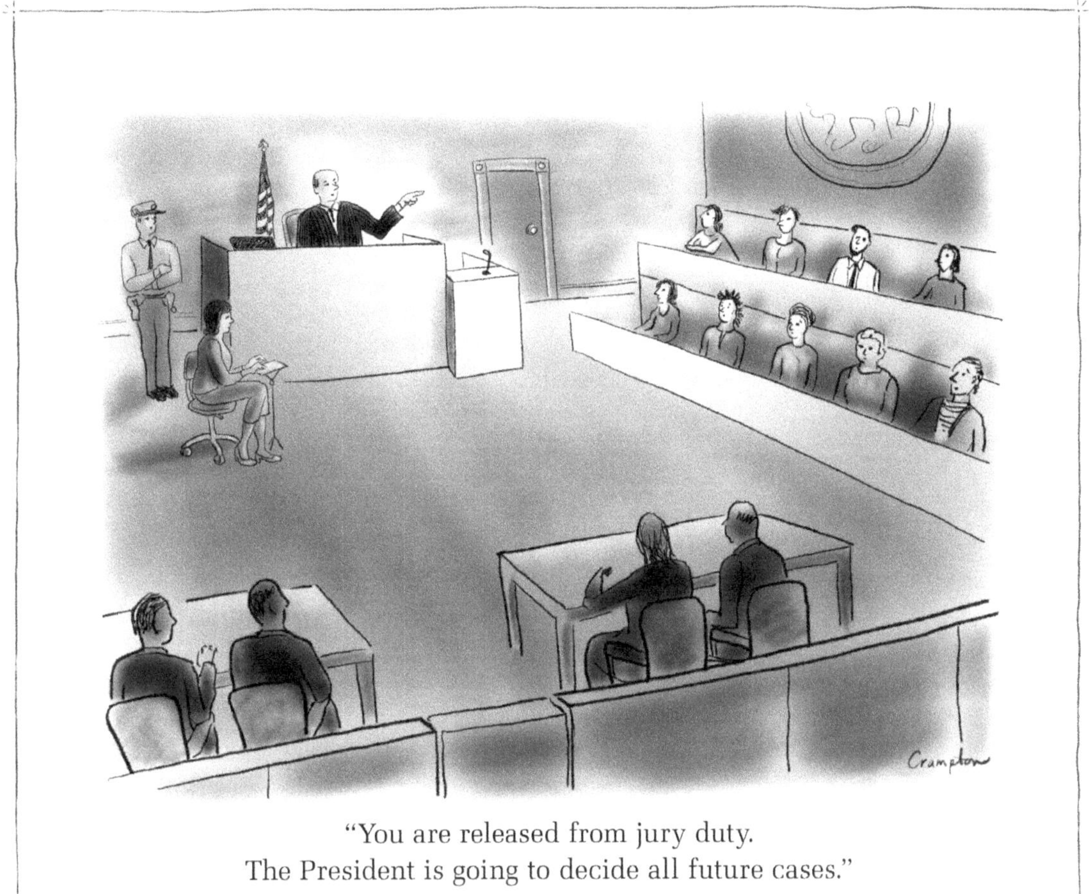

"You are released from jury duty.
The President is going to decide all future cases."

February 19, 2020
News broke that U.S. Attorney General Bill Barr recommends a shorter sentence for Roger Stone (convicted of obstruction, false statements and witness tampering). Barr may be intervening in ongoing cases of Trump's friends and enemies, including getting cases dismissed. He did release a misleading summary of the Mueller Report in 2019.

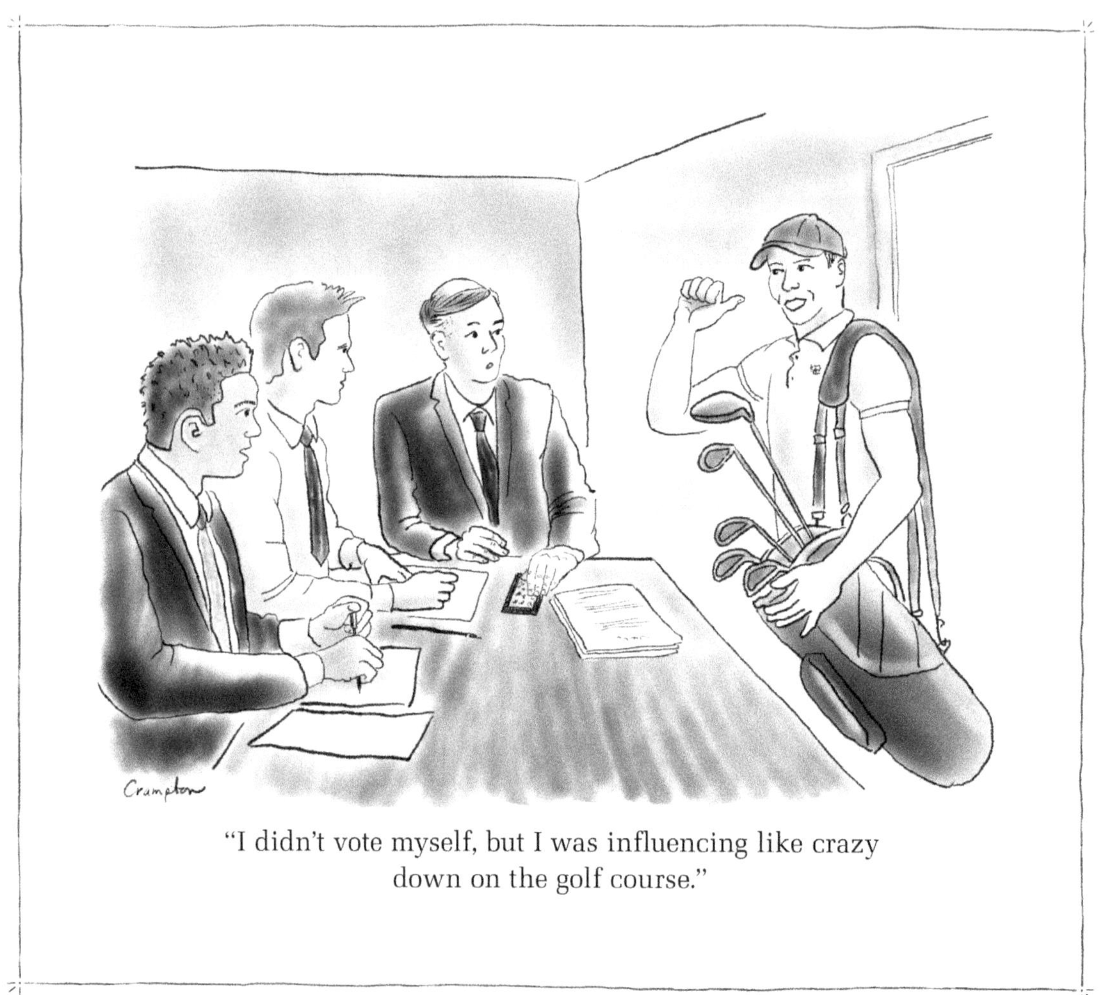

"I didn't vote myself, but I was influencing like crazy down on the golf course."

March 4, 2020
On Super Tuesday, the Bernie supporters who thronged to his rallies (and flamed me for supporting Hillary), mostly didn't turn out to vote in the primary election.

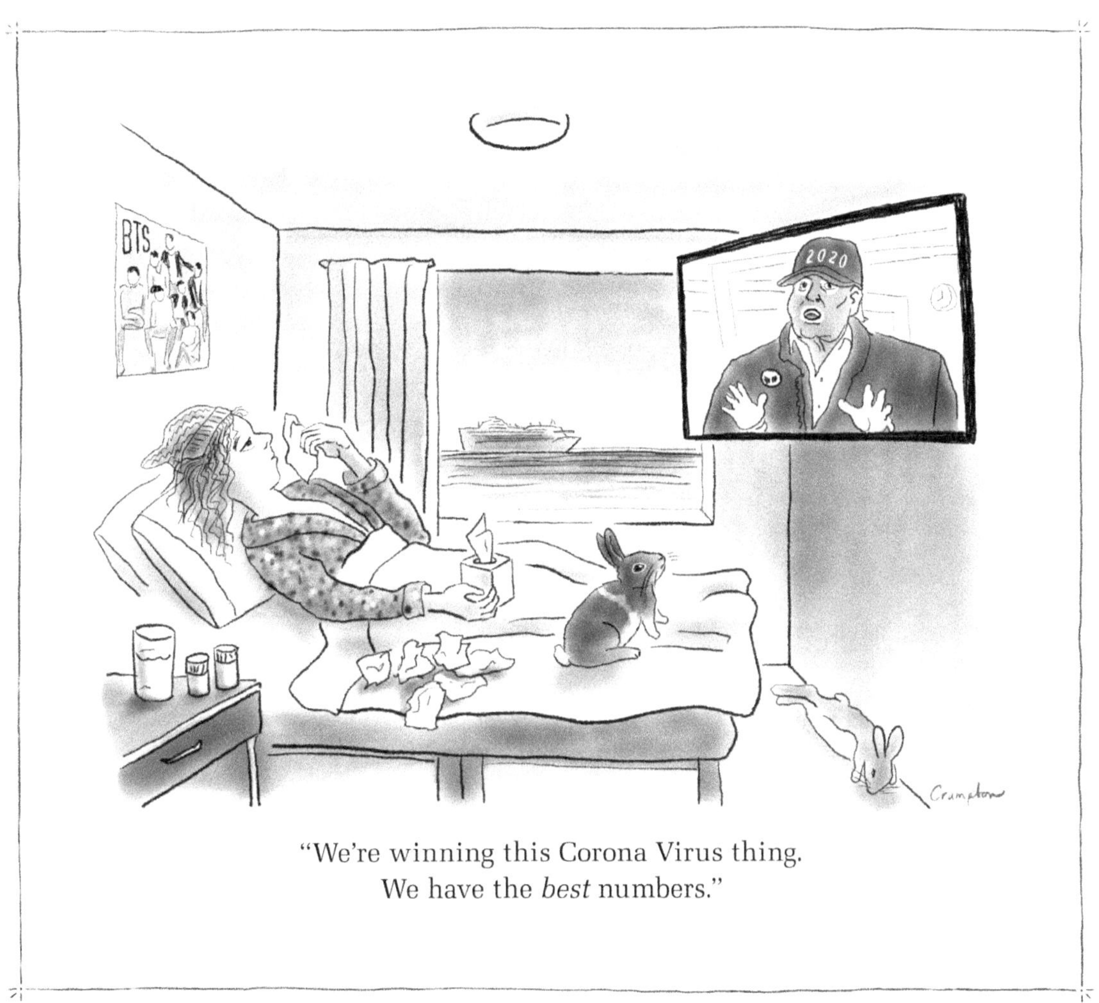

"We're winning this Corona Virus thing.
We have the *best* numbers."

March 8, 2020
I had Covid-19. Trump's appearances on TV were not reassuring, nor was the cruise ship, the Grand Princess, which was anchored offshore with uncounted infected people on it. *(Note: onboard 122 positive, 7 deaths)*

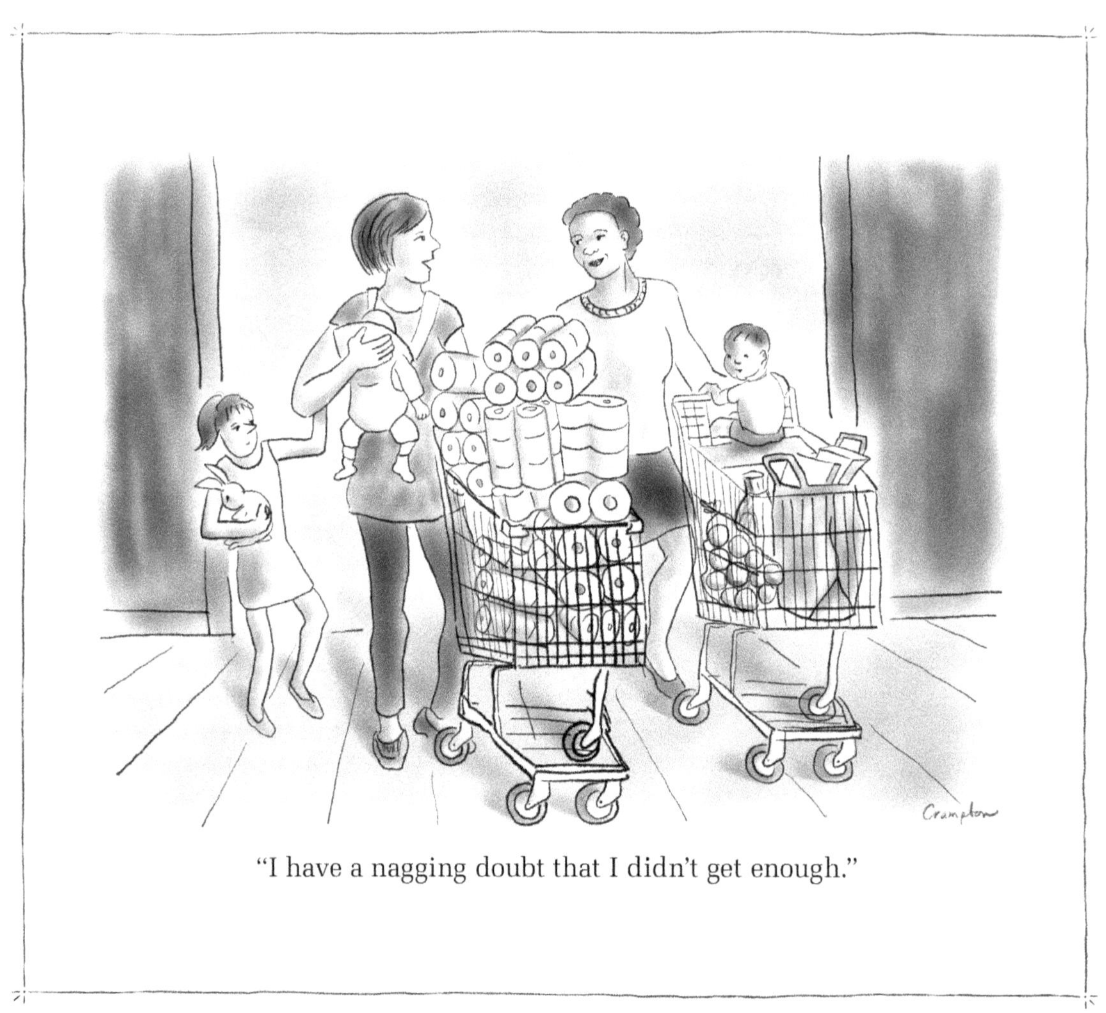

"I have a nagging doubt that I didn't get enough."

March 14, 2020
Americans hoard toilet paper in a panic because of the Pandemic. Some fight over it in stores.

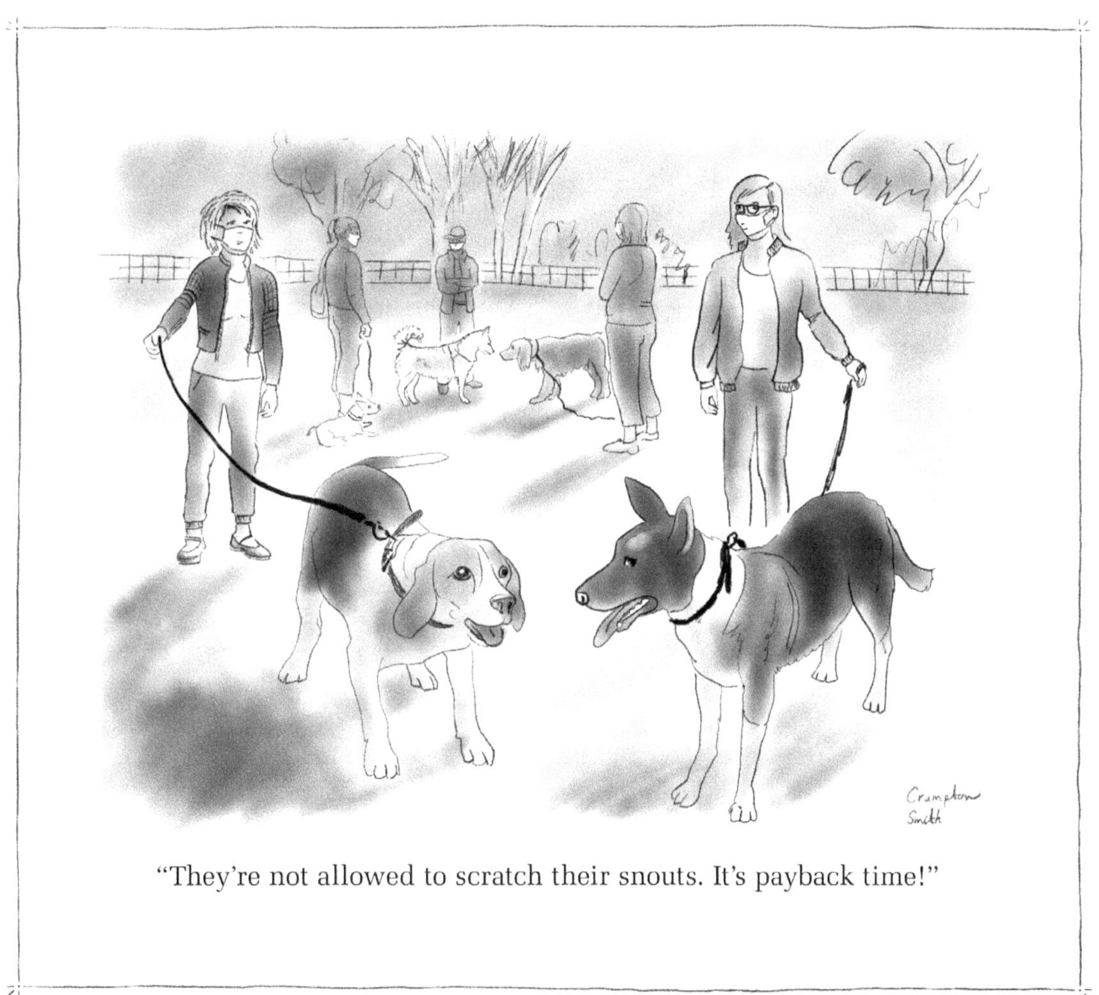

"They're not allowed to scratch their snouts. It's payback time!"

March 19, 2020
Bay Area residents, and later, all Californians, are ordered to shelter-at-home except for essential trips, in order to "flatten the curve". People who have masks wear them; others are sewing them. *Thanks to Kim Smith.*

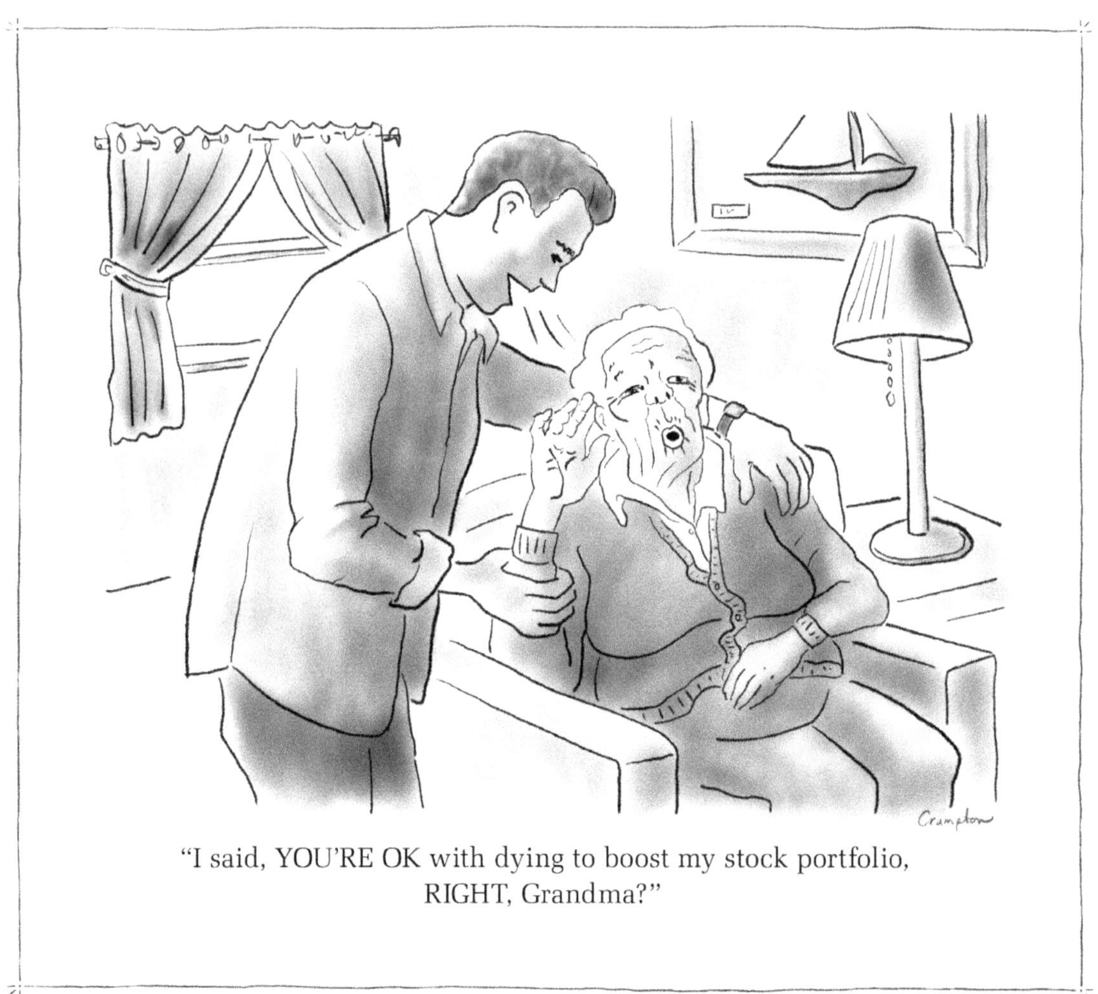

"I said, YOU'RE OK with dying to boost my stock portfolio, RIGHT, Grandma?"

March 24, 2020
Texas Lt. Governor Dan Patrick suggests that older Americans might be willing to sacrifice themselves for their children's economic future. President Trump and others float the idea of ending social distancing in about a week, even though the Pandemic is expected to get much worse.

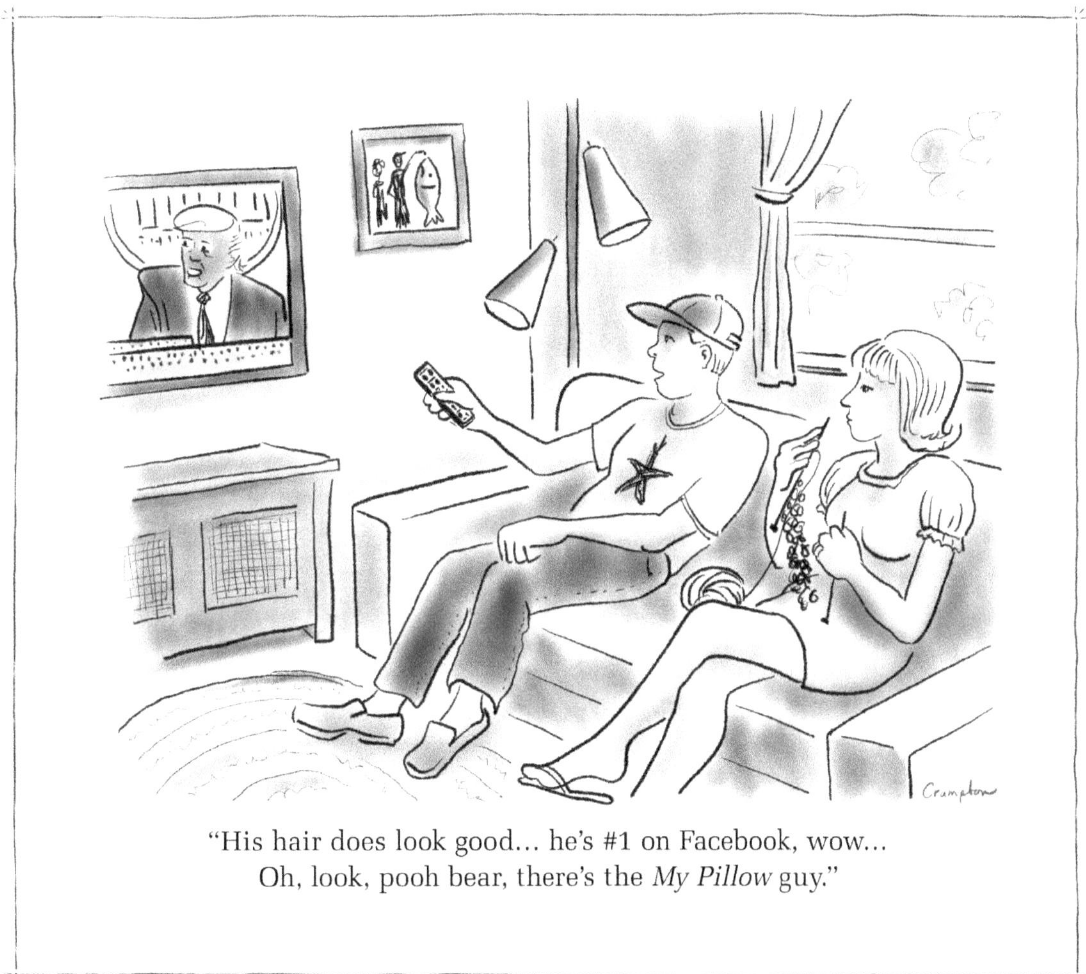

"His hair does look good... he's #1 on Facebook, wow...
Oh, look, pooh bear, there's the *My Pillow* guy."

April 2, 2020
Trump gives daily Coronavirus press briefings. His remarks include comments on his appearance, his great ratings (many people are now home from work, watching TV). He invites business leaders from Honeywell, Proctor & Gamble and other companies speak to the American people.

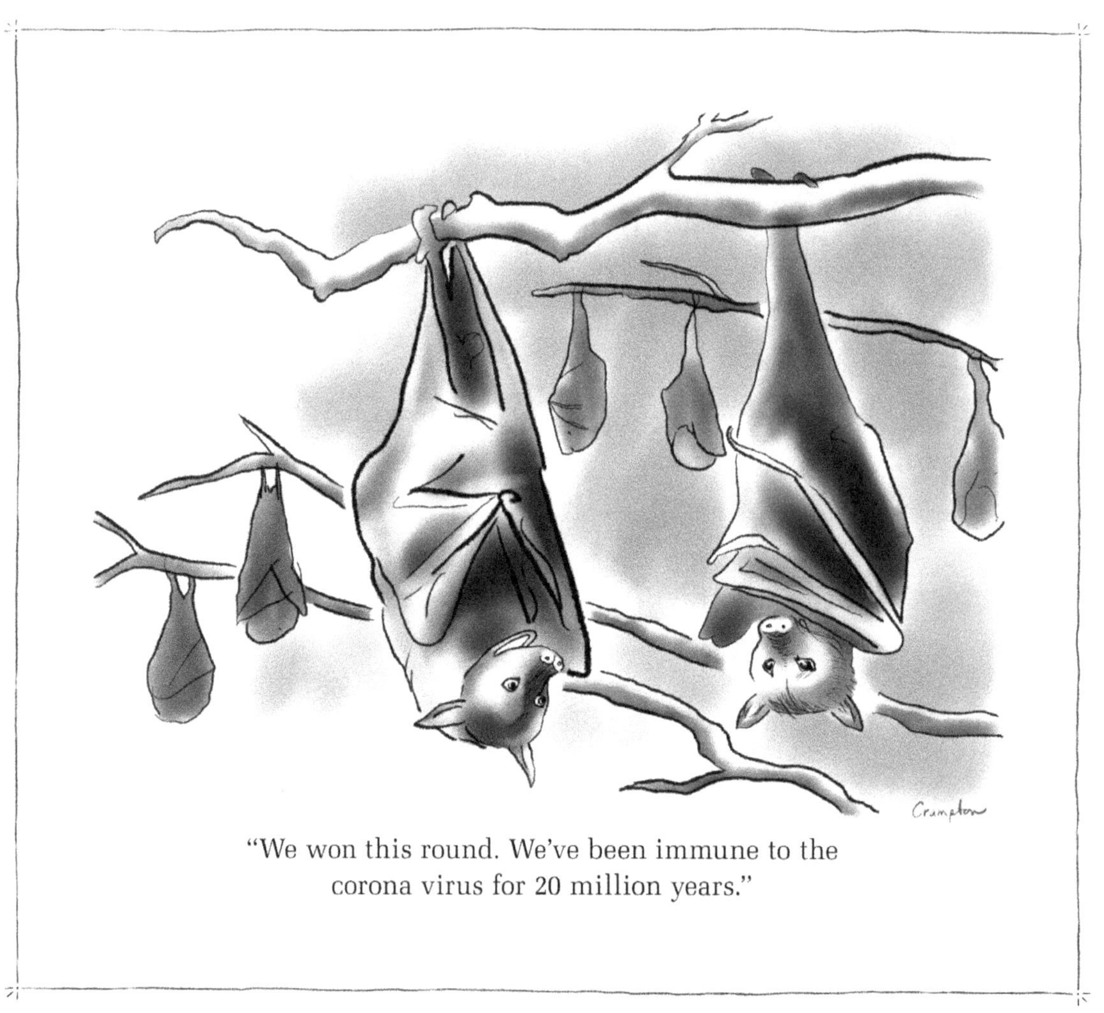

"We won this round. We've been immune to the corona virus for 20 million years."

April 4, 2020
The Covid-19 virus may have migrated from bats via an animal, a lab, or a wet market. My research shows that in flight, bats generate such high temperatures, that it enables them to kill viruses and build antibodies.

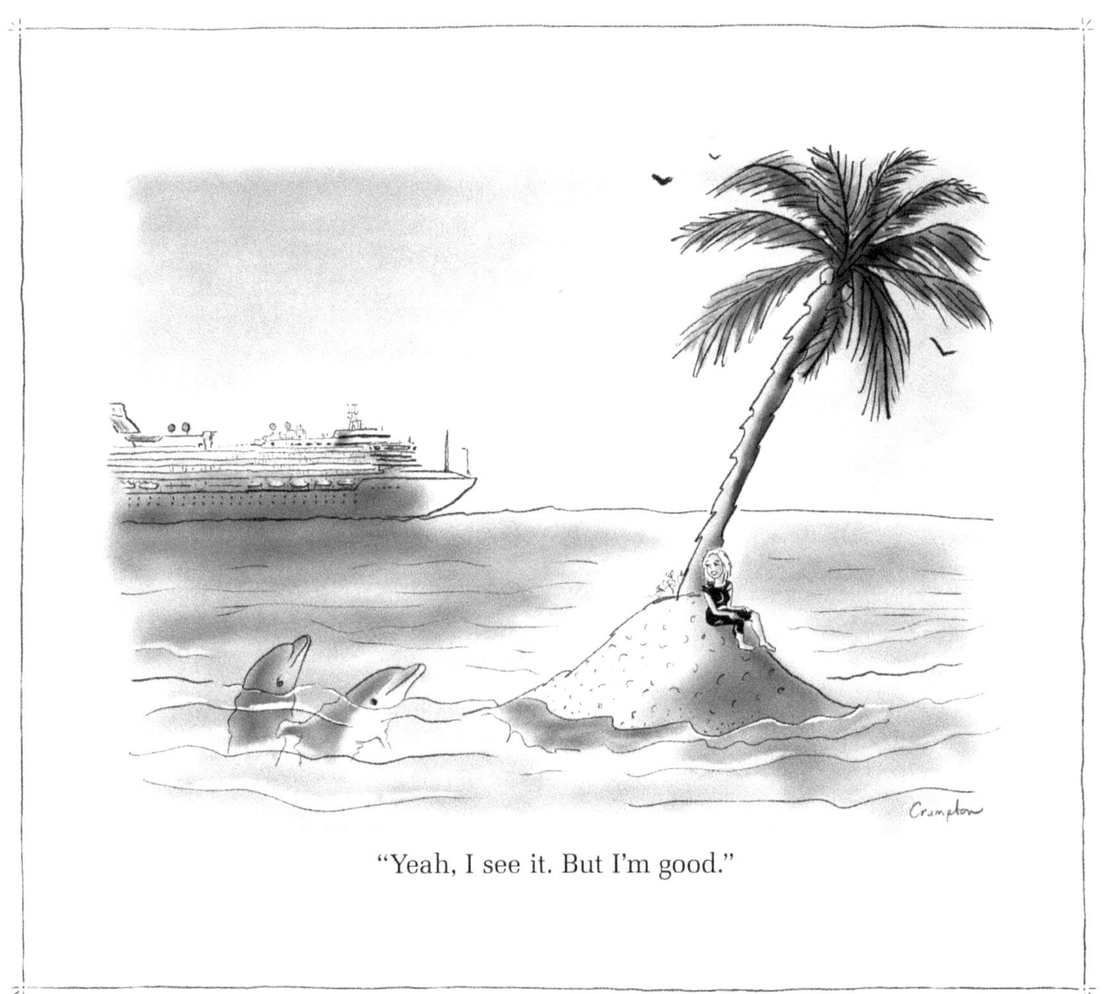

"Yeah, I see it. But I'm good."

April 14, 2020
More cruise ships are infected; some are not allowed to dock. The USS Theodore Roosevelt carrier was sidelined in Guam with 20% of sailors testing positive. Captain Brett Crozier was fired for warning Navy officials about this. *(Note: The Navy later recommended his reinstatement.)*

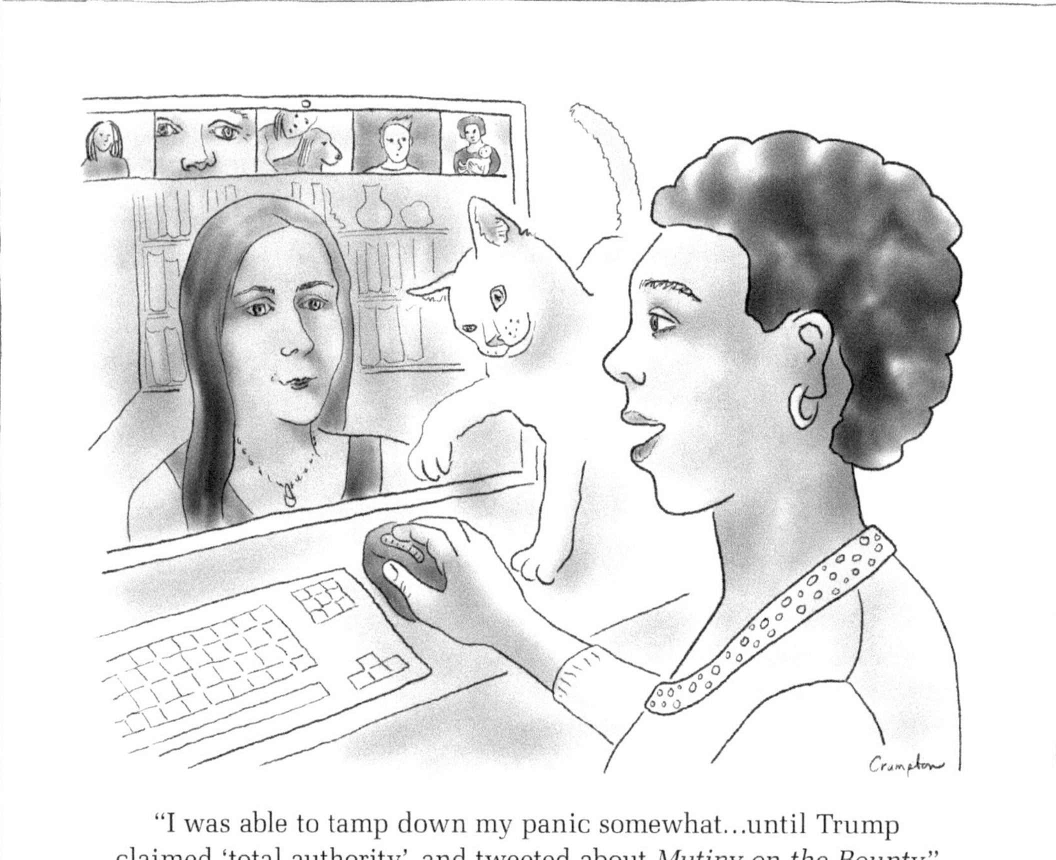

"I was able to tamp down my panic somewhat...until Trump claimed 'total authority', and tweeted about *Mutiny on the Bounty*."

April 16, 2020
People now work, attend classes or socialize using Zoom and similar online software.
Trump still holds daily gonzo TV press briefings.

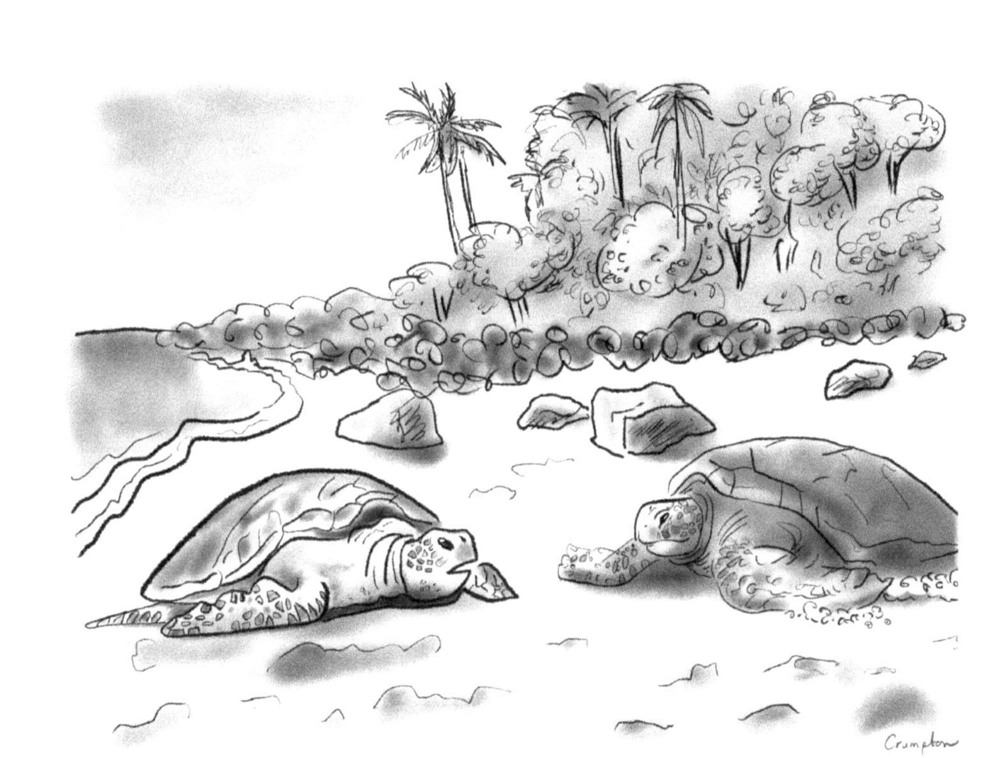

"Ya know what else is nice? Feeding without being chased down by suntan lotion-oozing, selfie-taking clowns."

April 25, 2020
Big right-wing donors stage multi-State protests against business- and beach-closures. Protesters carry guns, Confederate flags, and "liberty" signs. Hot weather causes mobs at some beaches. Hawaii closes their beaches.

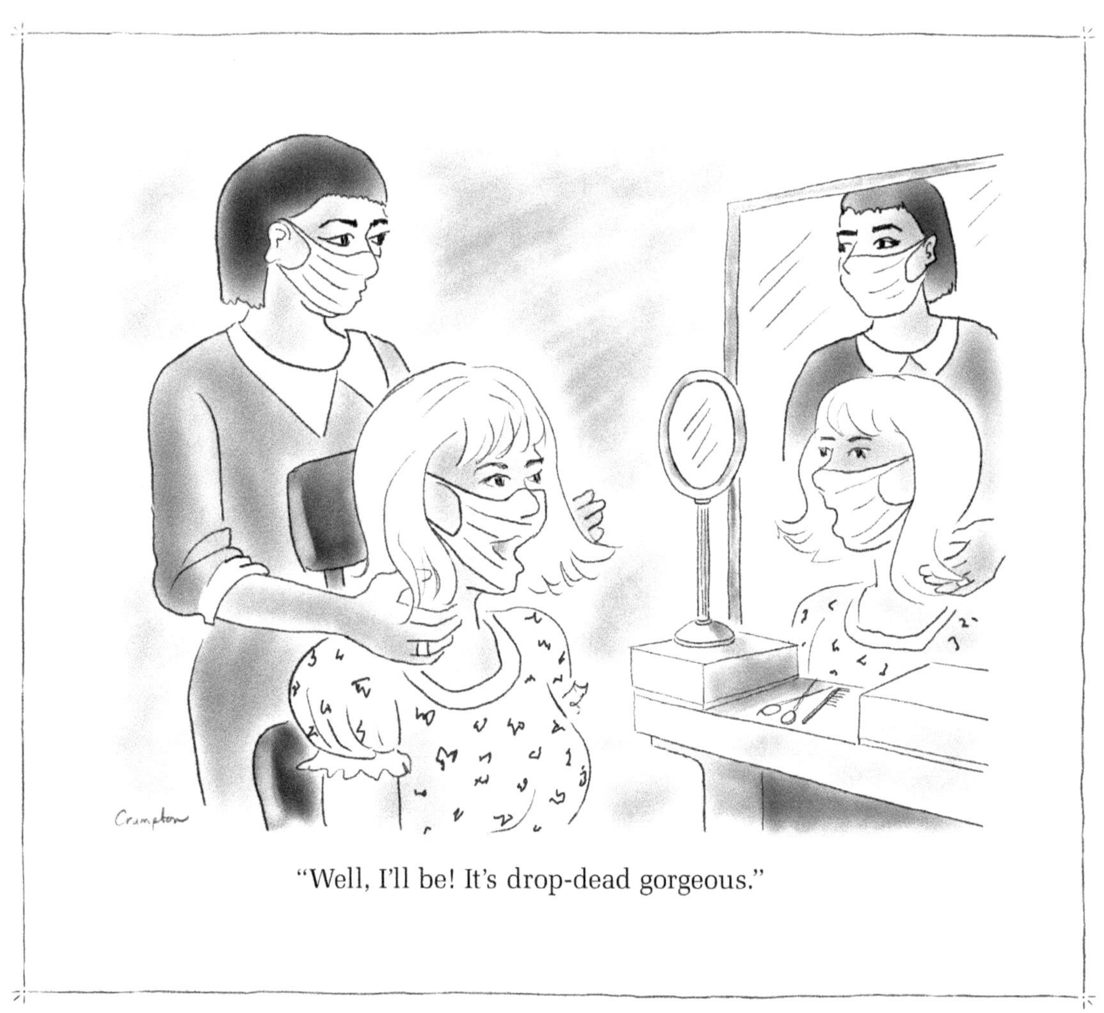

"Well, I'll be! It's drop-dead gorgeous."

April 28, 2020
Trump and Republican leaders plan to reopen many States even with a rising number of cases and no real testing or infection-tracing. People on social media object to being locked down for a hoax.

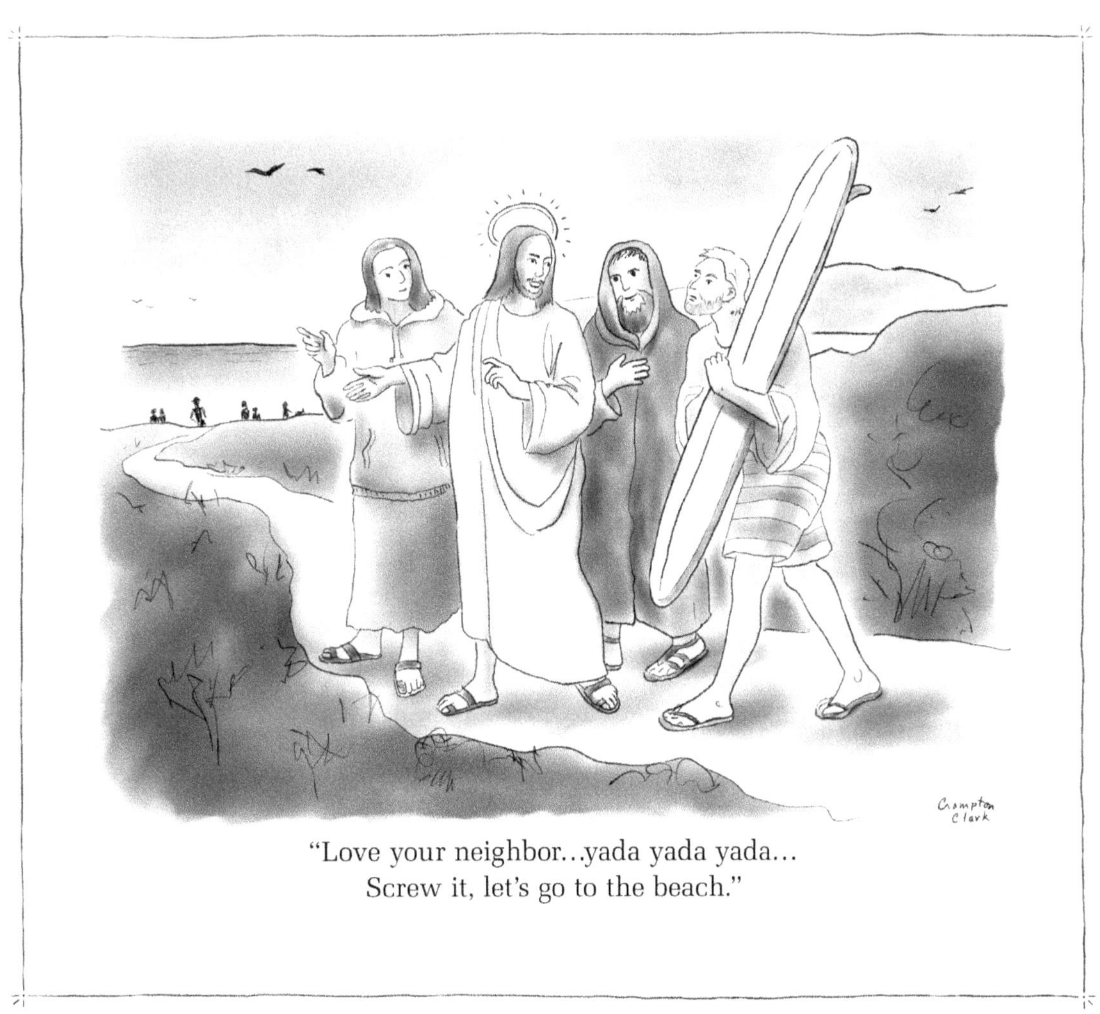

"Love your neighbor...yada yada yada...
Screw it, let's go to the beach."

May 5, 2020
Conservative Christians protest the closure of beaches in Huntington Beach and in other Southern California areas.
Thanks to Paula Clark.

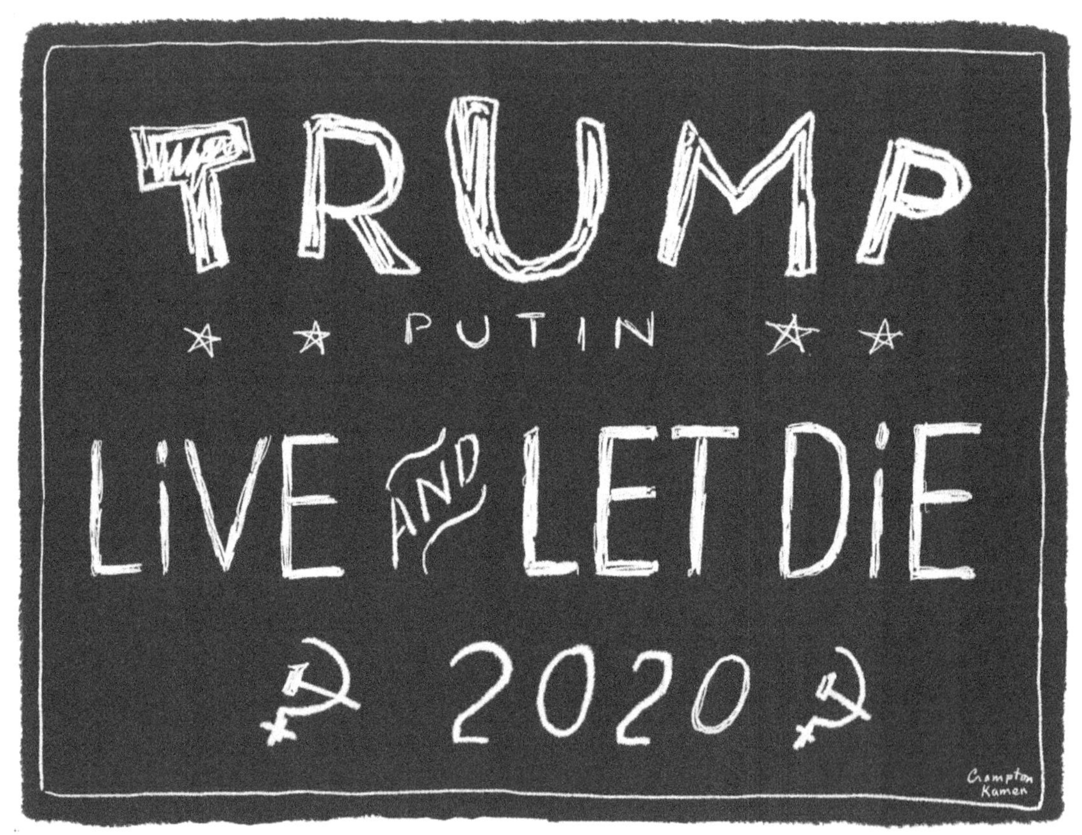

May 5, 2020
Campaign slogan idea by Ben Kamen, as found on Twitter, seems to just about sum up my feelings. Russia also has a run-away outbreak of the virus.

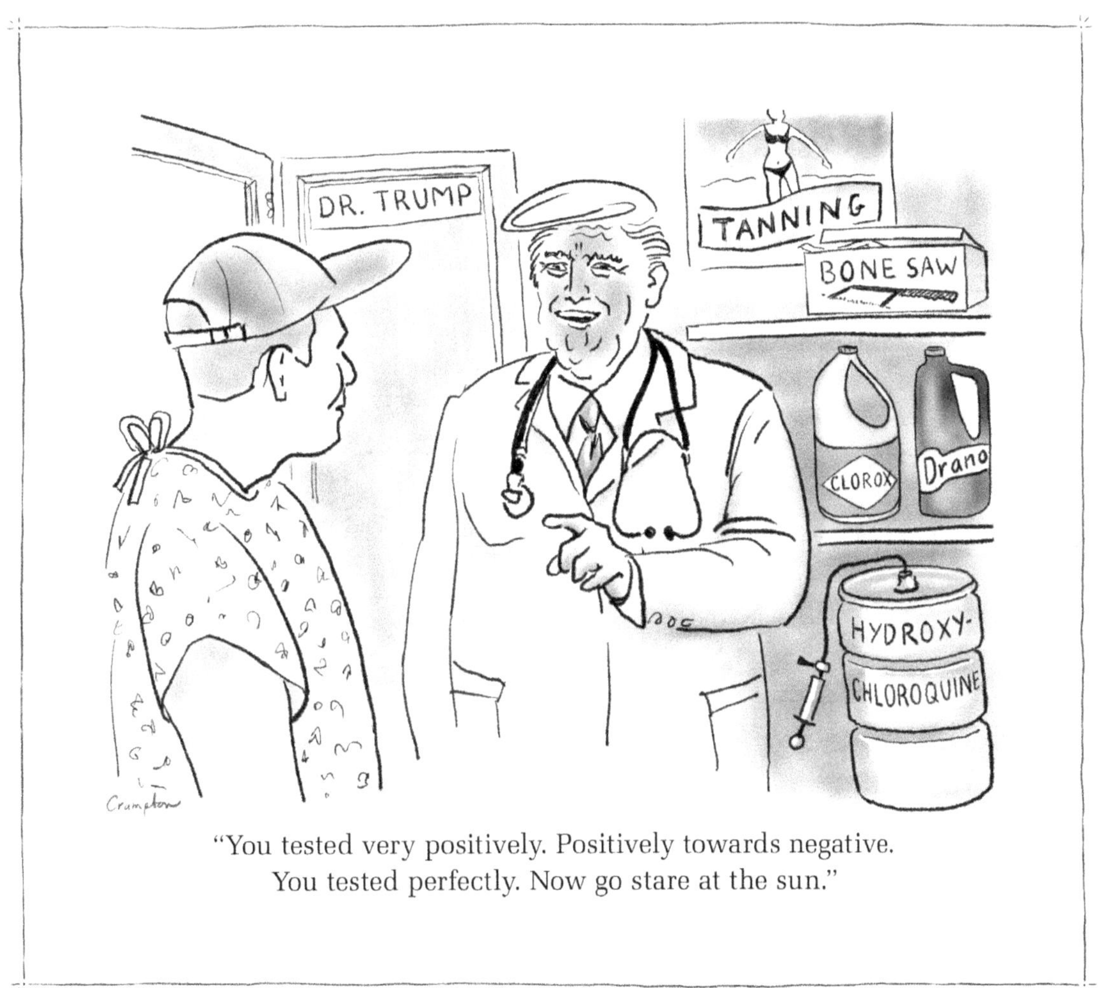

"You tested very positively. Positively towards negative. You tested perfectly. Now go stare at the sun."

May 25, 2020
This is mostly a quote from Trump. I added the "stare at the sun" because Trump famously looked directly at a solar eclipse in 2017. He suggests using UV light and disinfectant as treatments for Covid-19. People are reportedly seeking cures by drinking bleach and taking hydroxychloroquine.

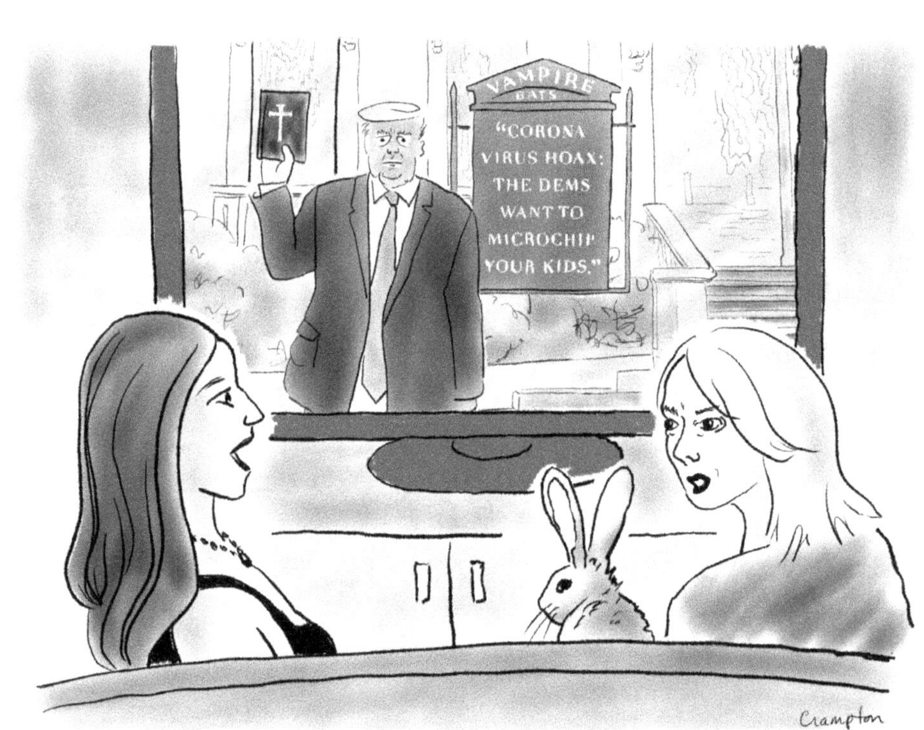

"It's supposed to look like he's warding off vampires. The base believes liberal elites drink a drug made from the blood of stolen children. Trump is using N.S.A. phone records to find evidence of it to lock them up. So, yeah, vampires."

June 5, 2020
Unmarked military personnel sprayed tear gas to break up a peaceful White House demonstration (a Black Lives Matter protest about the police-killing of George Floyd), in order to stage a Trump photo op.
This might be a good time to google "QAnon" and include keywords like "Pizza Parlor","adrenochrome".

IF YOU DON'T WANT TO WEAR A

FACE MASK

TO PROTECT OTHER PEOPLE,

YOU ARE

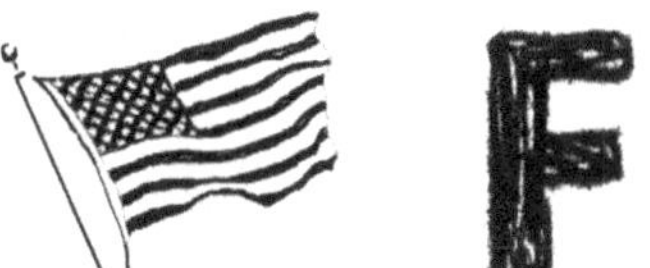

FREE

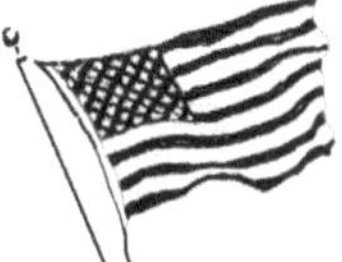

TO GO BACK TO THAT HOLE YOU CRAWLED OUT OF.

Crampton

June 12, 2020
Many States reopen (or never closed down). Mask-wearing is seen as a political act.

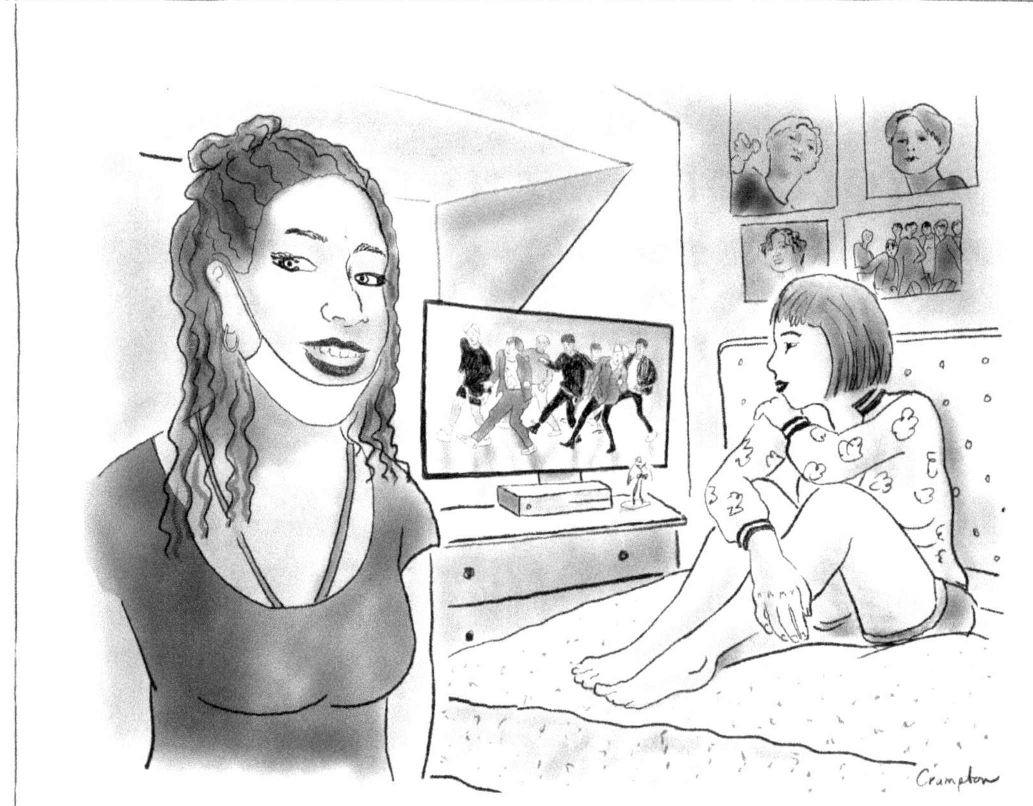

"My friends and I reserved hundreds of tickets to the Tulsa rally, but it was my dog's goldfish's funeral, so..."

June 22, 2020
TikTok teenagers, fans of the band BTS and other K-pop groups, fake-reserved many of the one million tickets for Trump's rally in Tulsa. *This action was possibly inspired by the TikTok videos by M. J. Laupp.*

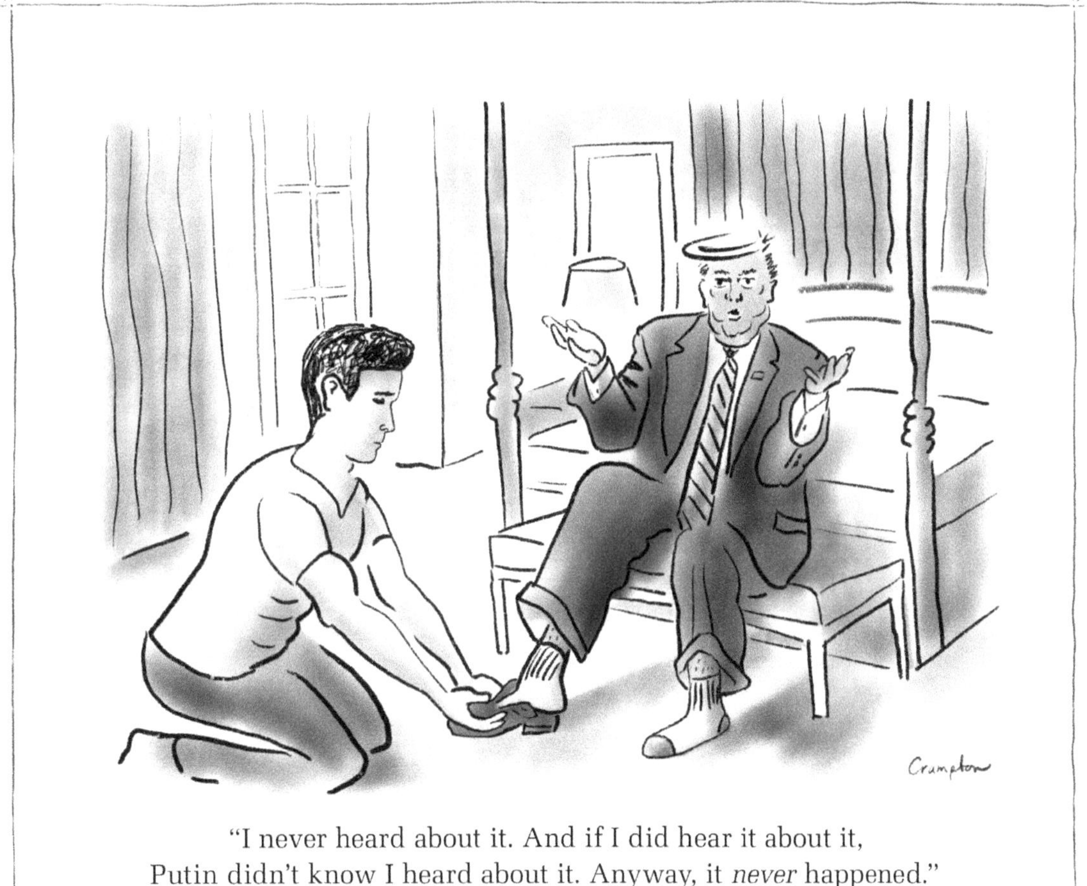

"I never heard about it. And if I did hear it about it, Putin didn't know I heard about it. Anyway, it *never* happened."

June 30, 2020
Russia paid bounties to Afghani's to kill U.S. soldiers, and reportedly, Trump knew about it.
Trump had friendly talks with Putin. He tried to get the G7 to re-admit Russia. Trump's valet had Coronavirus.

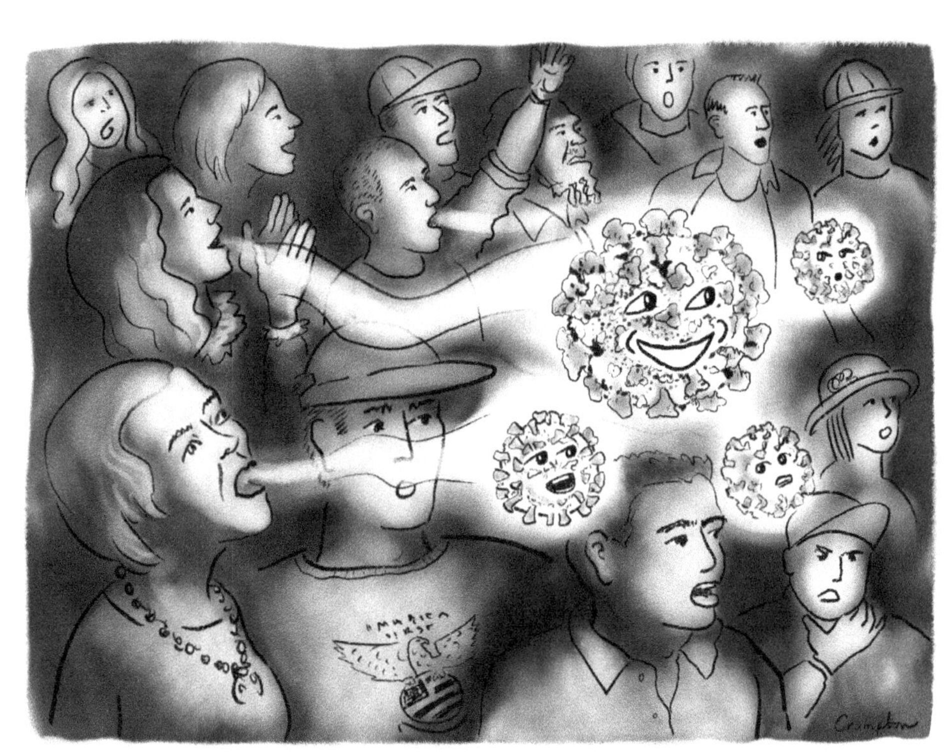

"Contact trace this, bitches!"

July 4, 2020
Trump holds a large, mask-less fireworks rally at Mt. Rushmore and another in Washington on July 4th. The weekend features national protests against masks. Most U.S. cities experience a high level of fireworks.

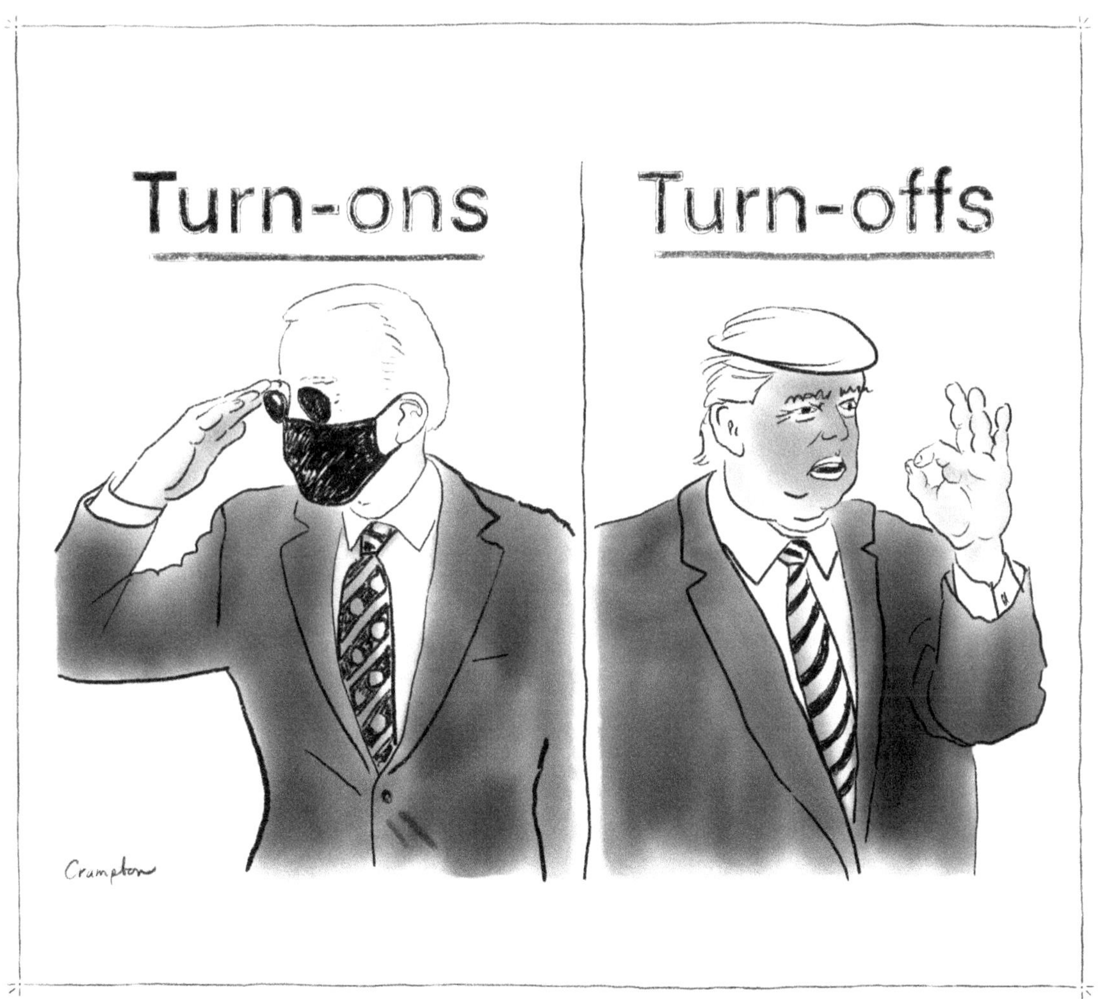

July 8, 2020
Inspired by Fourth of July appearances, at which former Vice President Biden salutes veterans, while Trump flashes the white power hand-sign.

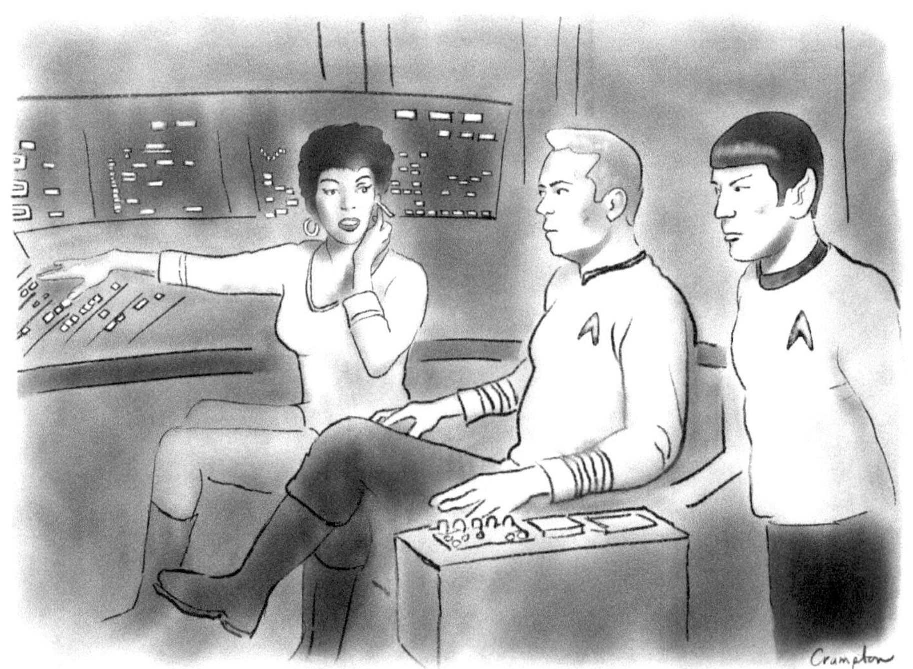

"Captain, I'm receiving white supremacist crap on all frequencies. Earth must be held captive by evil, manipulative warlords!"

July 13, 2020
Trump commutes Roger Stone's sentence, possibly for not spilling the beans about Trump's crimes. Rumors abound that the President is about to pardon others.

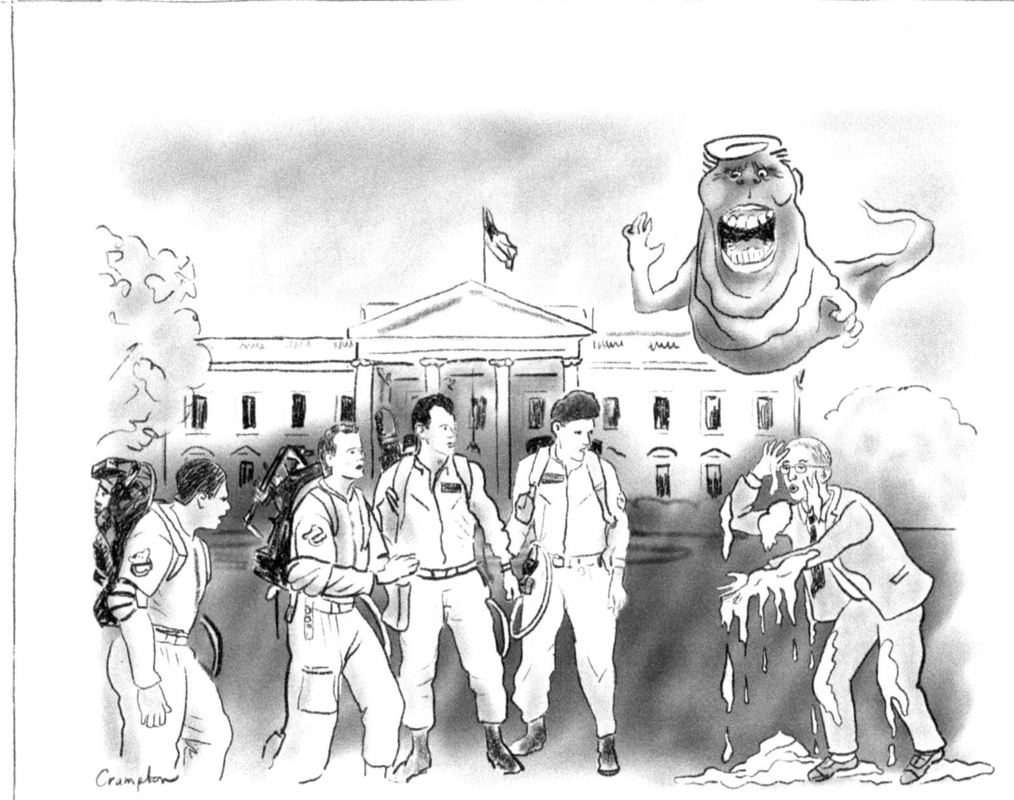

"Venkman, it looks like Doctor Fauci got slimed."

July 21, 2020
Doctor Anthony Fauci* says he's trying to walk a fine line not to contradict Trump. The White House releases a statement undermining Fauci, saying there is no reason to change one's behavior to avoid Covid-19.
Director of the National Institute of Allergy and Infectious Diseases

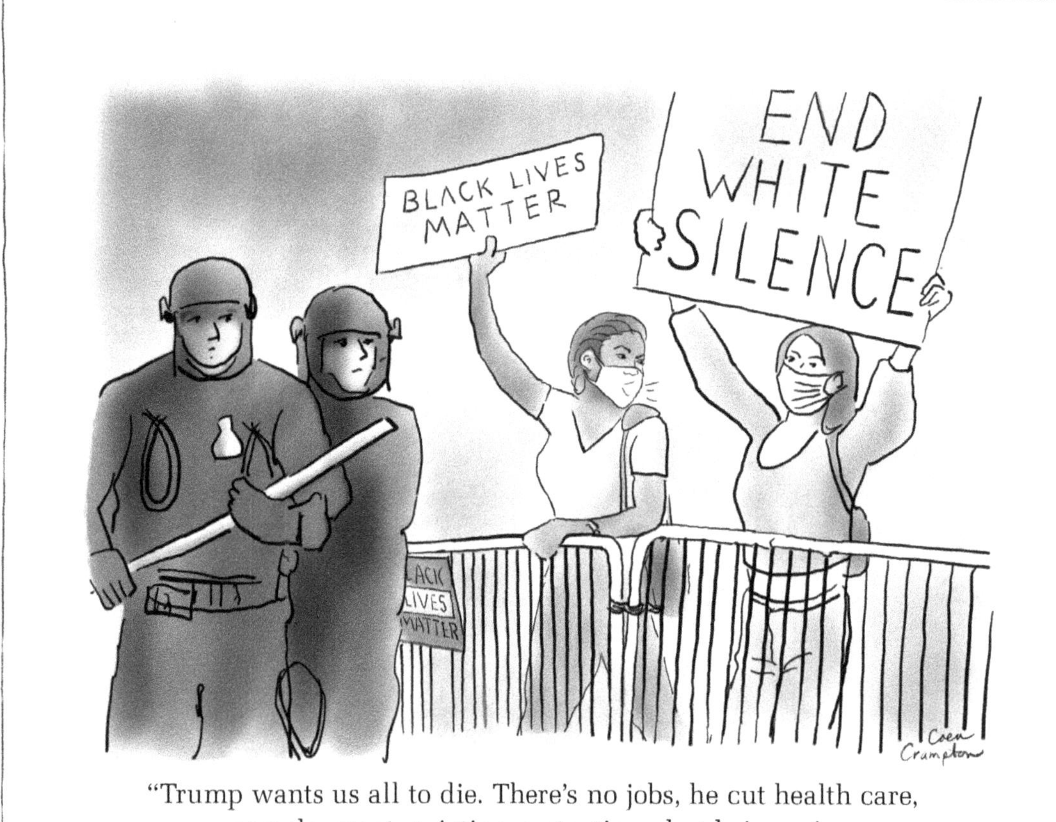

"Trump wants us all to die. There's no jobs, he cut health care, unemployment, eviction protection...but he's paving the rose garden for Melania's spike heels."

July 27, 2020
Secret (unmarked) government forces clash with Black Lives Matter protesters, including moms and dads with leaf-blowers, in Portland and elsewhere. The government isn't providing financial relief for Covid-19. Melania paves part of the White House Rose Garden and removes the crabapple trees. *Thanks to Lisa Coen.*

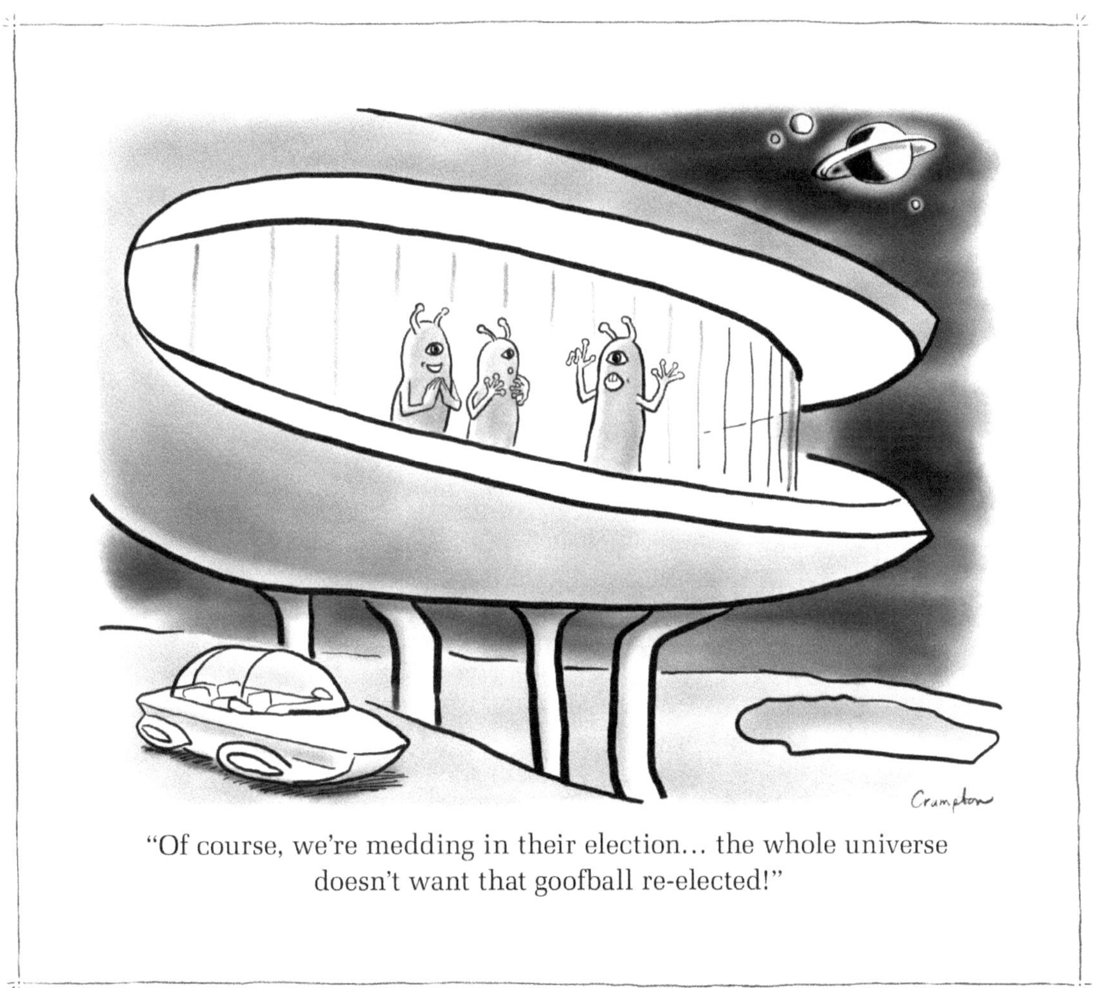

"Of course, we're medding in their election... the whole universe doesn't want that goofball re-elected!"

August 3, 2020
There are reports of various governments meddling in our upcoming election.

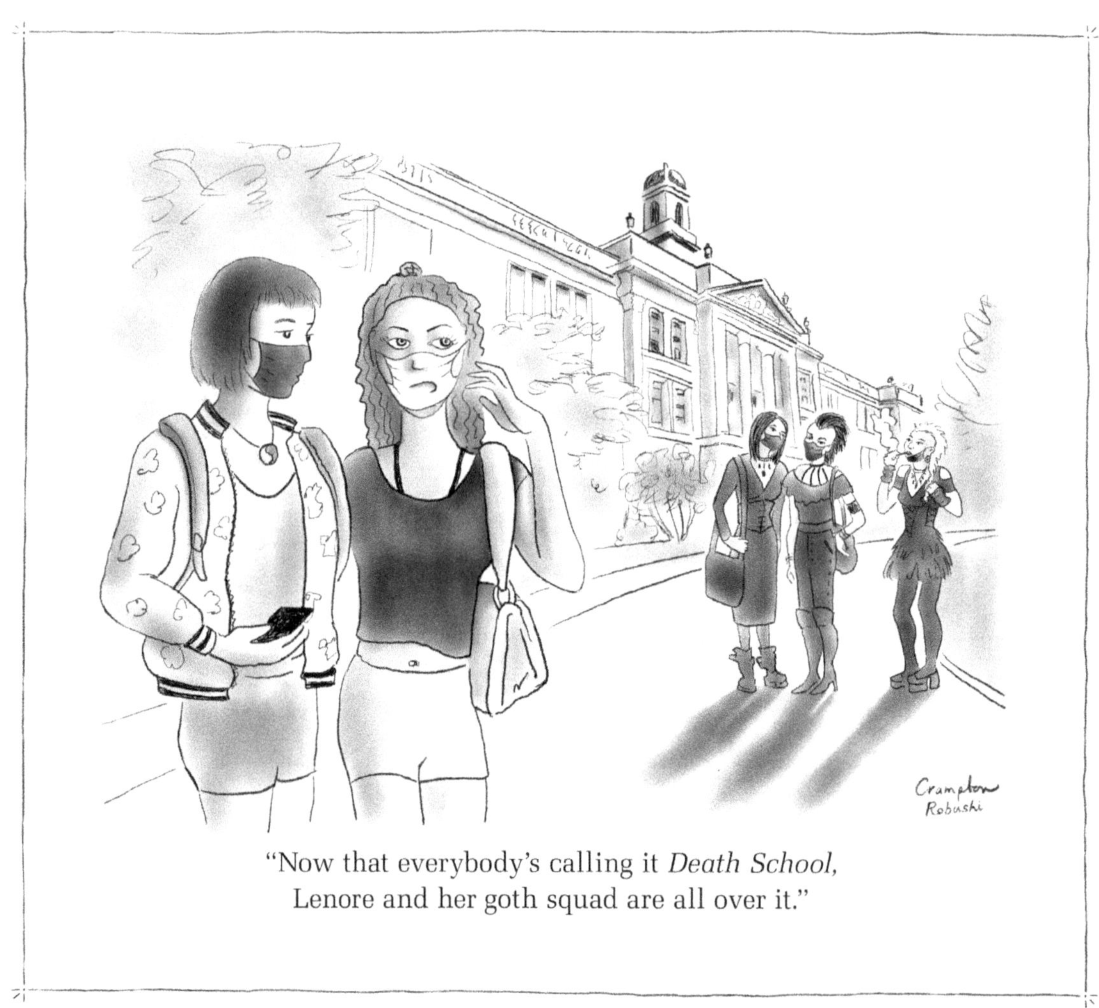

"Now that everybody's calling it *Death School,*
Lenore and her goth squad are all over it."

August 11, 2020
The virus is rampant. Many States reopen schools. *Thanks to Wendy Robushi.*

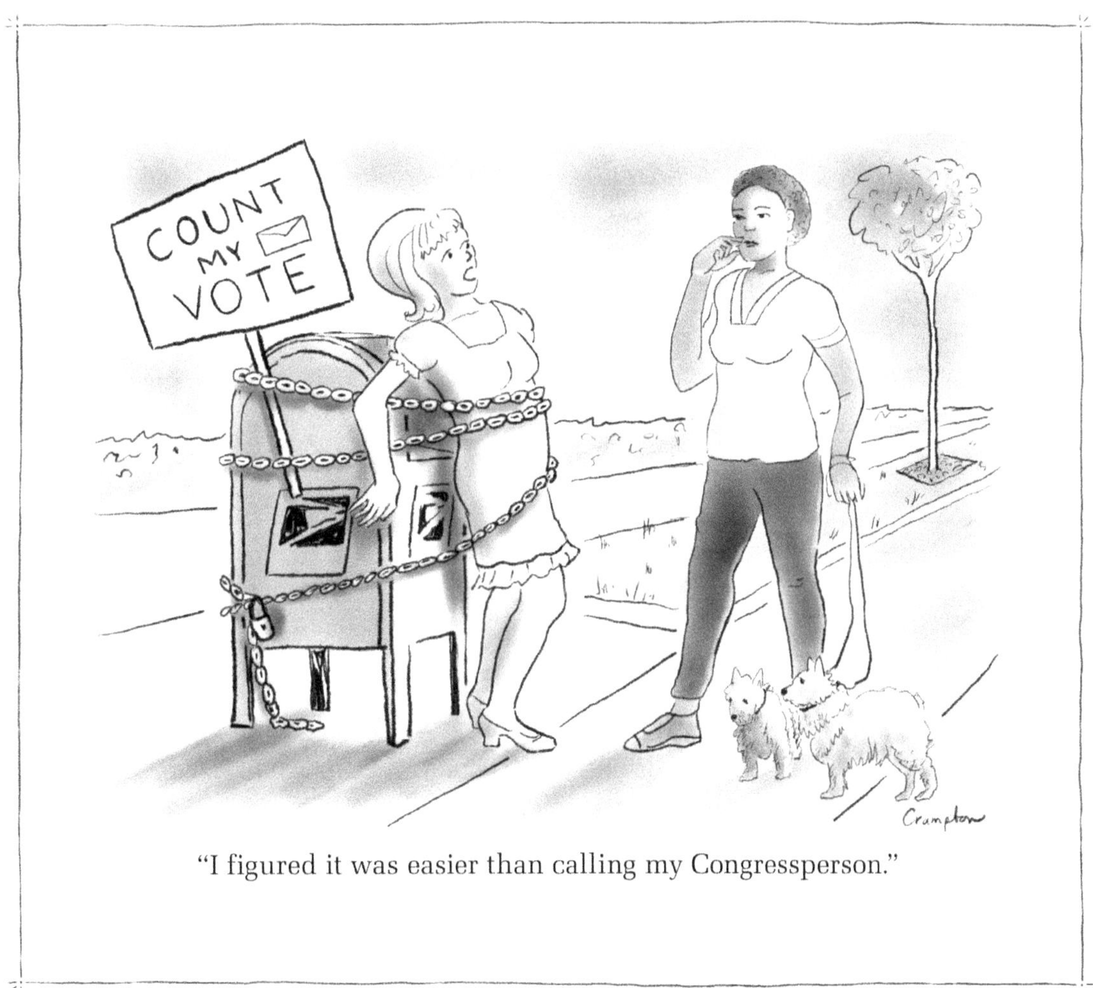

"I figured it was easier than calling my Congressperson."

August 17, 2020
Possibly because the Democratic Party encourages voters to use mail-in ballots for safety, Trump's new Postal Service head, Louis DeJoy, is accused of dismantling mail-sorting machines and removing physical mail boxes.

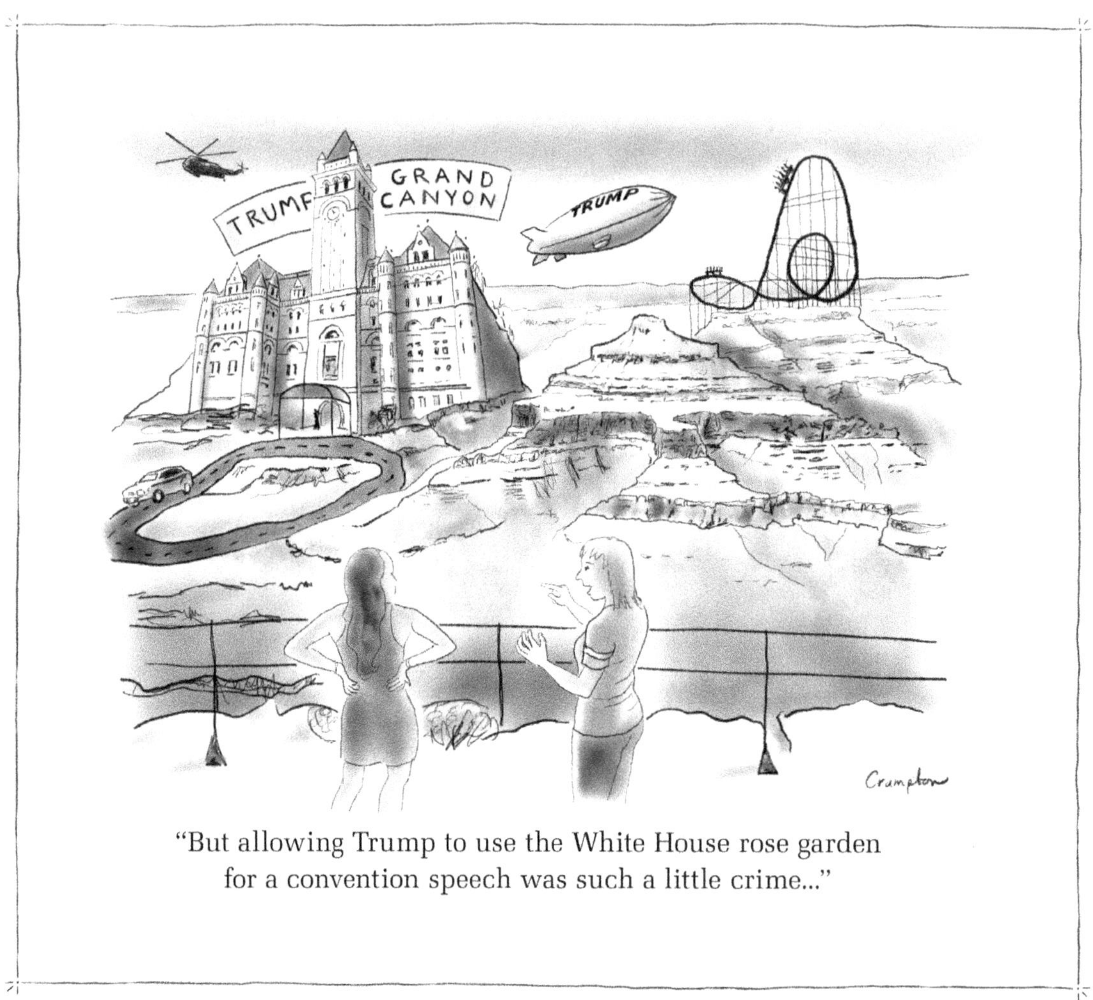

"But allowing Trump to use the White House rose garden for a convention speech was such a little crime..."

August 23, 2020
Trump plans to use the White House Rose Garden for his Republic National Convention speeches. This would violate the Hatch Act. *I imagined how a Trump Grand Canyon Hotel would look.*

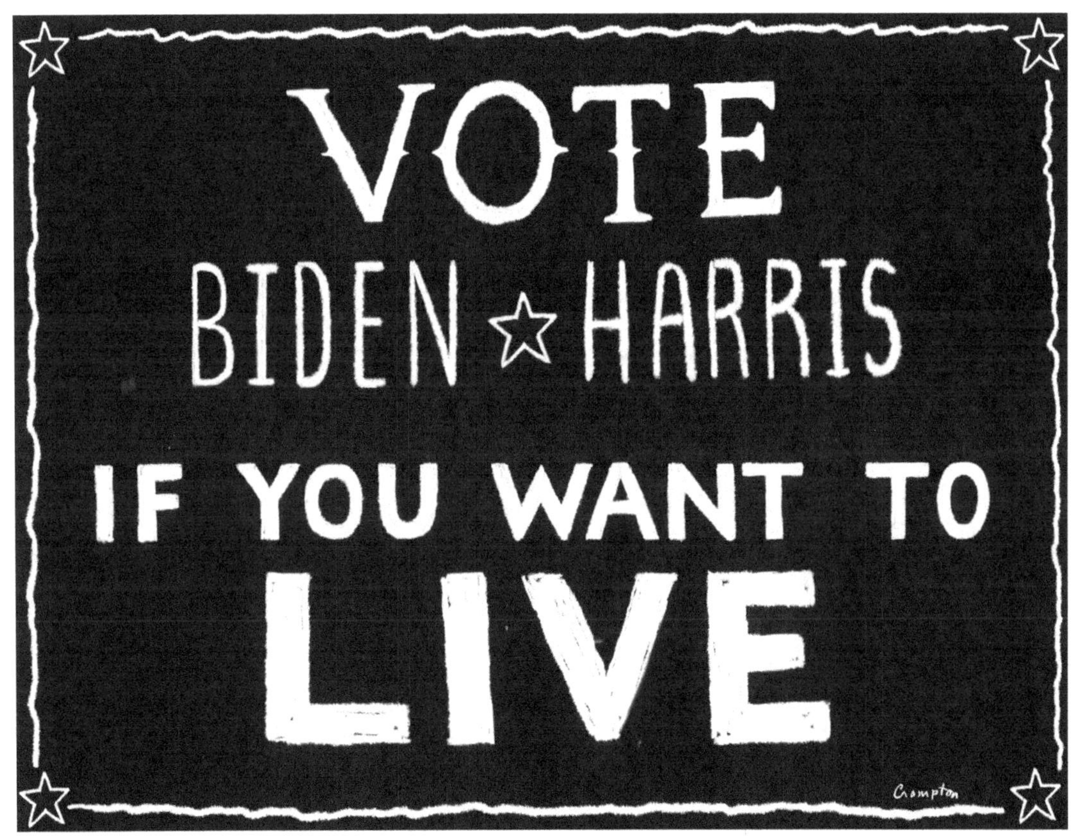

September 1, 2020
I saw this meme on Facebook... couldn't find the creator to credit them, but I drew a version for a campaign poster.

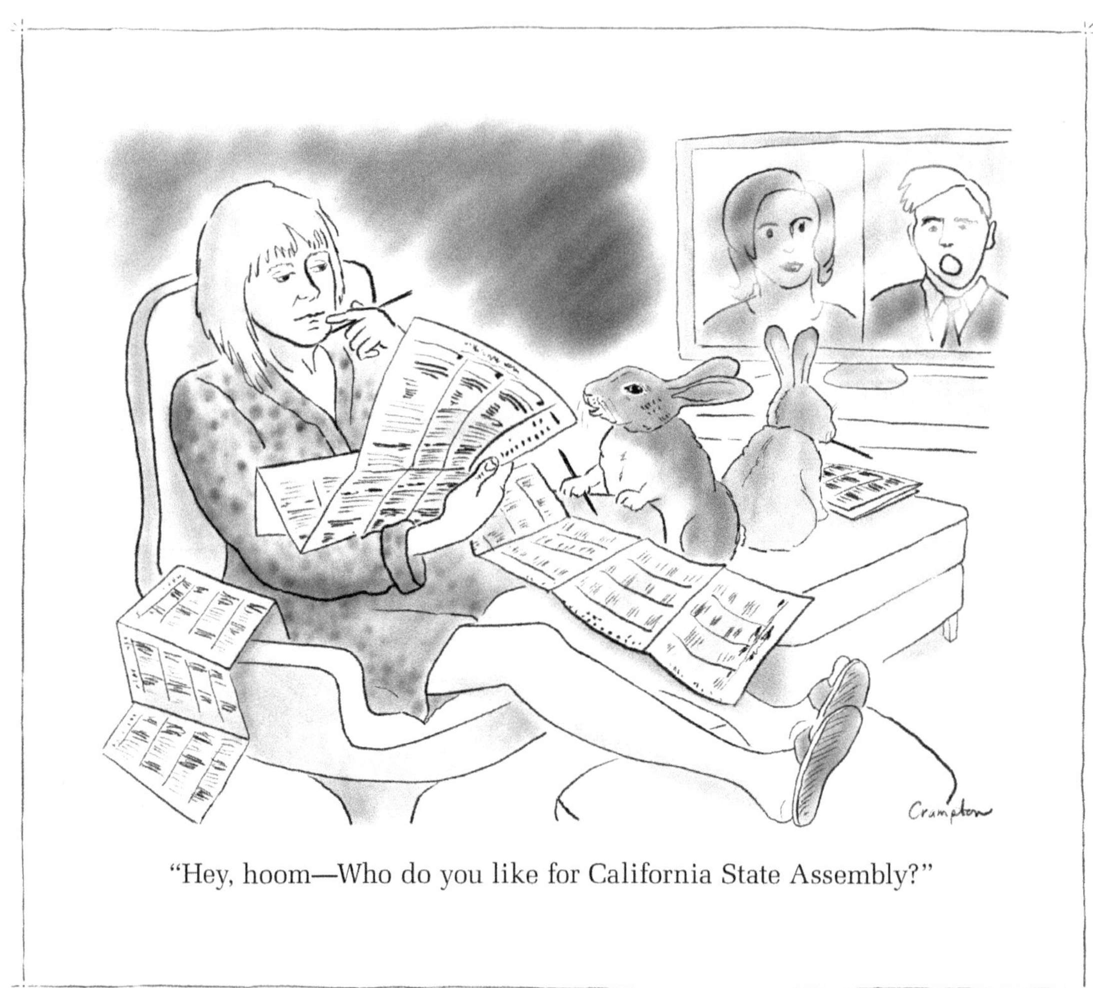

"Hey, hoom—Who do you like for California State Assembly?"

September 6, 2020
Trump repeatedly announces that dogs voted in California.

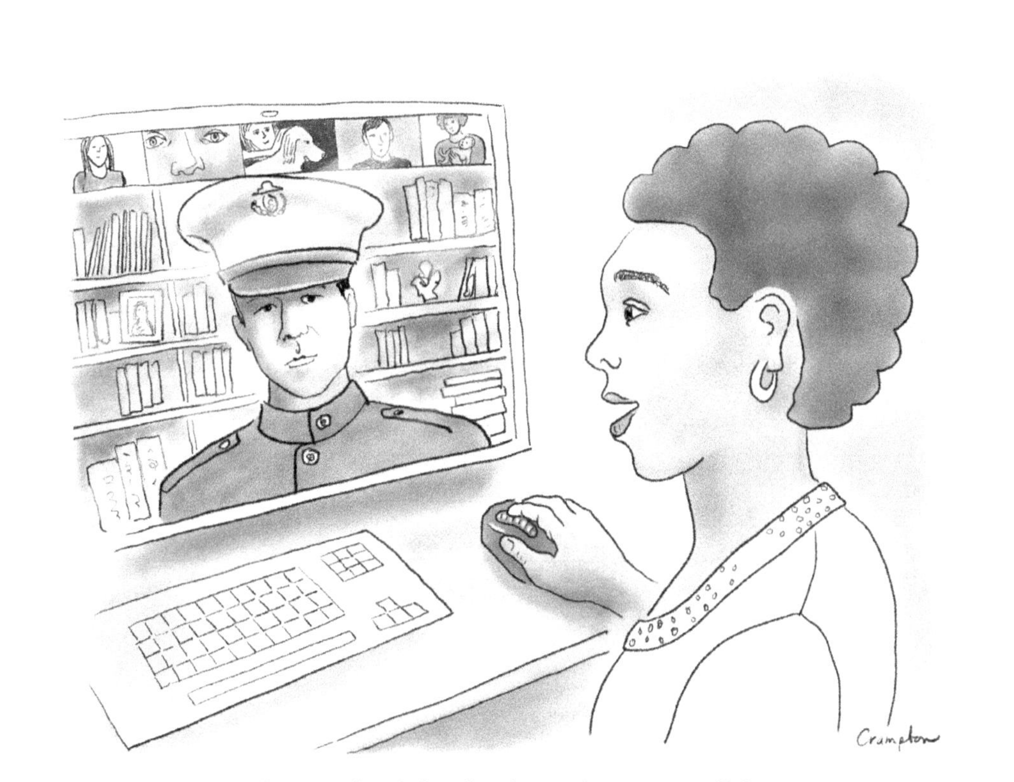

"The Commander in Chief thinks the military are all losers—except for Colonel Sanders, Captain Crunch, and the Three Musketeers."

September 10, 2020
Bob Woodward's book "Rage" includes anecdotes and actual audio tapes of Trump calling military personnel "losers and suckers".

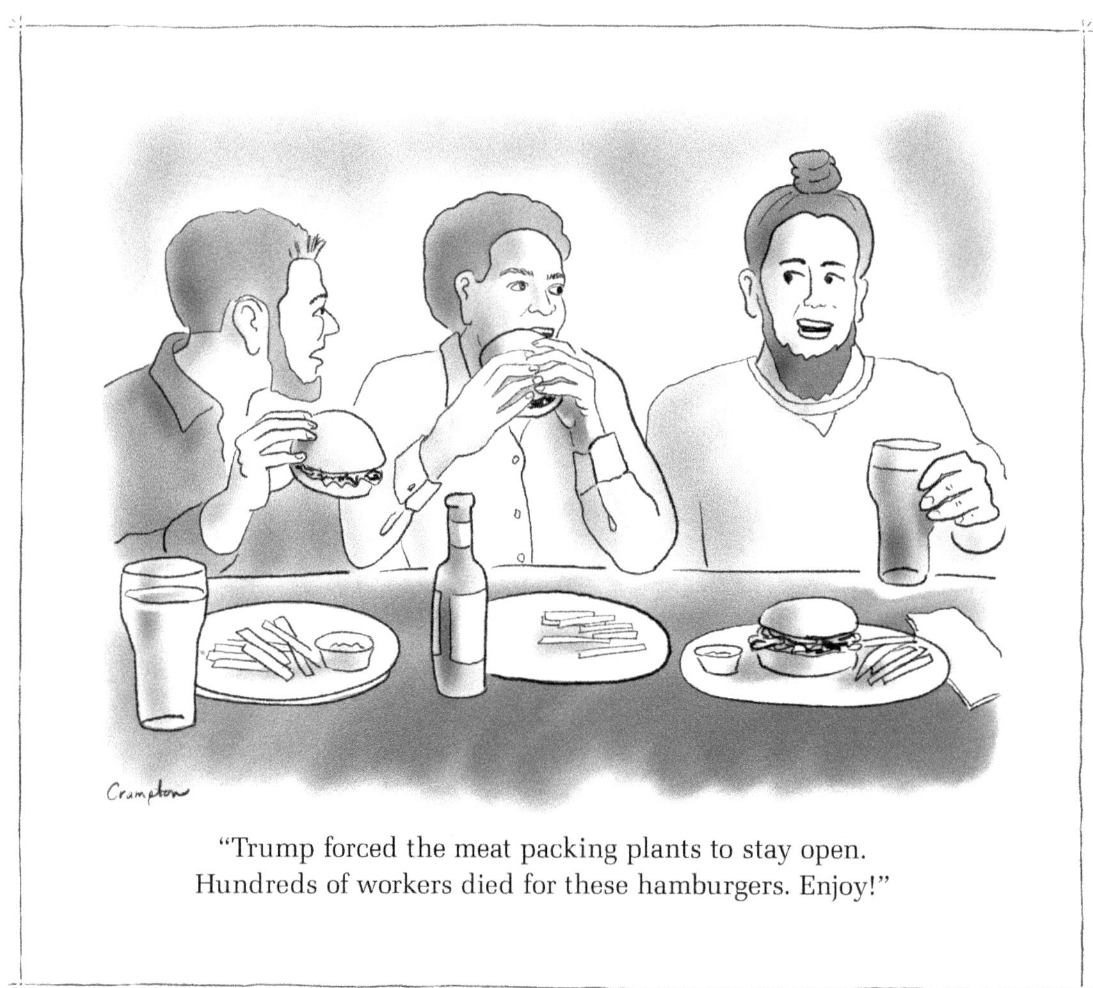

"Trump forced the meat packing plants to stay open. Hundreds of workers died for these hamburgers. Enjoy!"

September 21, 2020
Trump signs an executive order to keep the meat packing plants open—in some cases without testing, or any changes requested by the CDC* task force to ensure safety for the workers.
**Centers for Disease Control and Prevention*

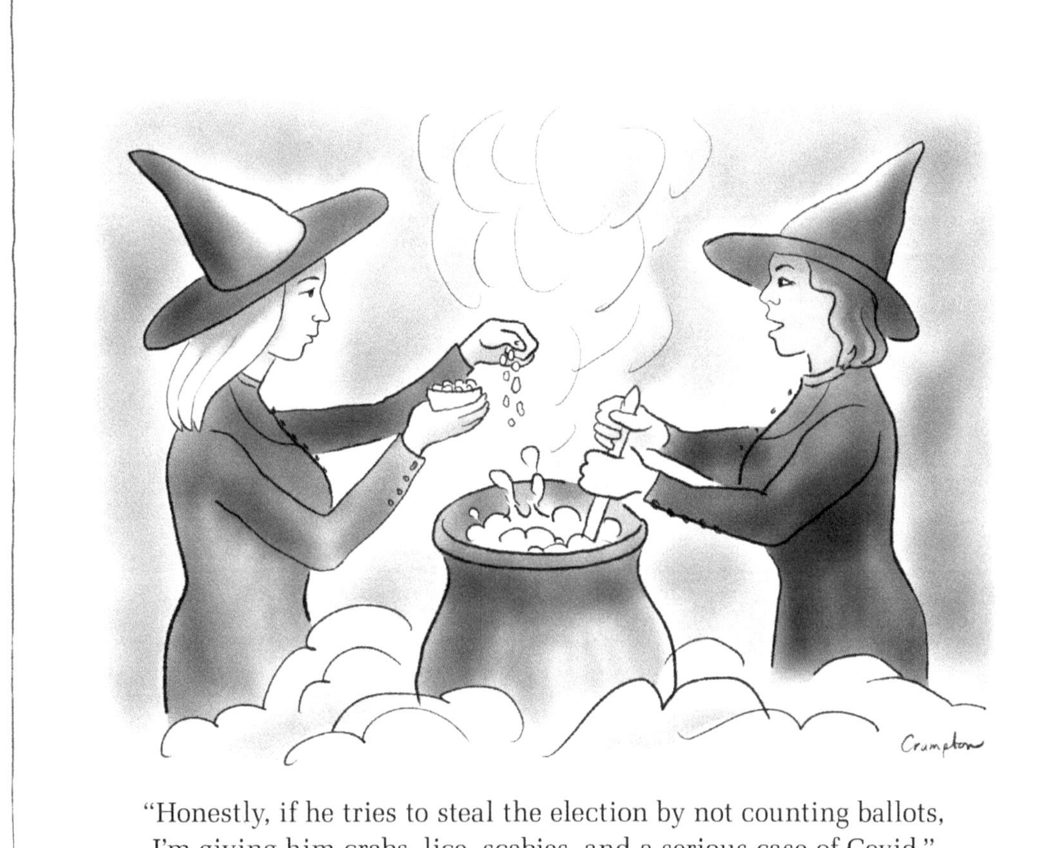

"Honestly, if he tries to steal the election by not counting ballots, I'm giving him crabs, lice, scabies, and a serious case of Covid."

September 24, 2020
Trump insists that the election will not be fair and he may not agree to a transition of power.
He denies intelligence reports that say that Russia is meddling again.
(Note: he did get Covid shortly after this was posted.)

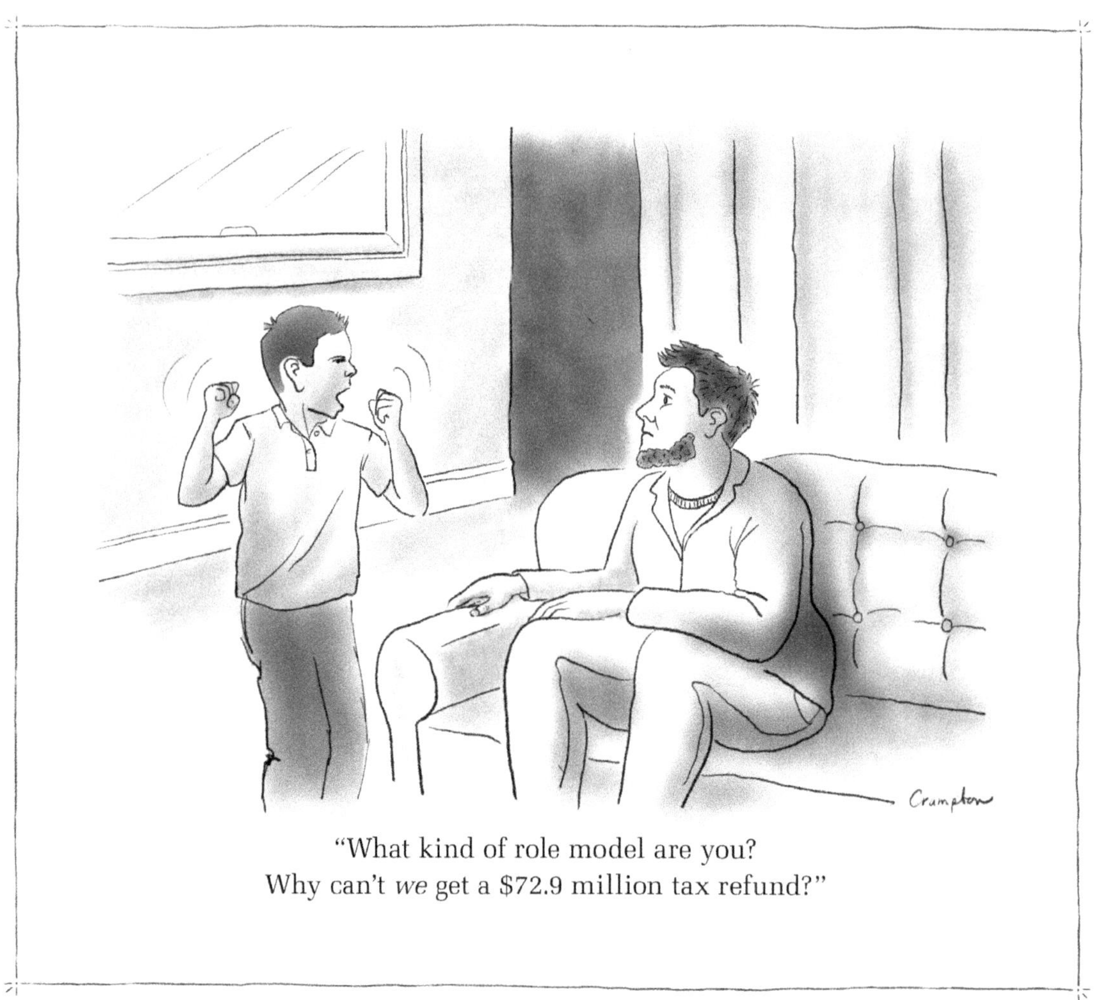

"What kind of role model are you?
Why can't *we* get a $72.9 million tax refund?"

September 20, 2020
The "New York Times" obtains Trump's taxes. He paid $750 a year since he has been president.
In 2010, he received a huge tax refund and said that he "could not believe how stupid the government was for giving someone like him that much money back."

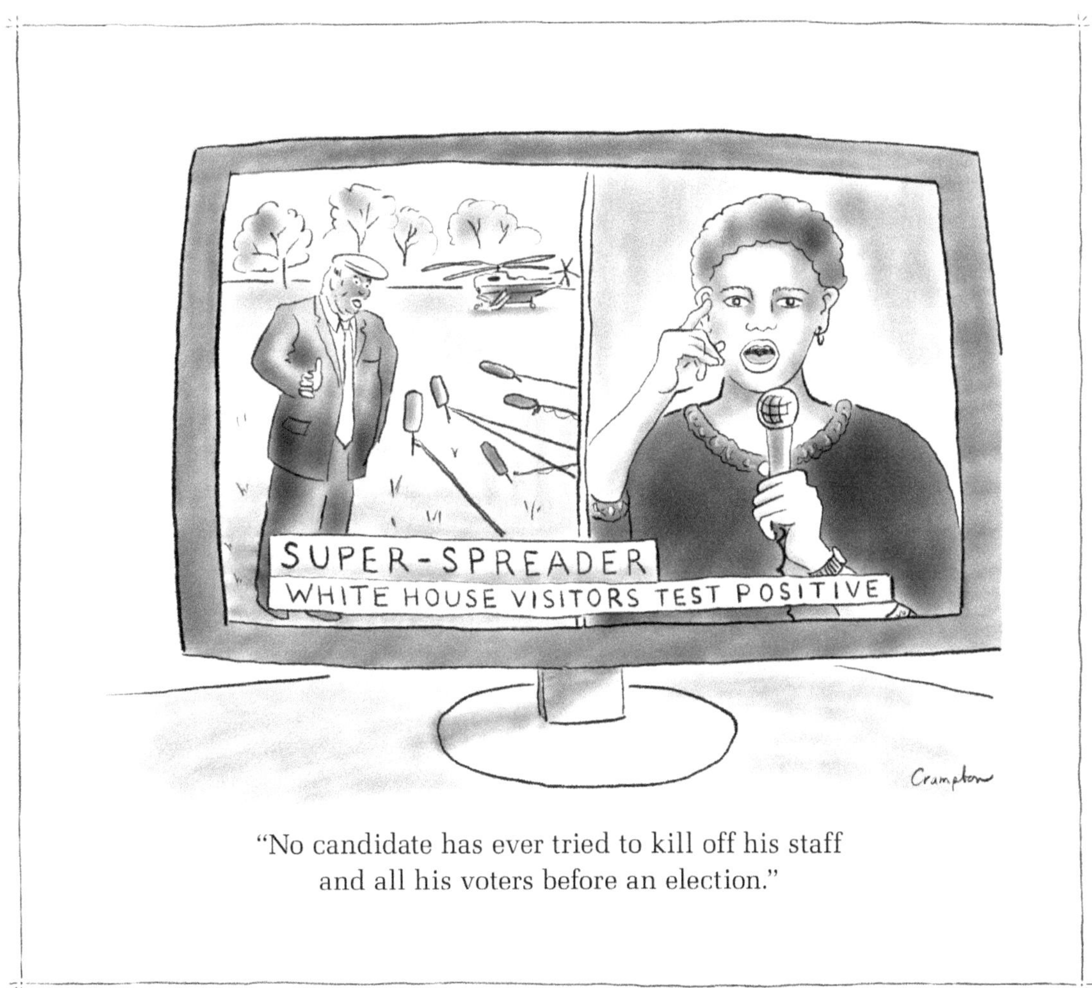

"No candidate has ever tried to kill off his staff and all his voters before an election."

October 8, 2020
Trump had Covid-19 and briefly went to the hospital to receive experimental treatments and oxygen.
He continues to hold rallies without any social distancing or masking, and ridicules journalists for wearing masks.

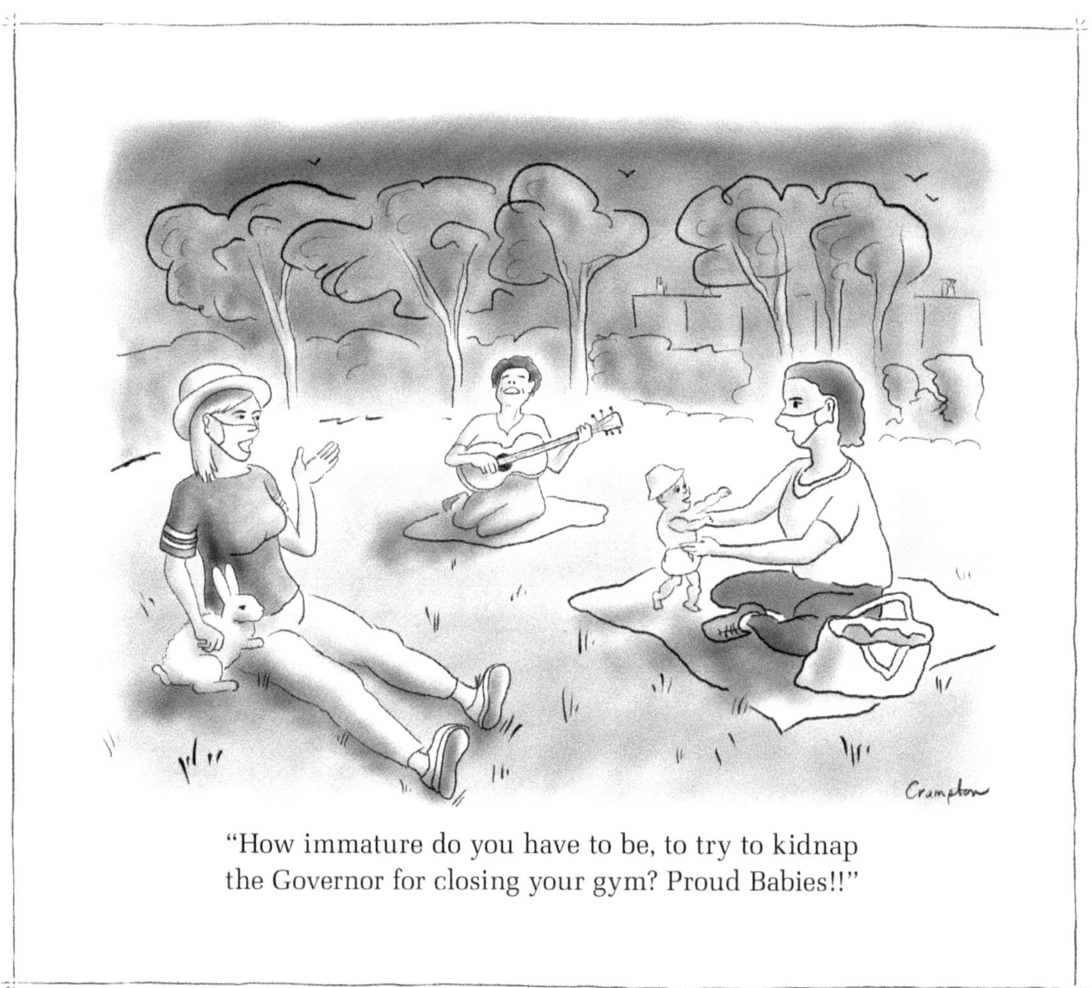

"How immature do you have to be, to try to kidnap the Governor for closing your gym? Proud Babies!!"

October 20, 2020
In the Presidential debate, when asked to denounce white supremacy, Trump asks the militia group "Proud Boys" to "stand back and stand by". The Wolverine Watchmen planned to kidnap Michigan Governor Gretchen Whitmer over her strict lockdown policies. A similar threat was made against the Wichita Mayor, Brandon Whipple.

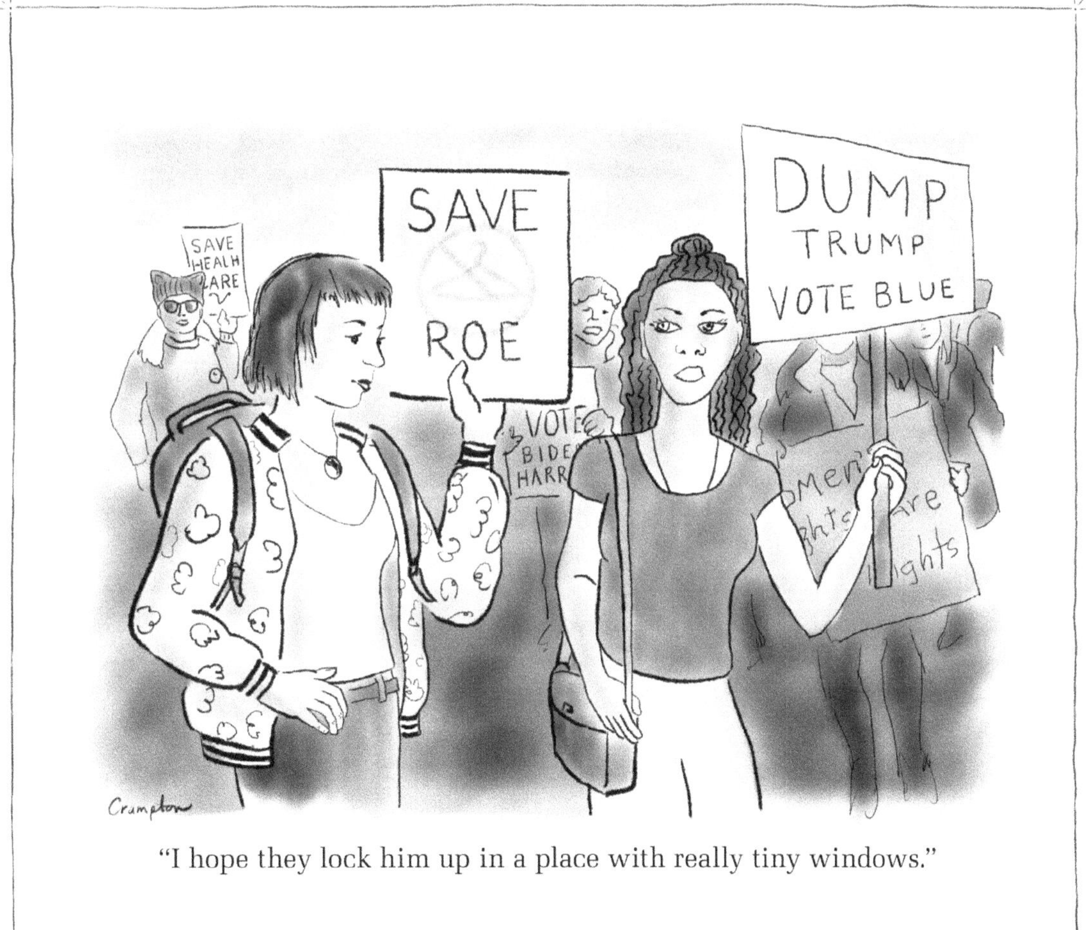

"I hope they lock him up in a place with really tiny windows."

October 23, 2020
During the debate, to answer a question about climate change, Trump claims that Democrats "want to take buildings down because they want to make bigger windows into smaller windows". This is incorrect.

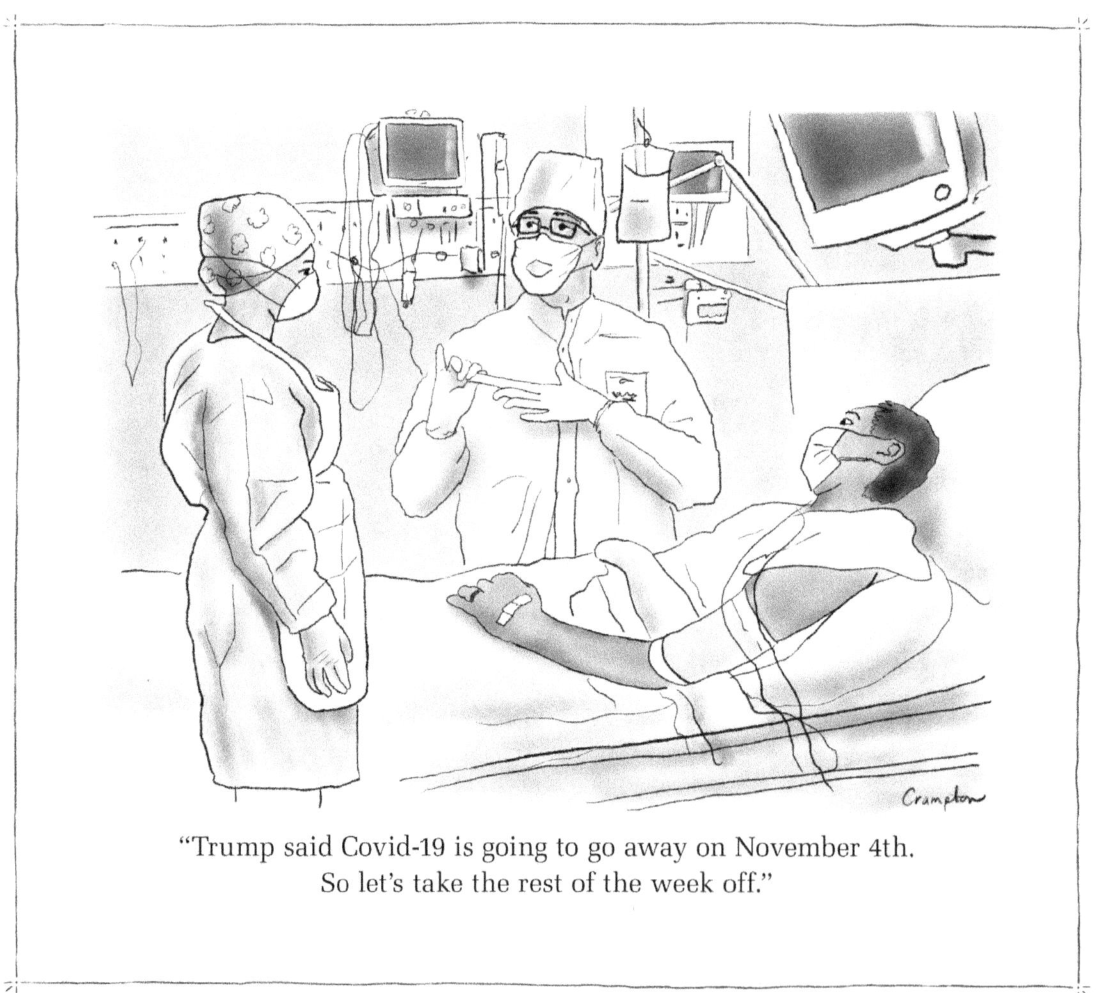

"Trump said Covid-19 is going to go away on November 4th.
So let's take the rest of the week off."

November 4, 2020
Trump stated that Covid-19 was a hoax to win the election. Election ballots are still being counted.
Thanks to @gore_won.

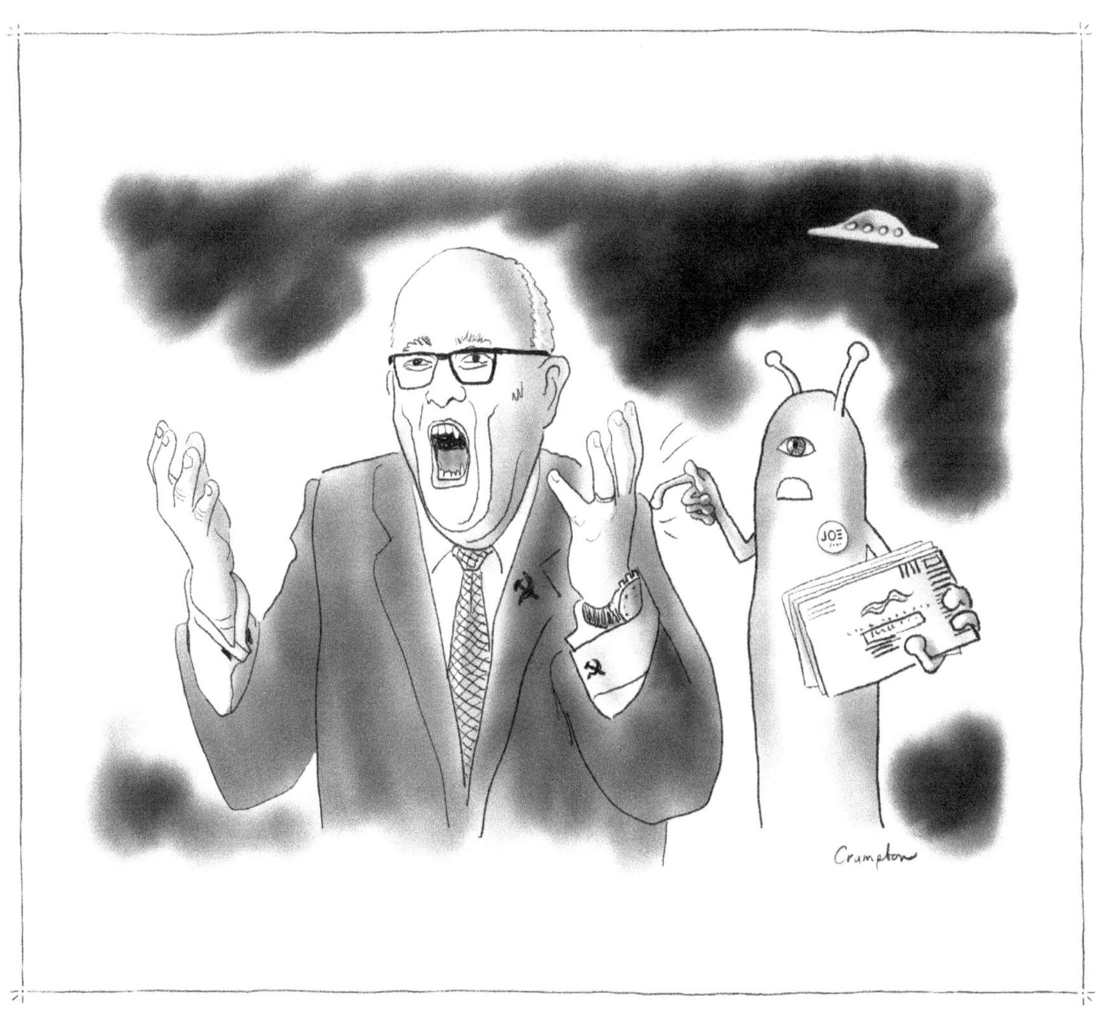

November 6, 2020
The President's lawyer, Rudy Giuliani, claims that ballots marked for Biden came from dead people and from Mars.
(Note: At a Philadelphia rally on 11-04-2020)

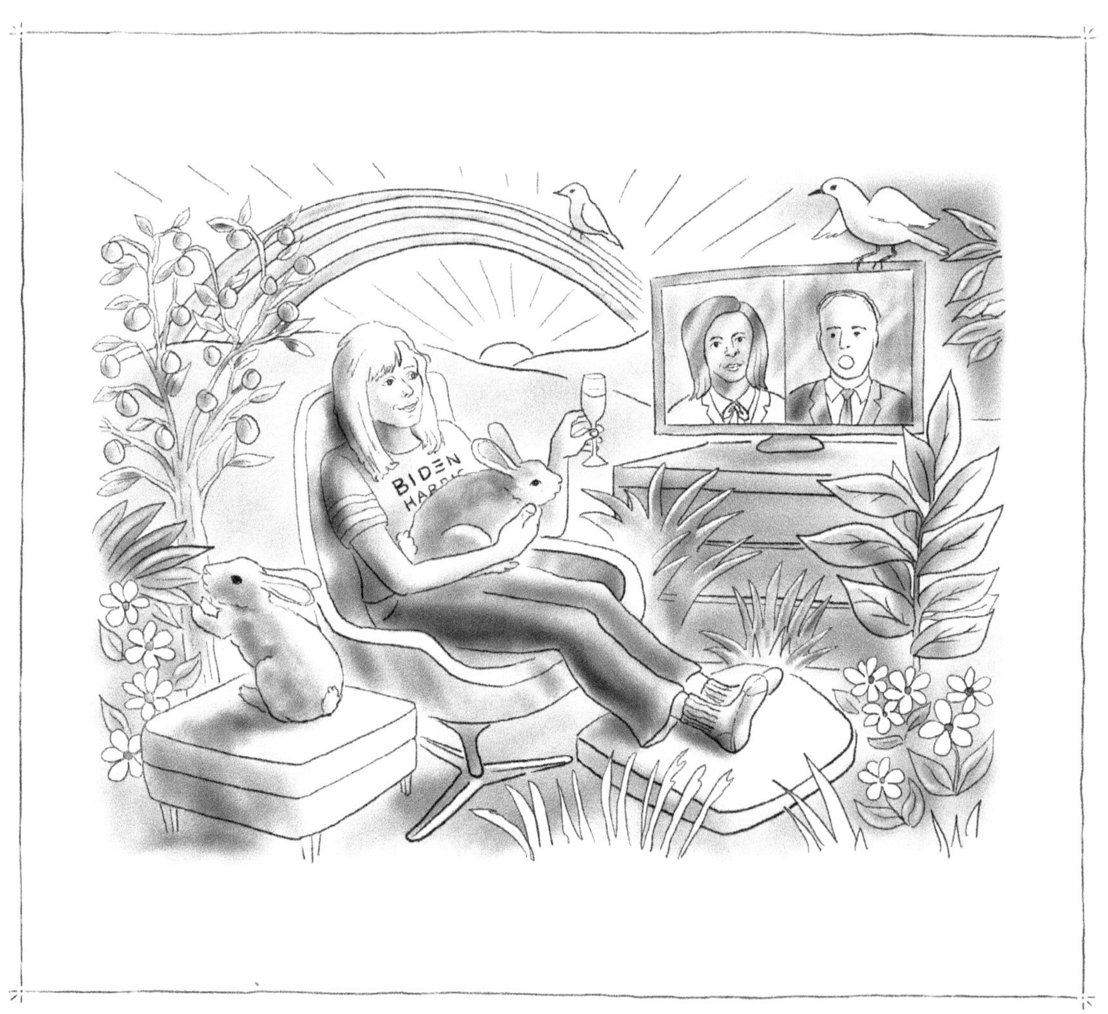

November 11, 2020
It took a few days to count all the mail-in ballots. Many Democrats voted by mail in order to socially distance. Biden/Harris won the Electoral College and won the popular vote by 7 million more votes.

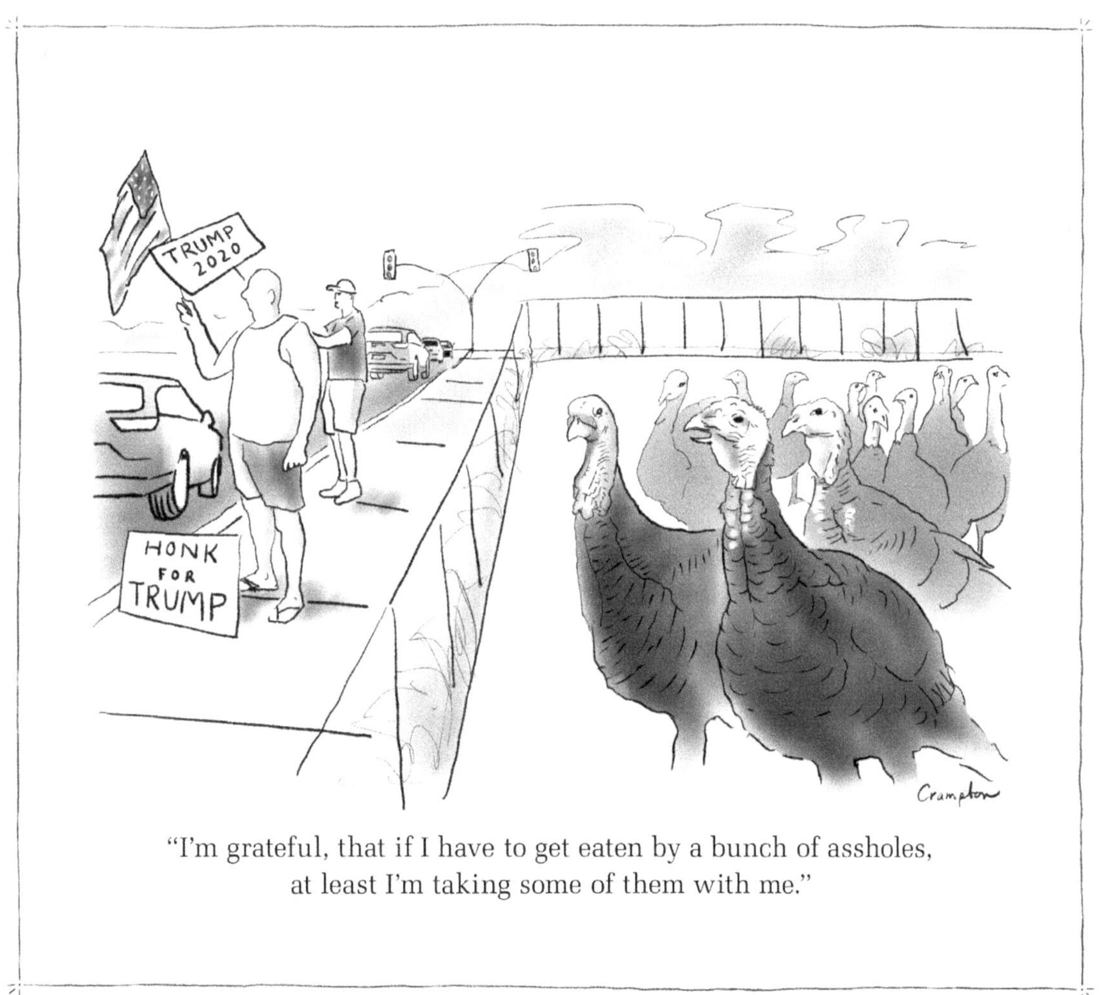

"I'm grateful, that if I have to get eaten by a bunch of assholes, at least I'm taking some of them with me."

November 18, 2020
The CDC urges folks not to have traditional Thanksgiving gatherings, but many people expect to travel around the country and dine indoors anyway. *Your cartoonist is a life-long vegetarian.*

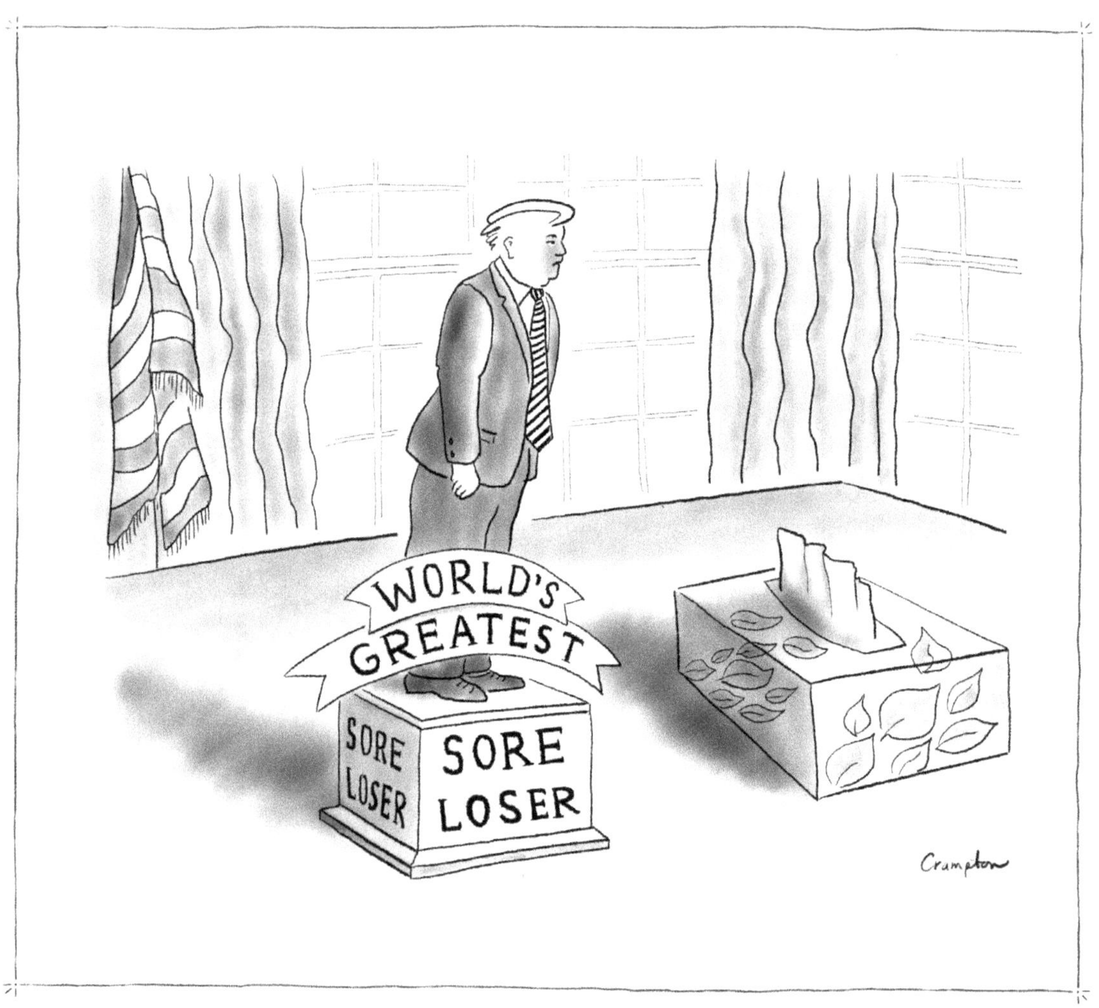

November 11, 2020
More than a week after Biden's victory, Trump will still not concede. He's holding up the transition process. Most Republican politicians remain silent about this.

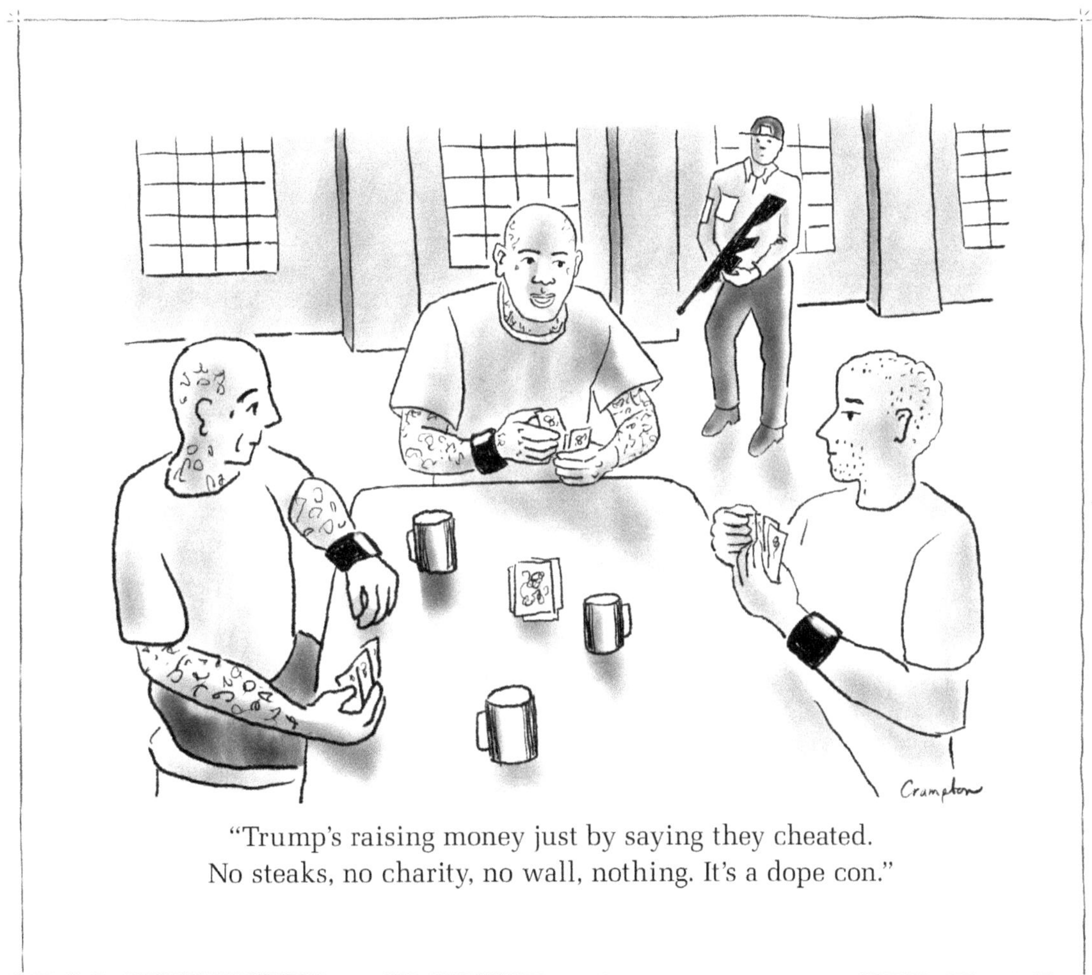

"Trump's raising money just by saying they cheated.
No steaks, no charity, no wall, nothing. It's a dope con."

December 3, 2020
Trump raised $170,000,000 since the election by denying that he lost. He refuses to concede and accuses Democrats of "ballot-harvesting" or dumping ballots.

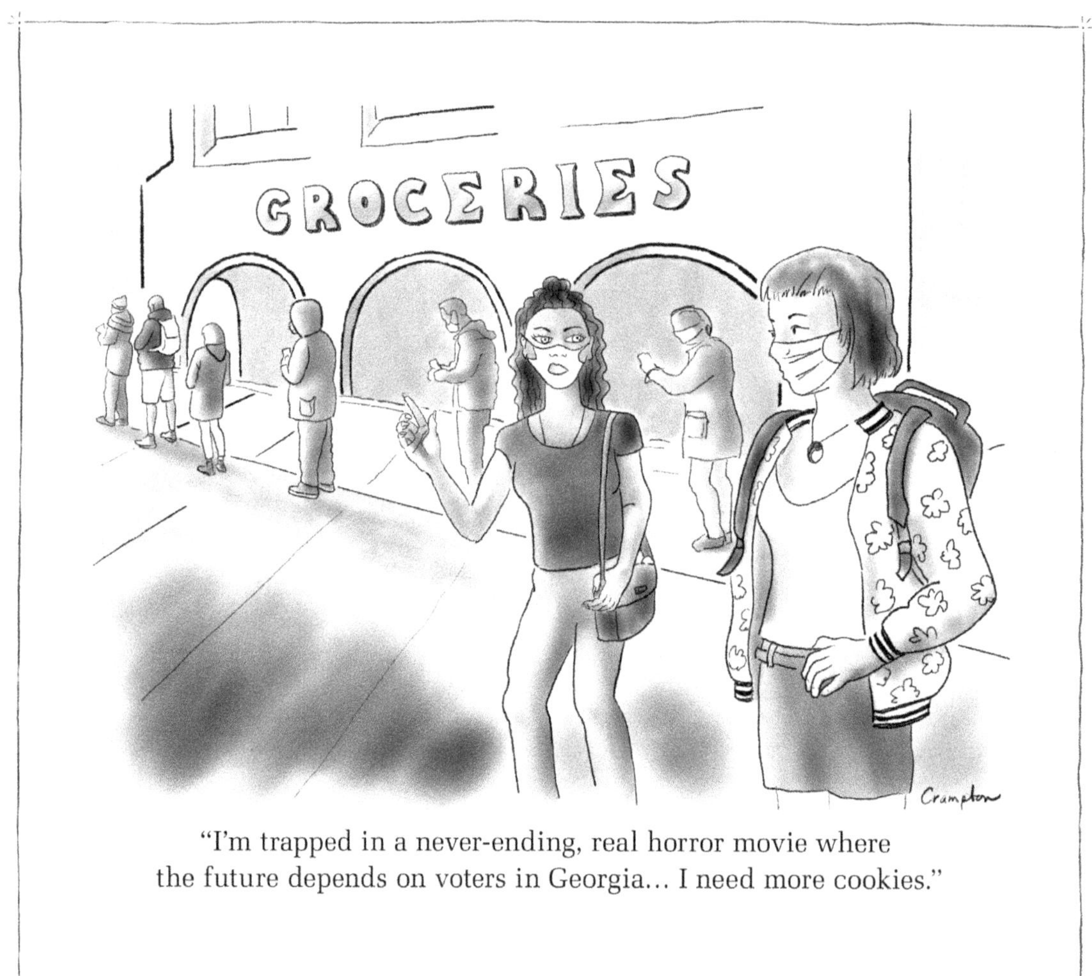

"I'm trapped in a never-ending, real horror movie where the future depends on voters in Georgia… I need more cookies."

December 11, 2020
Trump filed at least sixty cases to turn over the election. Texas sued the border States and 17 State Attorney Generals, and 105 Congress-people signed on. The Supreme Court refused to hear the case. All eyes are on two Senate runoff races in Georgia which will determine who wins the Senate.

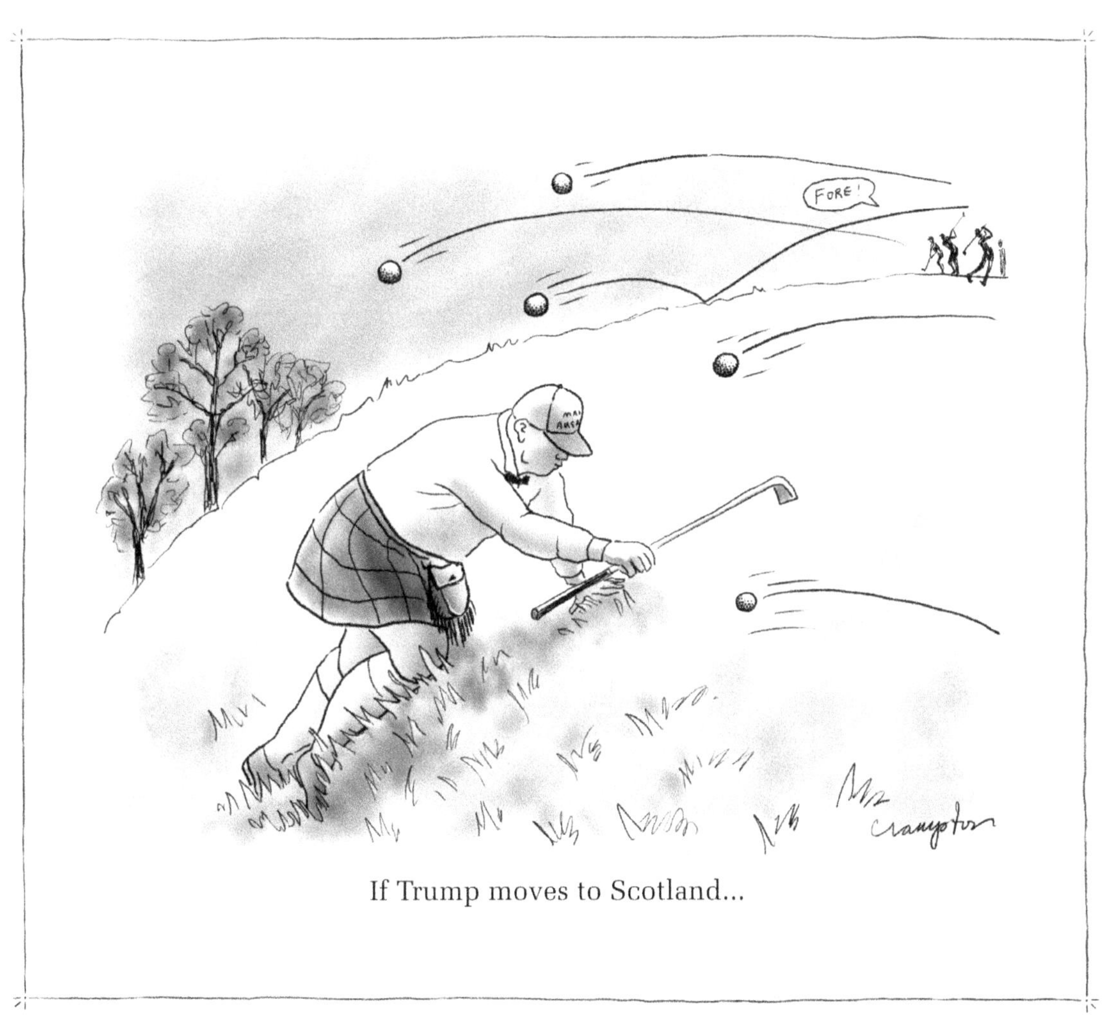

If Trump moves to Scotland...

December 18, 2020
Thinking about where Trump could move now that he will be leaving the White House.

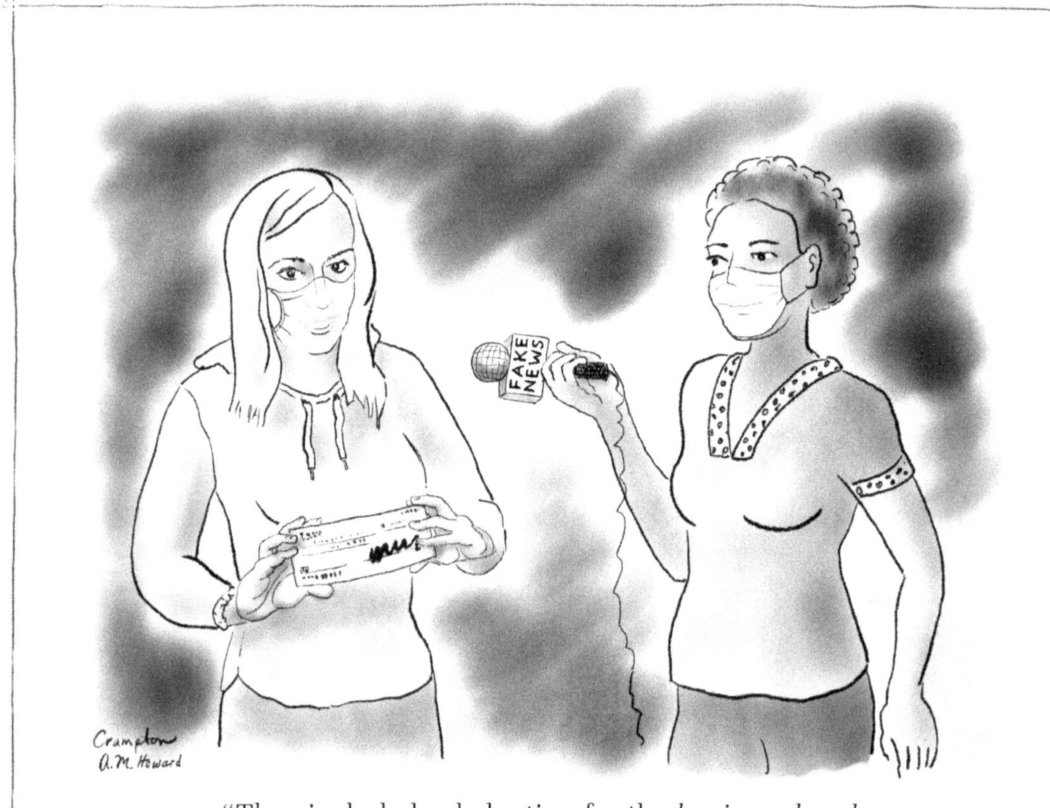

"They included a deduction for the *business lunch*, so with my $600, I'm going to buy a three-martini lunch, talk about unemployment, and then write it off."

December 25, 2020
The government plans to send out $600 pandemic relief checks to all Americans. Trump's signature will be on it.
Written by, and features the likeness of A. M. Howard.

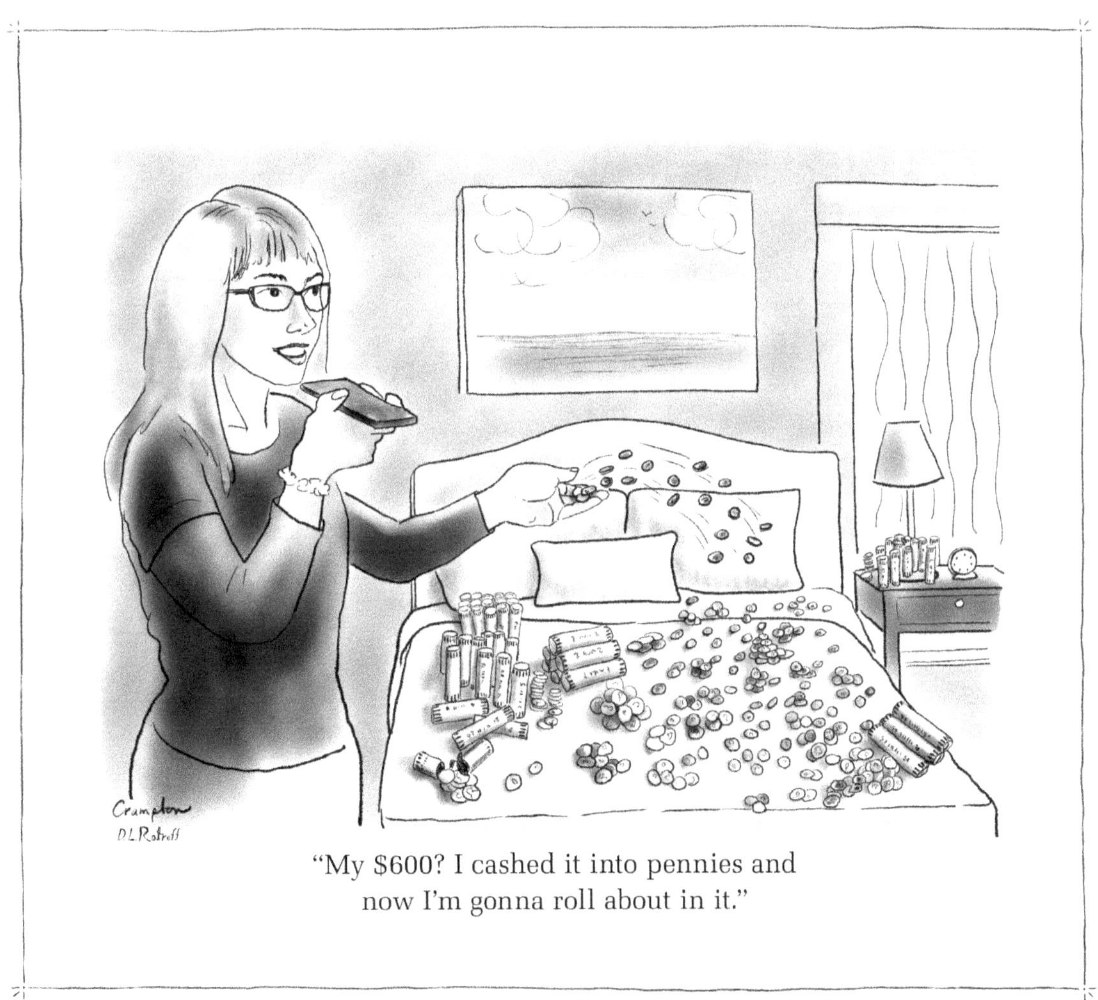

"My $600? I cashed it into pennies and now I'm gonna roll about in it."

December 25, 2020
The government plans to send out $600 pandemic relief checks to all Americans.
Written by, and features the likeness of D. L. Ratroff.

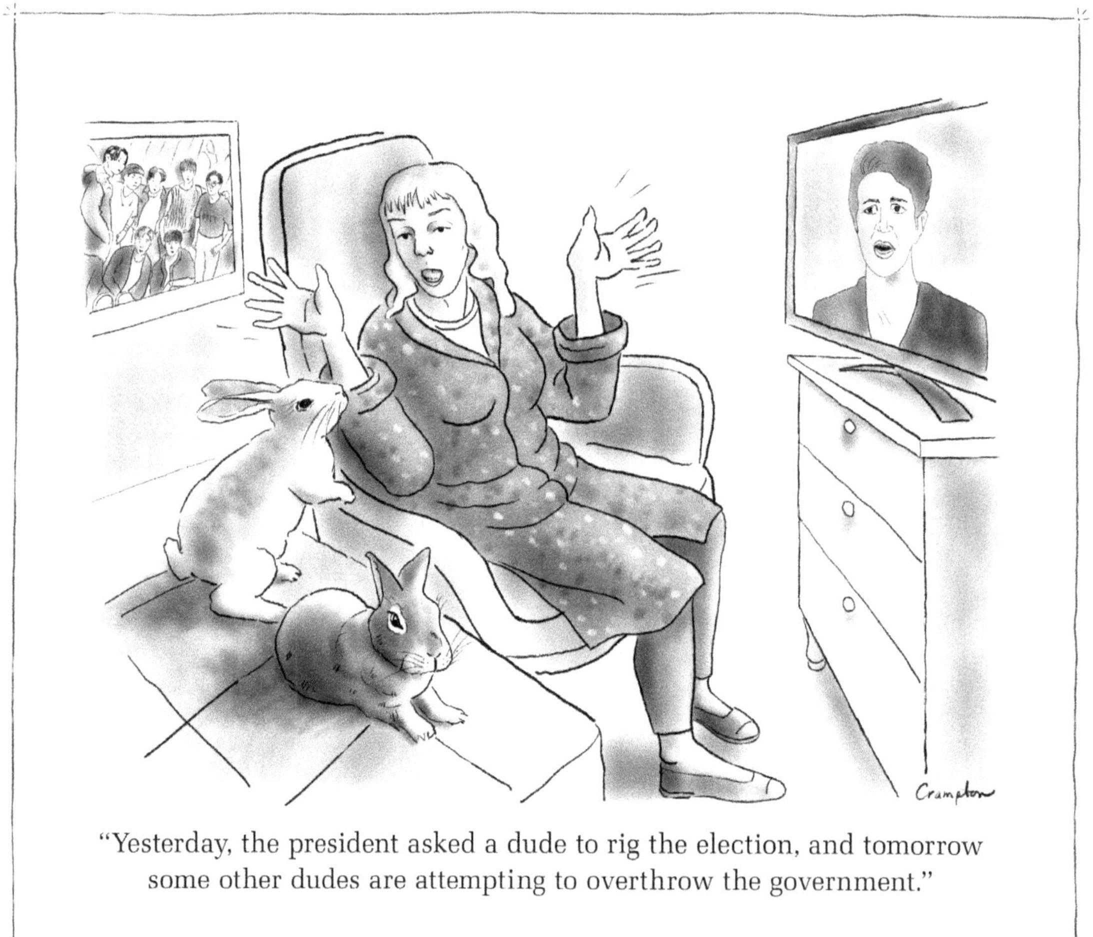

"Yesterday, the president asked a dude to rig the election, and tomorrow some other dudes are attempting to overthrow the government."

January 6, 2021
Drawn and posted the night before the mob invaded the Capitol. Those on the social media app Parler, knew "It will be wild". *(Note: 174 Capitol Police were beaten or injured. Five people died. Four officers later committed suicide. Two pipe bombs failed to go off. A gallows was carried and rioters chanted "Hang Mike Pence".)*

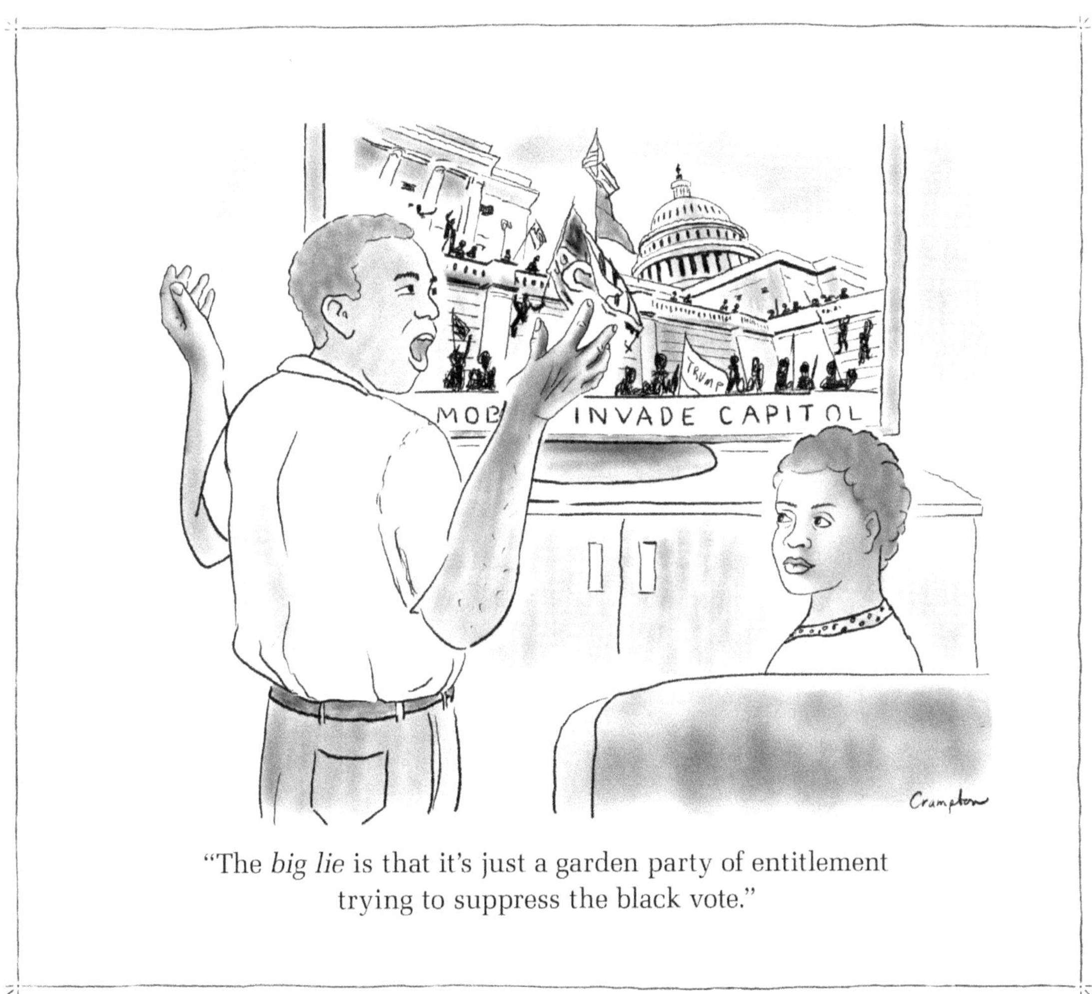

"The *big lie* is that it's just a garden party of entitlement trying to suppress the black vote."

January 14, 2020
Trump circulates "The Big Lie", accusing Democrats of election fraud. White Capitol rioters were allowed to simply go home. Black Lives Protesters were treated harshly last summer. Republicans said that it was just a tourist visit and that Antifa caused the violence. The House adopts an article of Impeachment against Trump for Incitement of Insurrection.

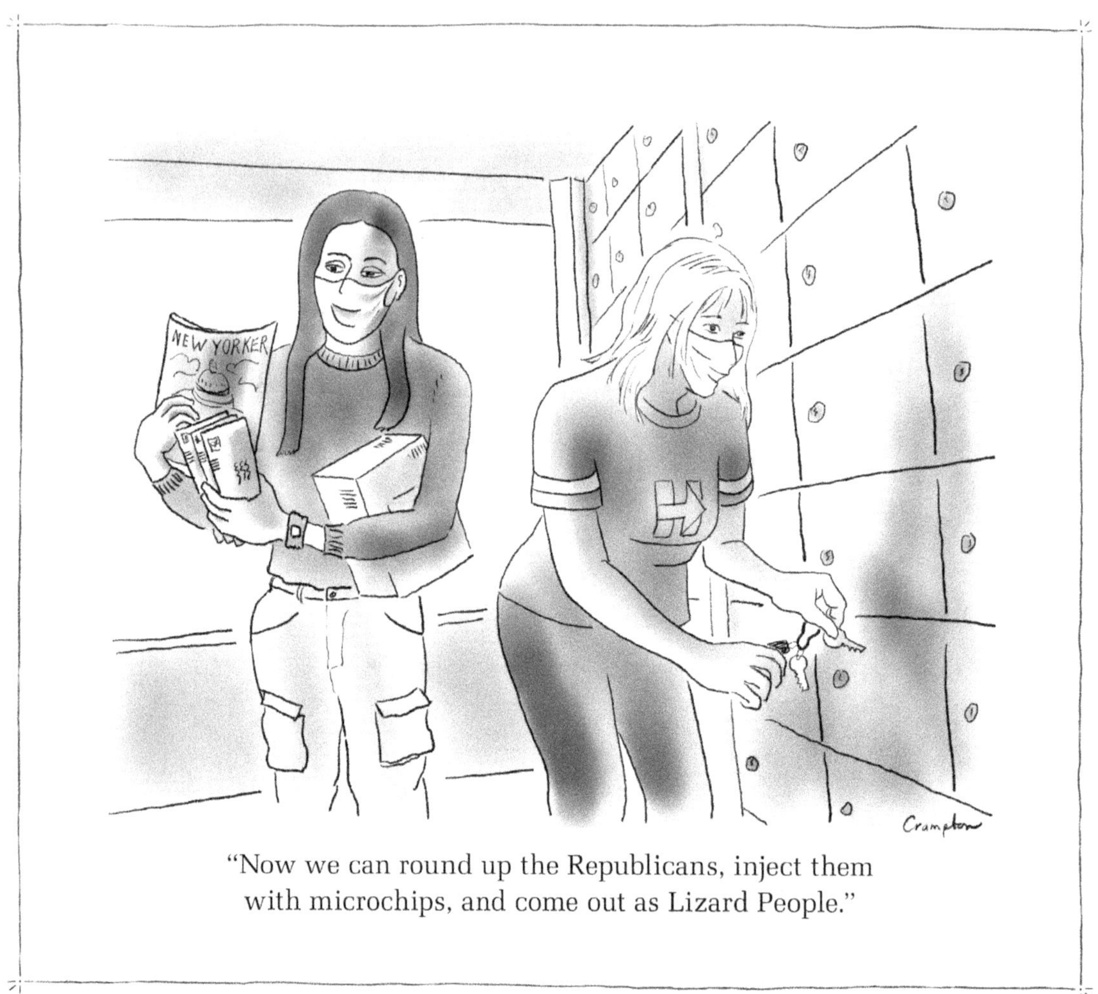

"Now we can round up the Republicans, inject them with microchips, and come out as Lizard People."

January 19, 2020
It appears that Joe Biden will be inaugurated as the 46th President on January 20th. Republicans joke online about Democrats rounding them up, taking their guns, injecting them with a suspicious vaccine–and worse. Did you look up QAnon?

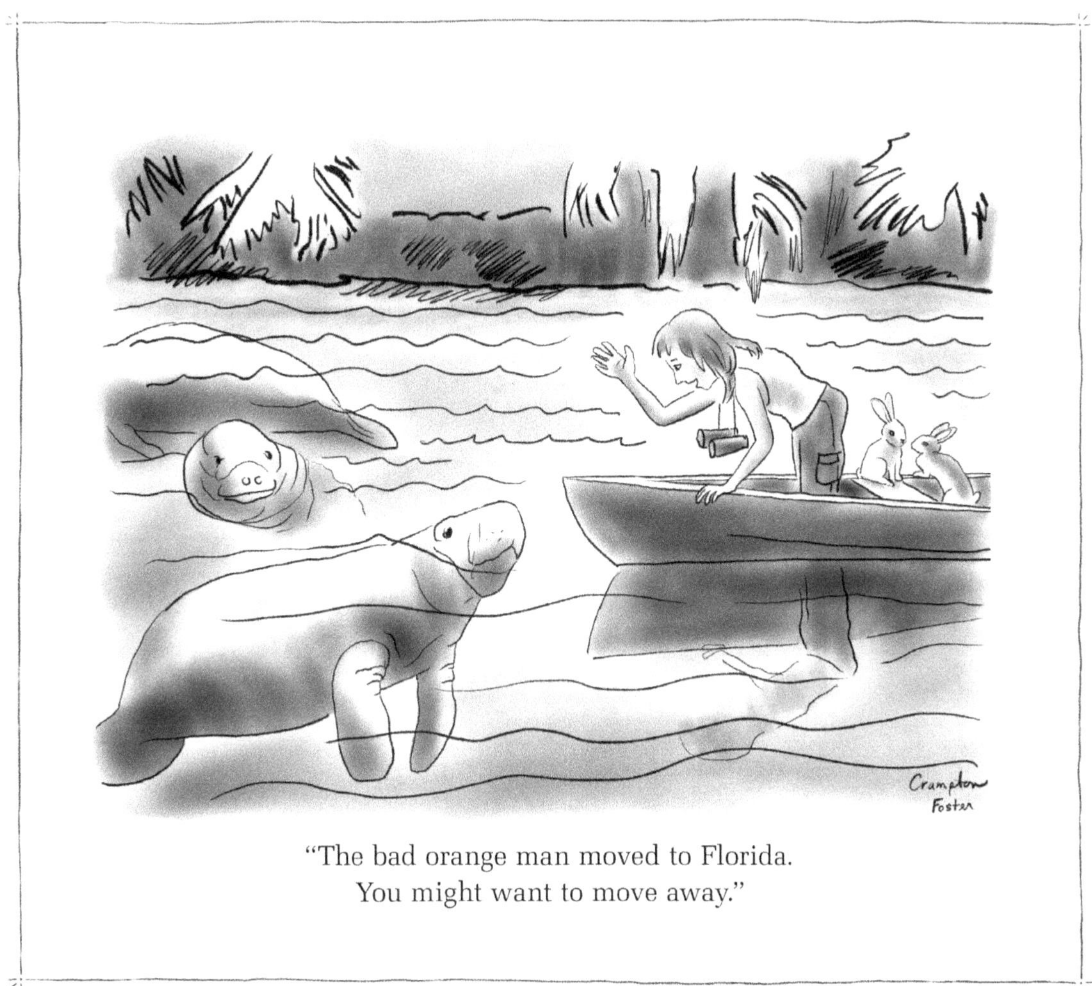

"The bad orange man moved to Florida.
You might want to move away."

January 27, 2021
A photo circulates on social media of a live manatee with the word "TRUMP" incised on it's skin.
A second Trump Impeachment Trial is underway. *Thanks to Michael Foster.*

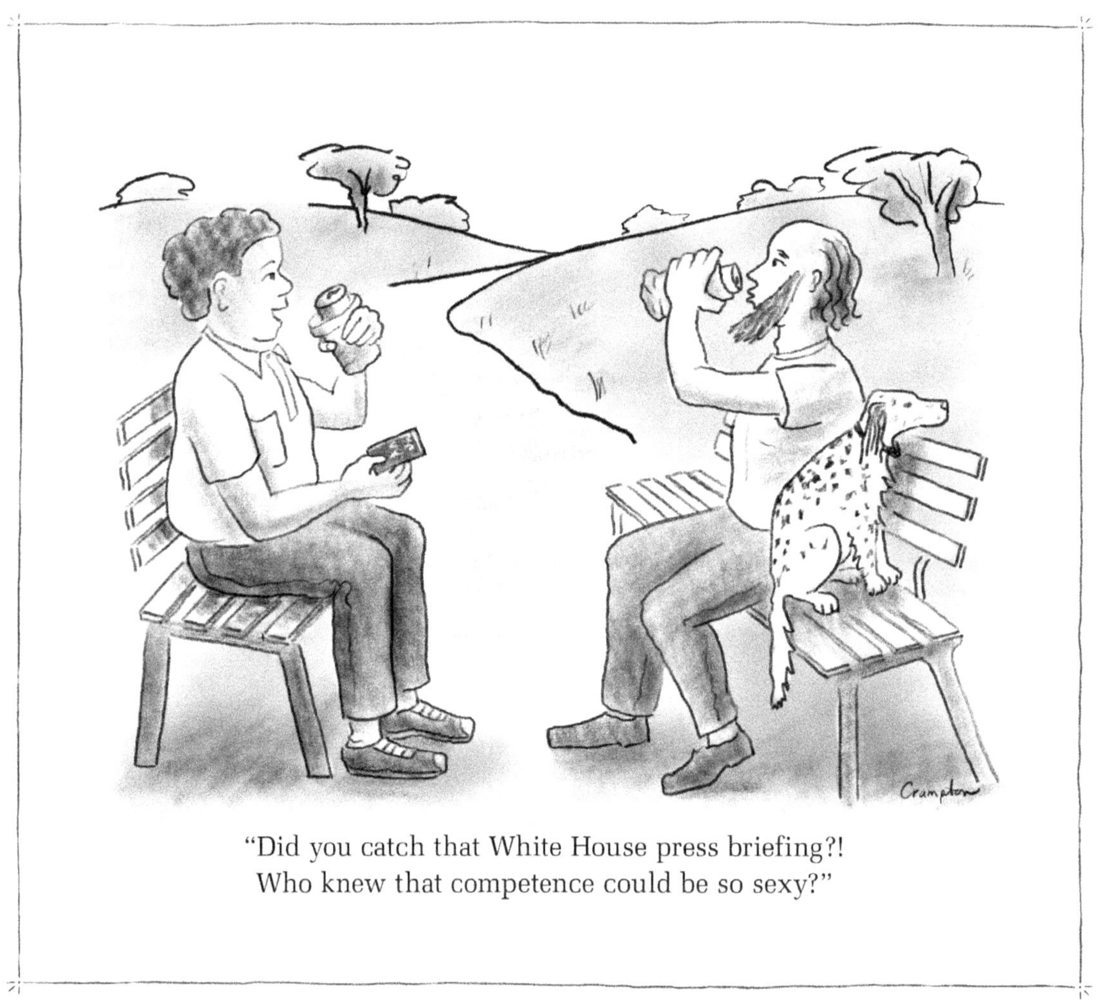

"Did you catch that White House press briefing?!
Who knew that competence could be so sexy?"

January 29, 2021
The Biden administration begins regular, normal press briefings with an articulate and prepared press secretary, Jen Psaki. Everything about the briefings seems so strangely calm.

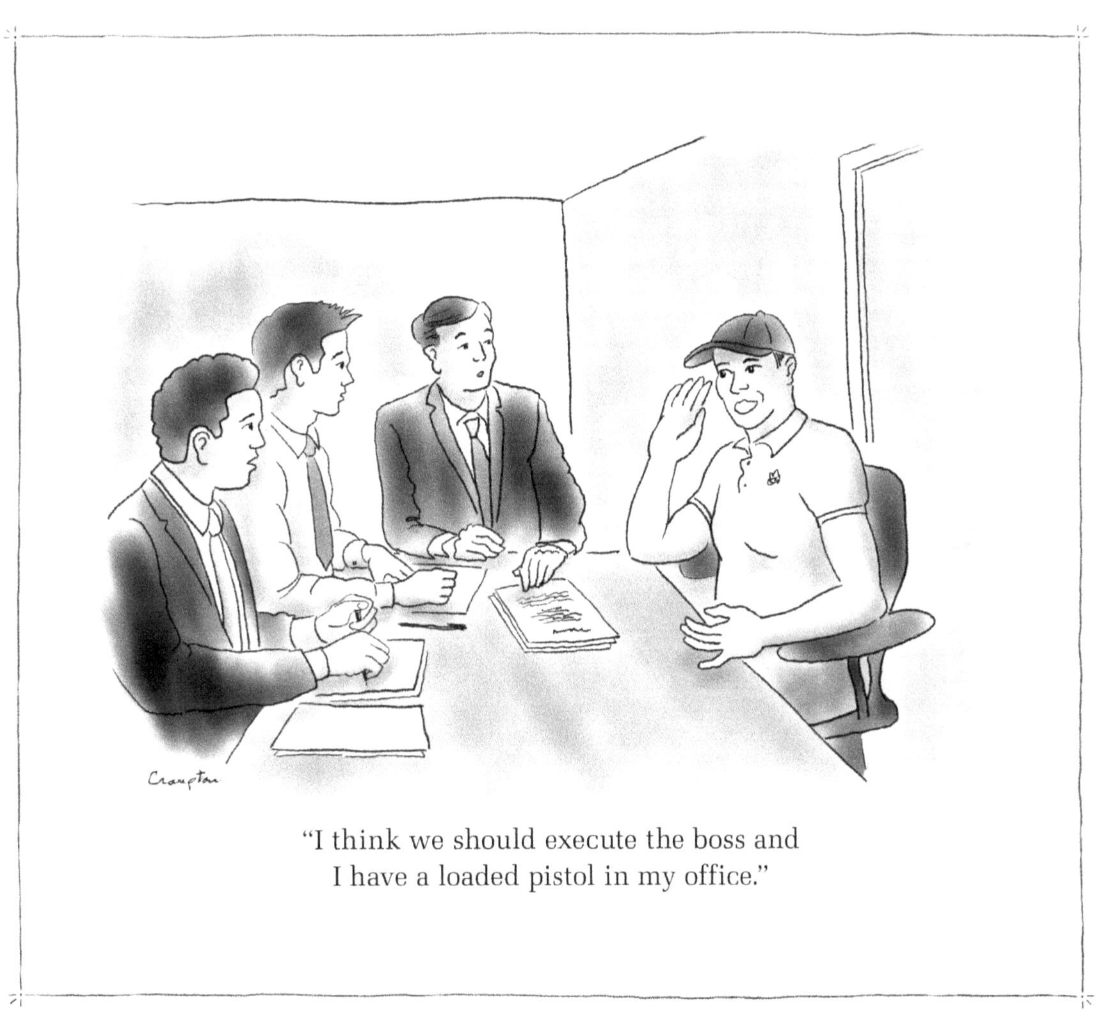

"I think we should execute the boss and
I have a loaded pistol in my office."

February 4, 2021
Republicans bypass the new metal detectors in the Capitol. Representative Andy Harris tries to carry a gun onto the House floor. Majority Leader, Nancy Pelosi, proposes stiff fines. In 2019, before she was elected to the House, Marjorie Taylor Greene called Pelosi a traitor who deserved execution.

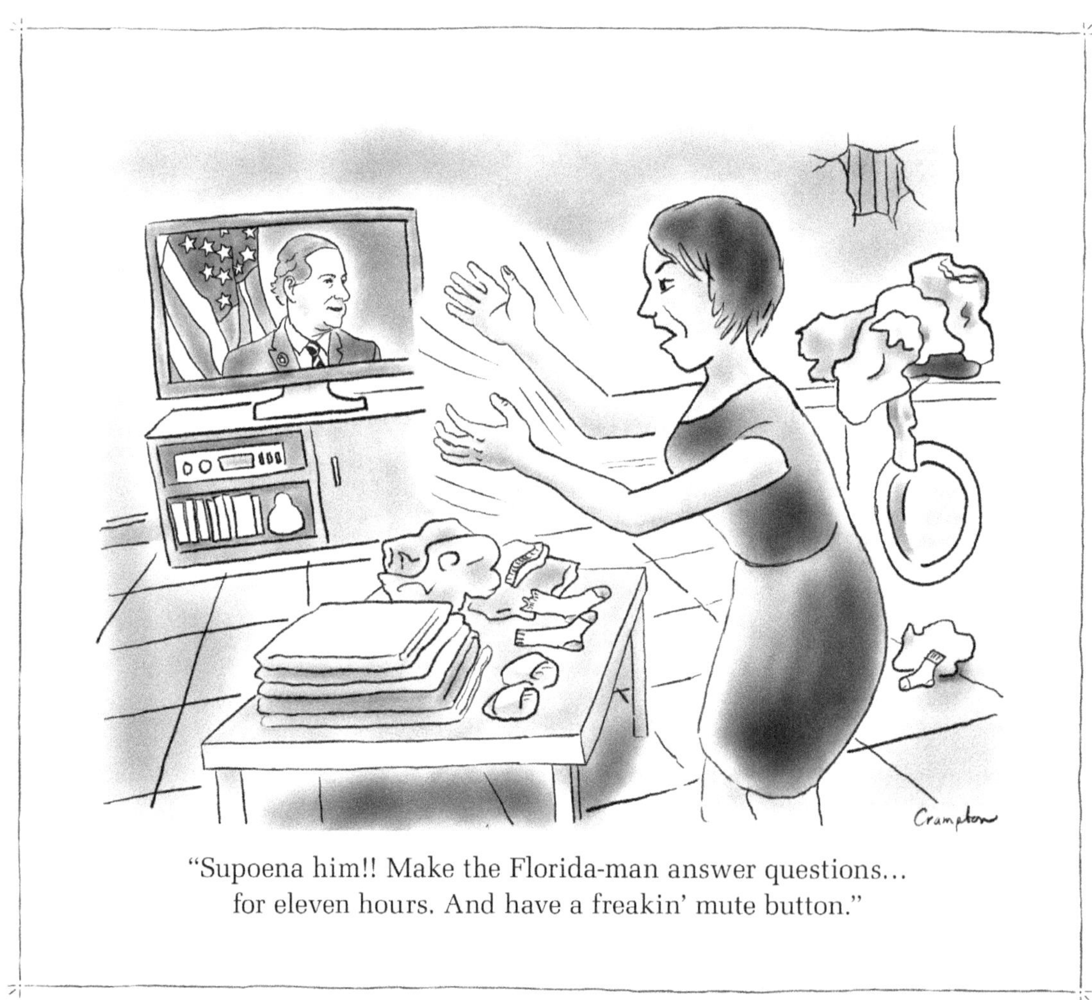

"Supoena him!! Make the Florida-man answer questions...
for eleven hours. And have a freakin' mute button."

February 8, 2021
This was inspired by my desire to watch Trump grilled by Congress. Hillary Clinton, as Secretary of State, testified for eleven hours about the attack on Benghazi, Libya.

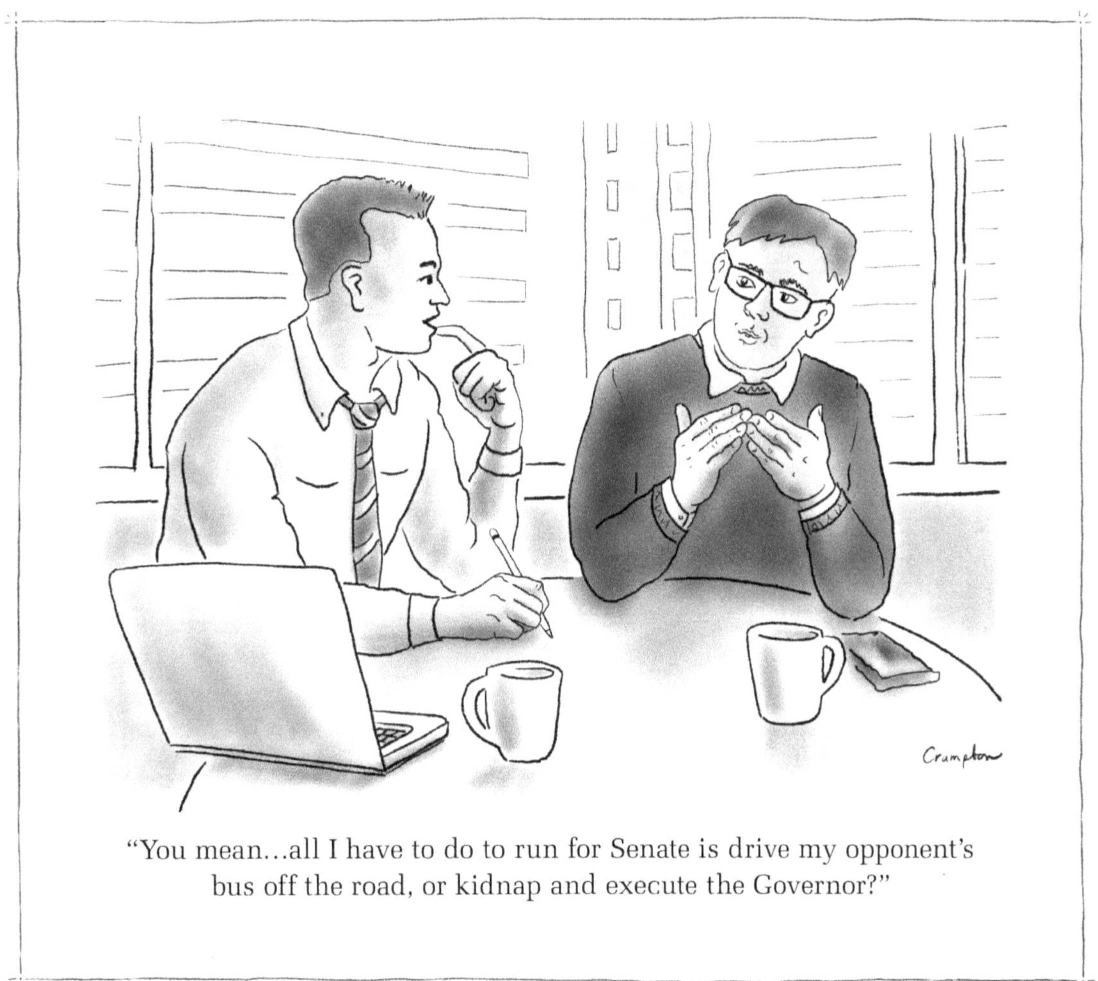

"You mean...all I have to do to run for Senate is drive my opponent's bus off the road, or kidnap and execute the Governor?"

February 11, 2021
Senate Republicans voted not to impeach President Trump. Earlier, a militia planned to kidnap and execute Governor Whitmer. In October, a 50-vehicle "Trump Train" aggressively harassed and rammed a Biden/Harris campaign bus in Texas causing them to cancel events.

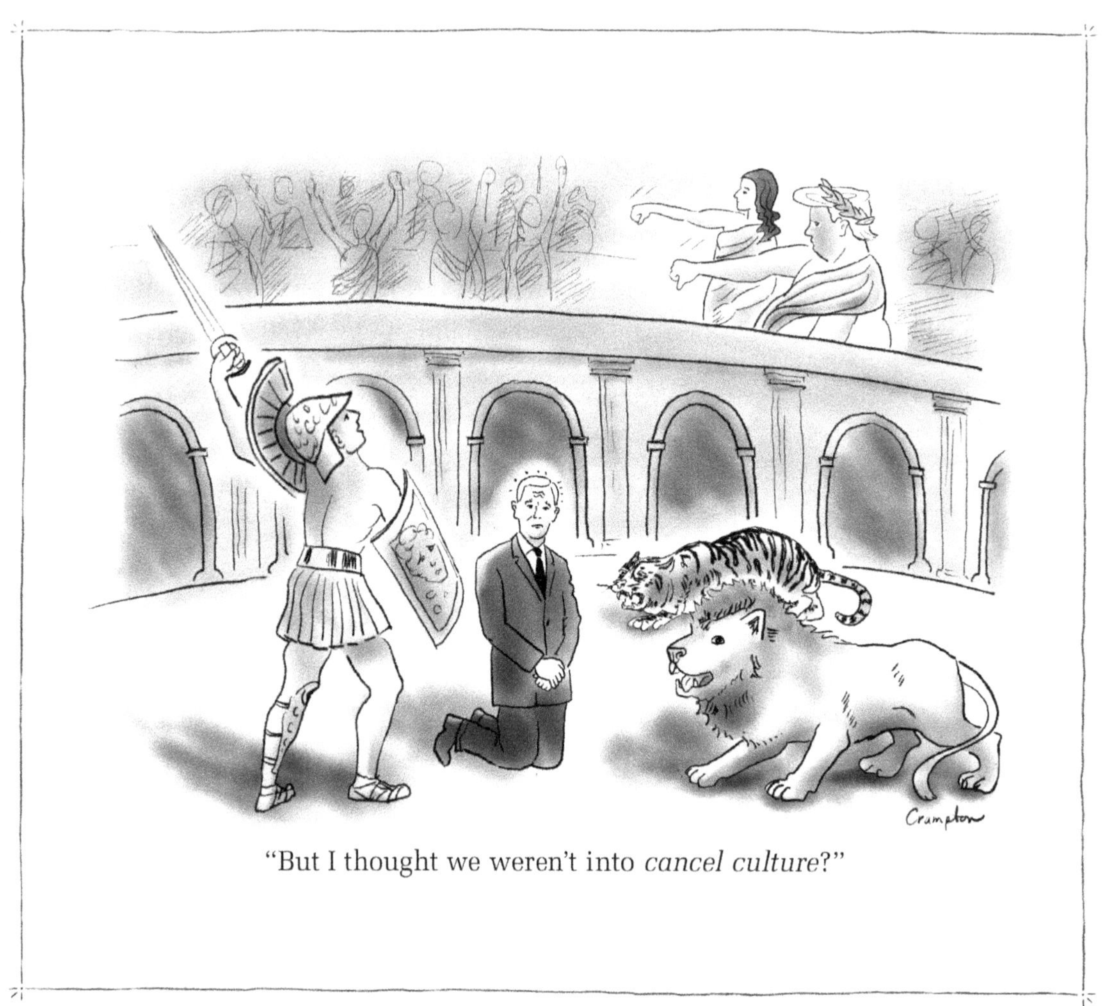

"But I thought we weren't into *cancel culture*?"

February 15, 2021
Republicans complain that Democrats practice "cancel culture". This seems hypocritical, since we learned in the Impeachment Trial that the mob came within a minute of reaching and possibly lynching Vice President Pence.

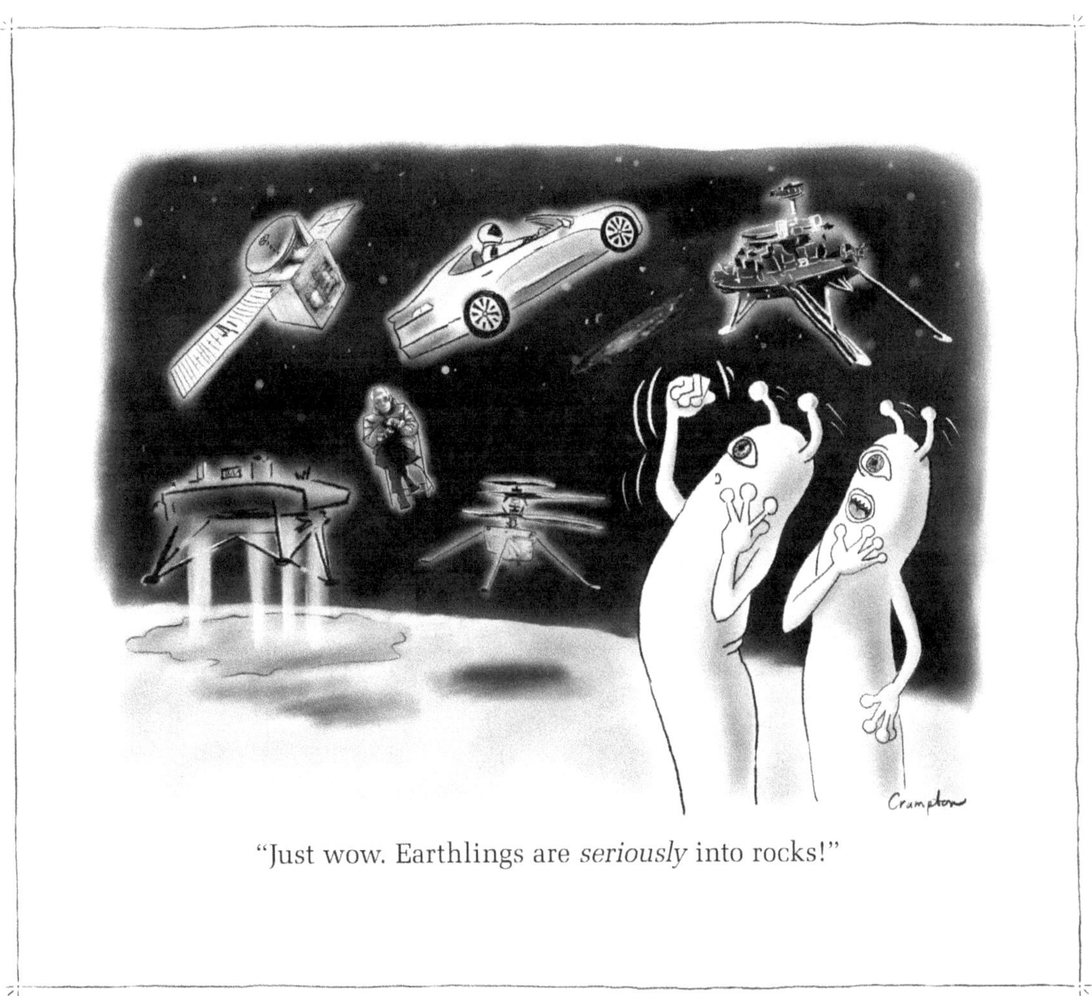

"Just wow. Earthlings are *seriously* into rocks!"

February 26, 2012
In one week, China, the U.A.E., and the U.S.A., all sent missions to Mars. The U.S.A. landed a rover with a drone on the surface. This drawing includes the Tesla car sent to Mars, and the Bernie-Sanders-with-mittens meme.

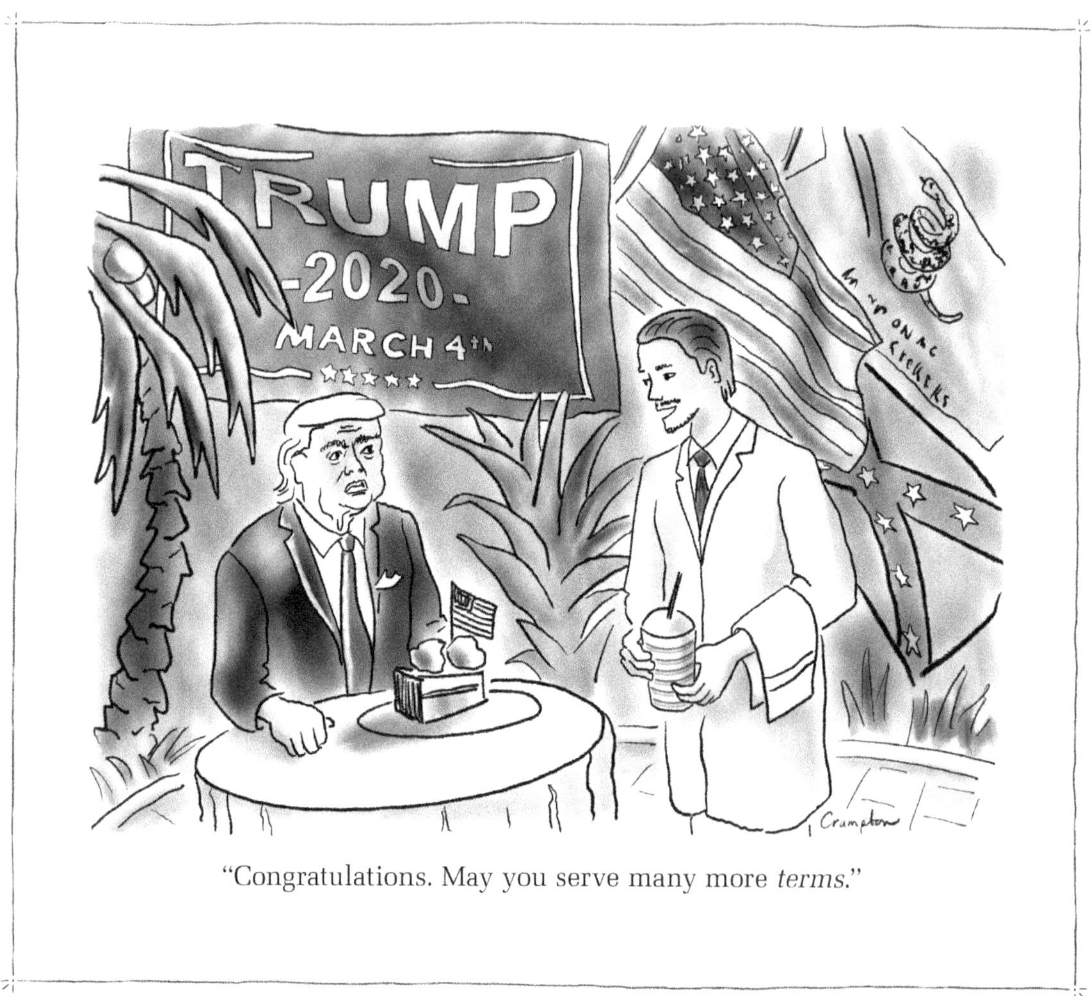

"Congratulations. May you serve many more *terms*."

March 5, 2021
QAnon predicted that on March 4th, Trump would be inaugurated for a second term, after right-wing extremists blow up the Capitol. The House of Representatives did not to come to work on March 4th.

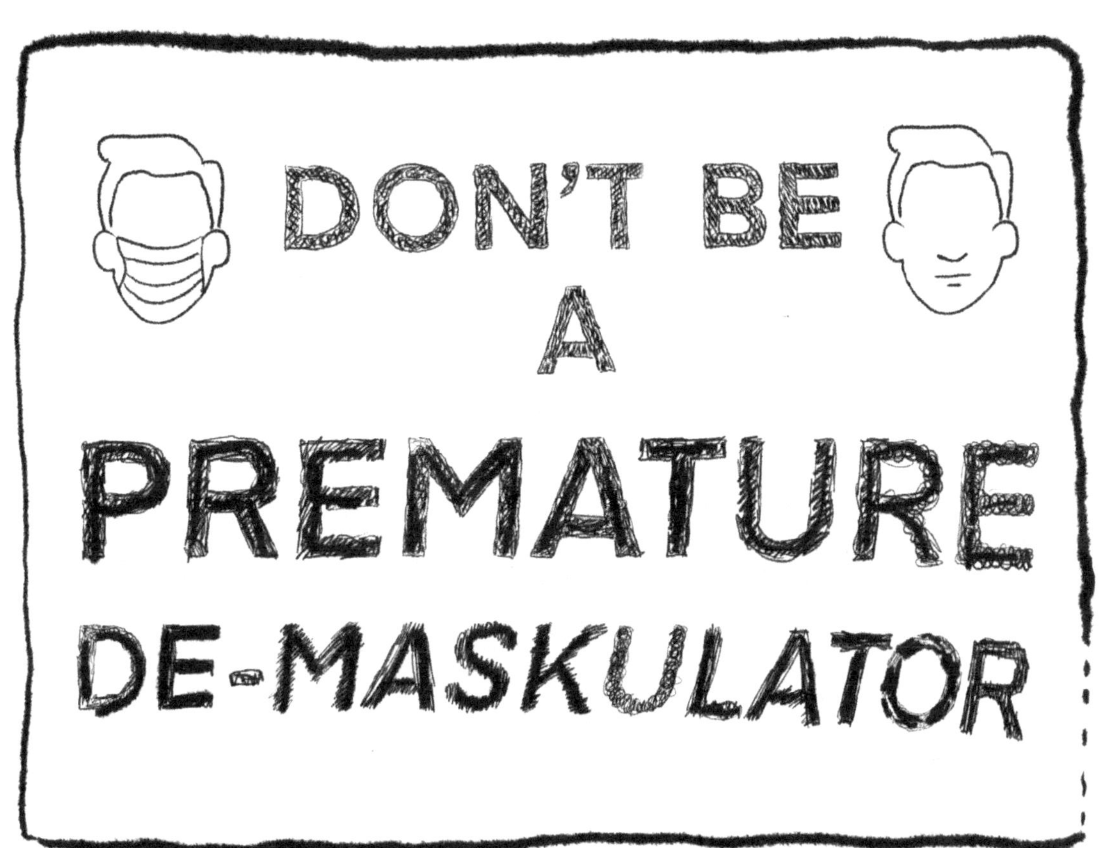

March 10, 2021
People in most States can't seem to keep their masks on, even for one more month, during the race to vaccinate. States are opening up.

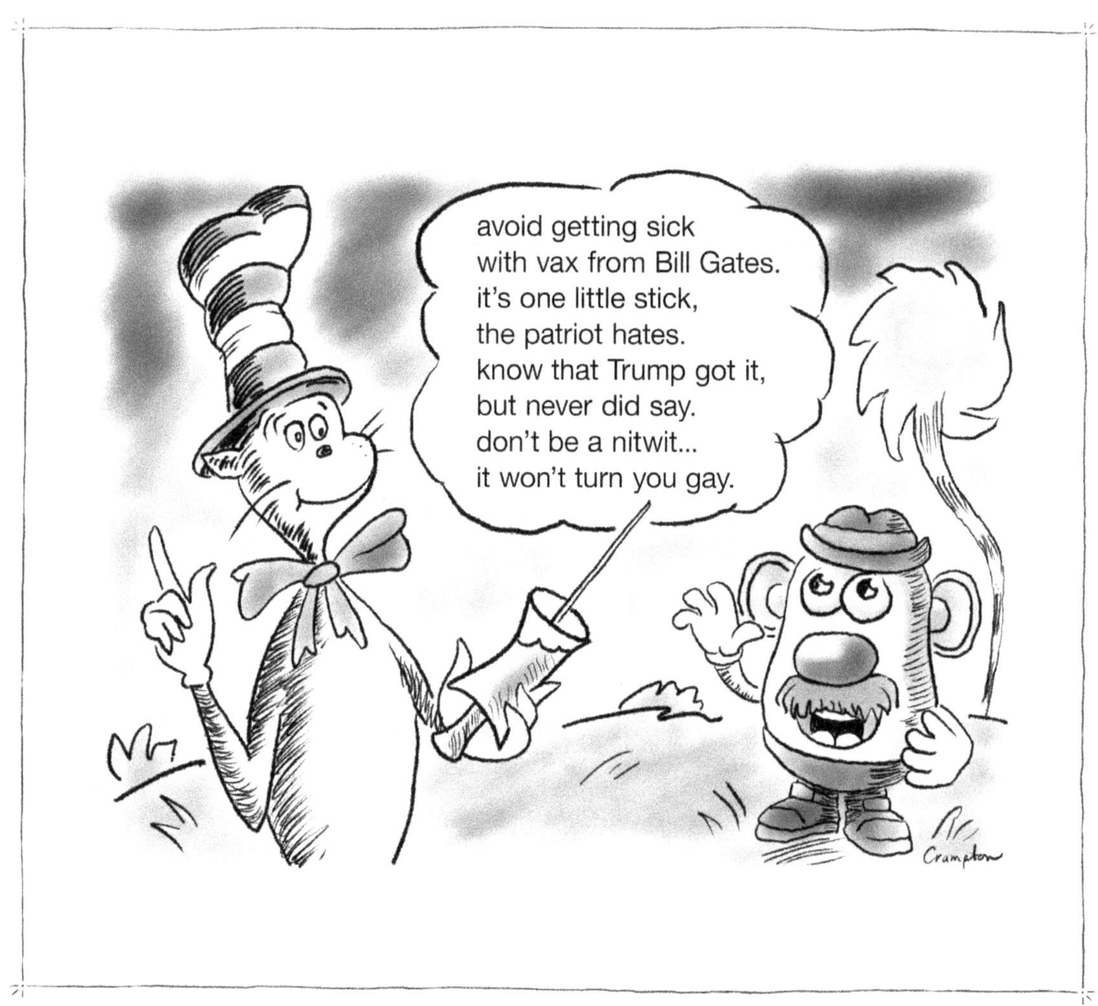

March 17, 2021
Congress passes Biden's Covid-19 Relief Bill with no GOP votes. Republicans on "Fox News" and elsewhere debate nonstop about whether Mr. Potato Head and Dr. Seuss are being cancelled by the "Libs".

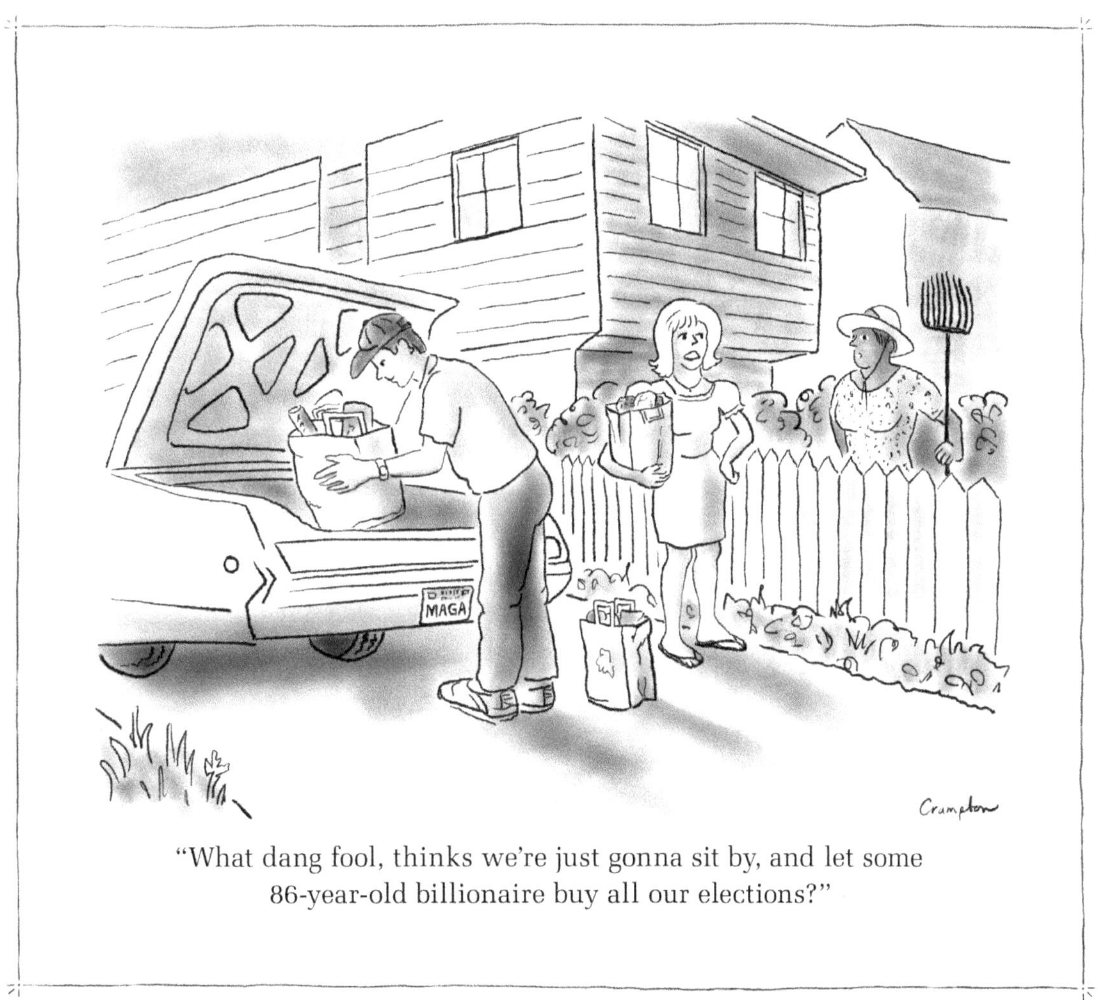

"What dang fool, thinks we're just gonna sit by, and let some 86-year-old billionaire buy all our elections?"

April 1, 2021
Georgia passed a bunch of new restrictive voting laws which make it harder for Democrats to vote. In a leaked Zoom audio, conservative donor, David Koch, admits that Republican voters are not fans of these laws either.

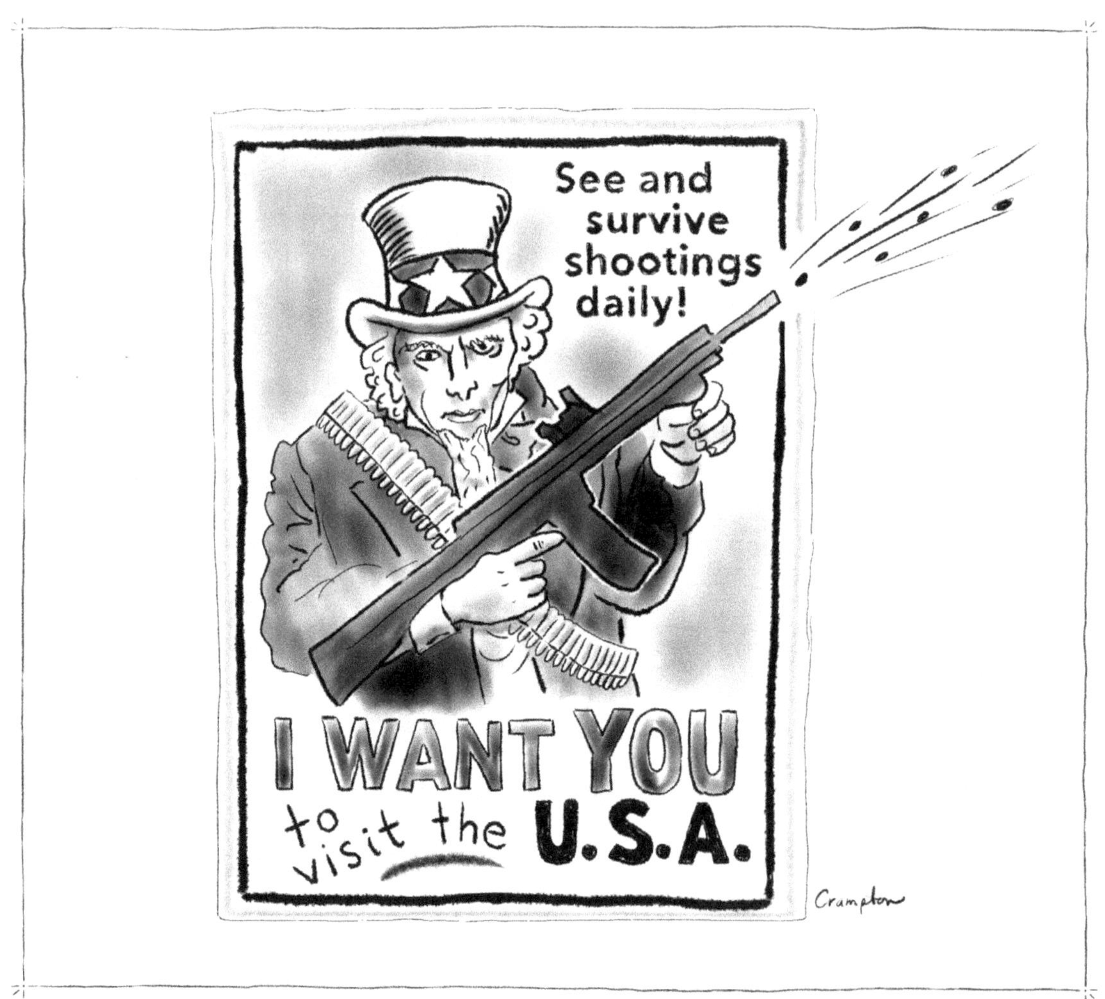

April 9, 2021
Millions vaccinated, States re-opening, and suddenly mass-shooter events are back on a daily basis.
I wonder how the country looks to potential tourists.

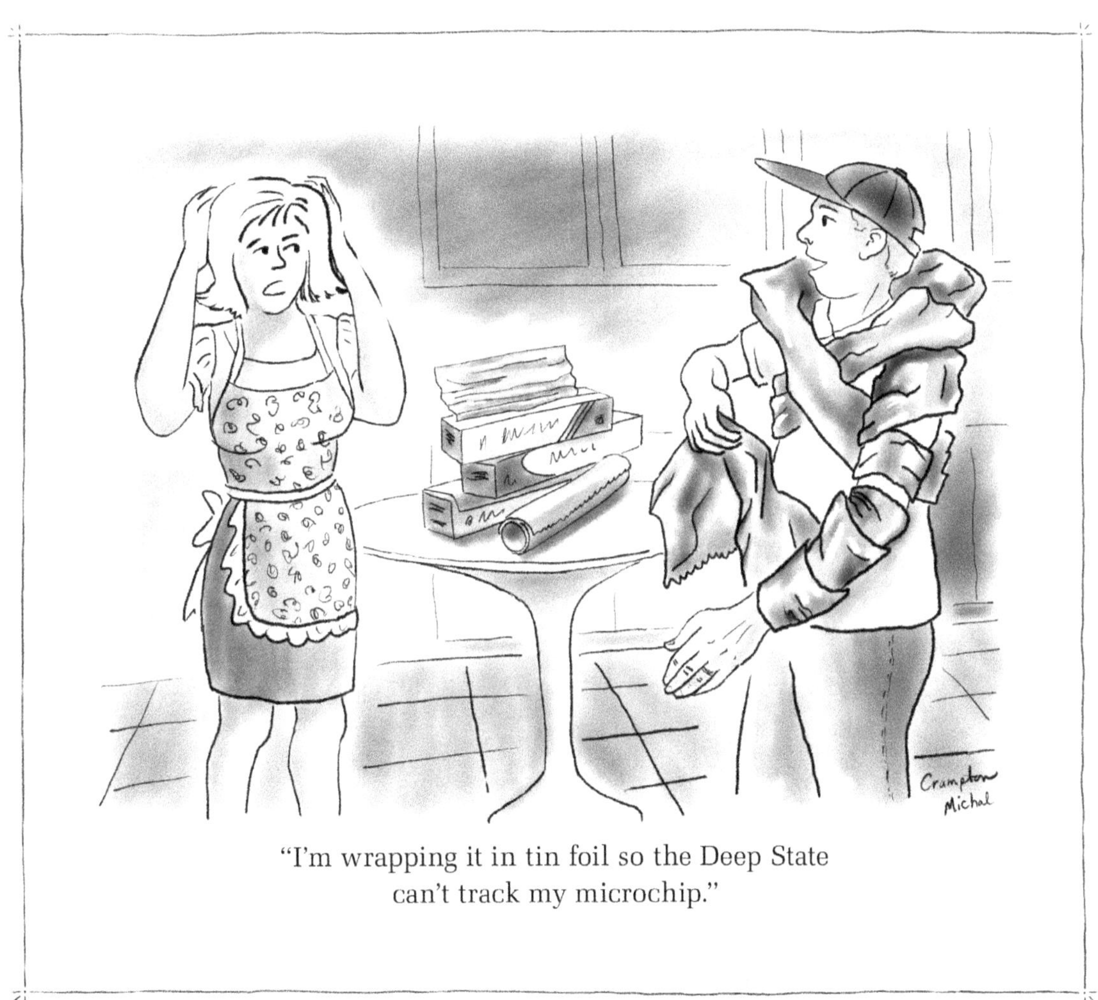

"I'm wrapping it in tin foil so the Deep State can't track my microchip."

April 13, 2021
Lots of Republican men won't take the vaccine. *Thanks to Gene Michal.*

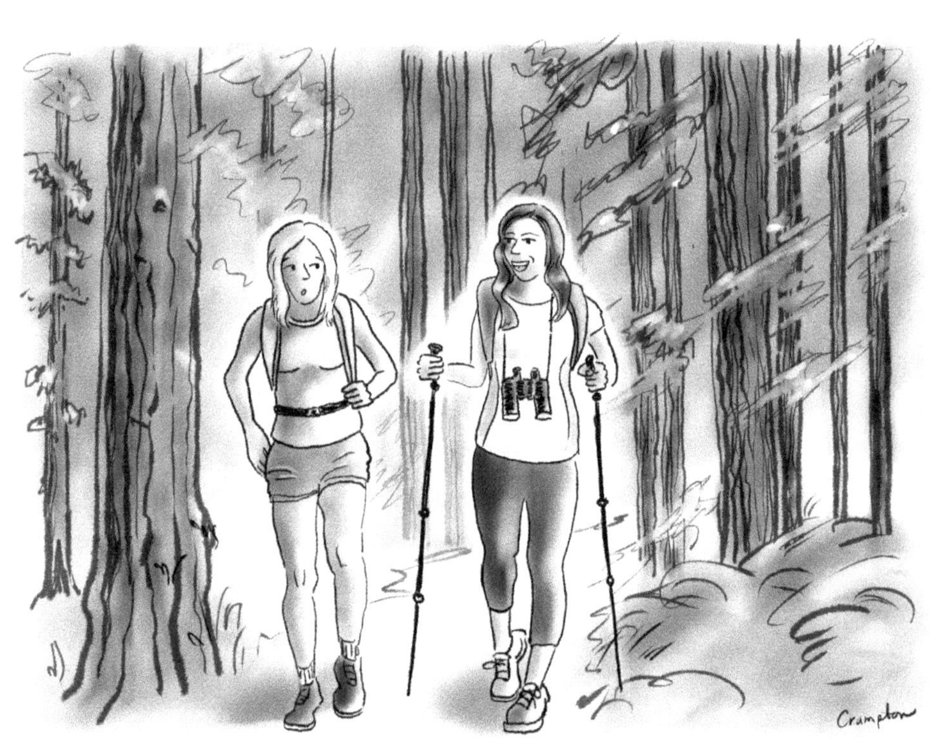

"How much d'you wanna bet, that the dudes who won't wear a mask, won't wear a condom either?"

April 21, 2021
Covid-19 hospitalizations are still growing in the States that are wide-open. In others, people won't wear masks.

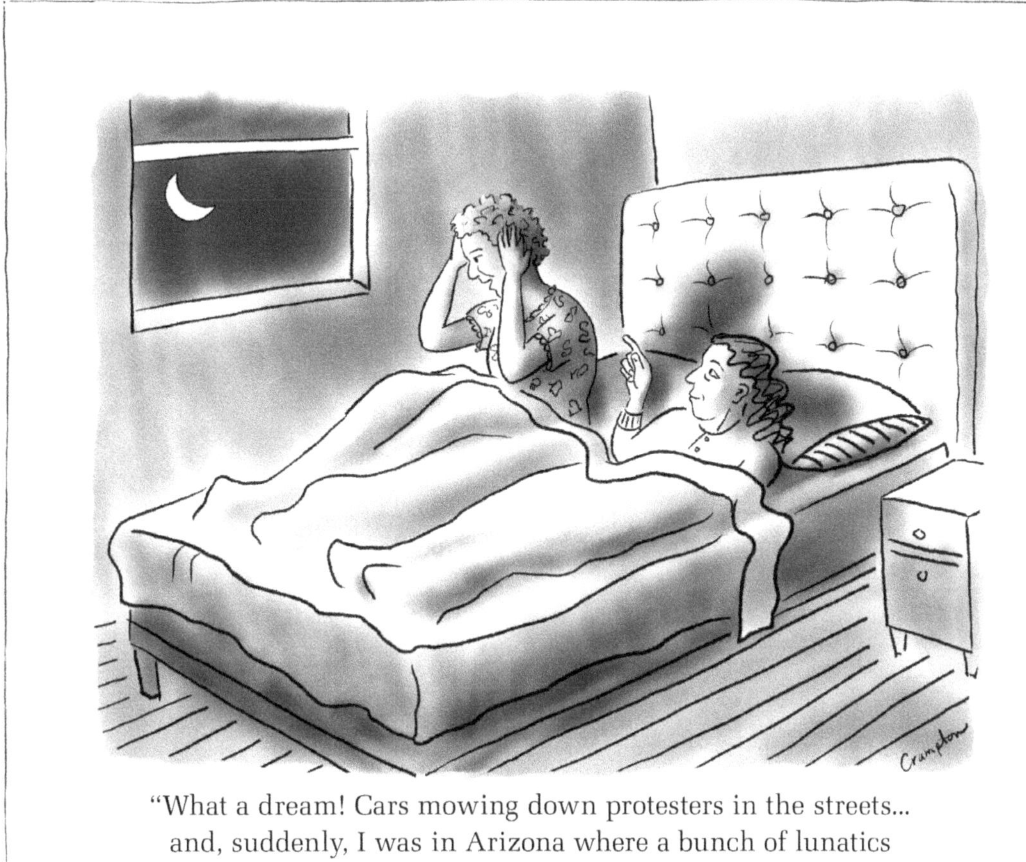

"What a dream! Cars mowing down protesters in the streets... and, suddenly, I was in Arizona where a bunch of lunatics were recounting the ballots..."

April 29, 2021
Florida and Oklahoma pass new laws to protect drivers who run over protesters with their vehicle. And yes, Arizona Republicans and QAnon enthusiasts are unofficially recounting official ballots.

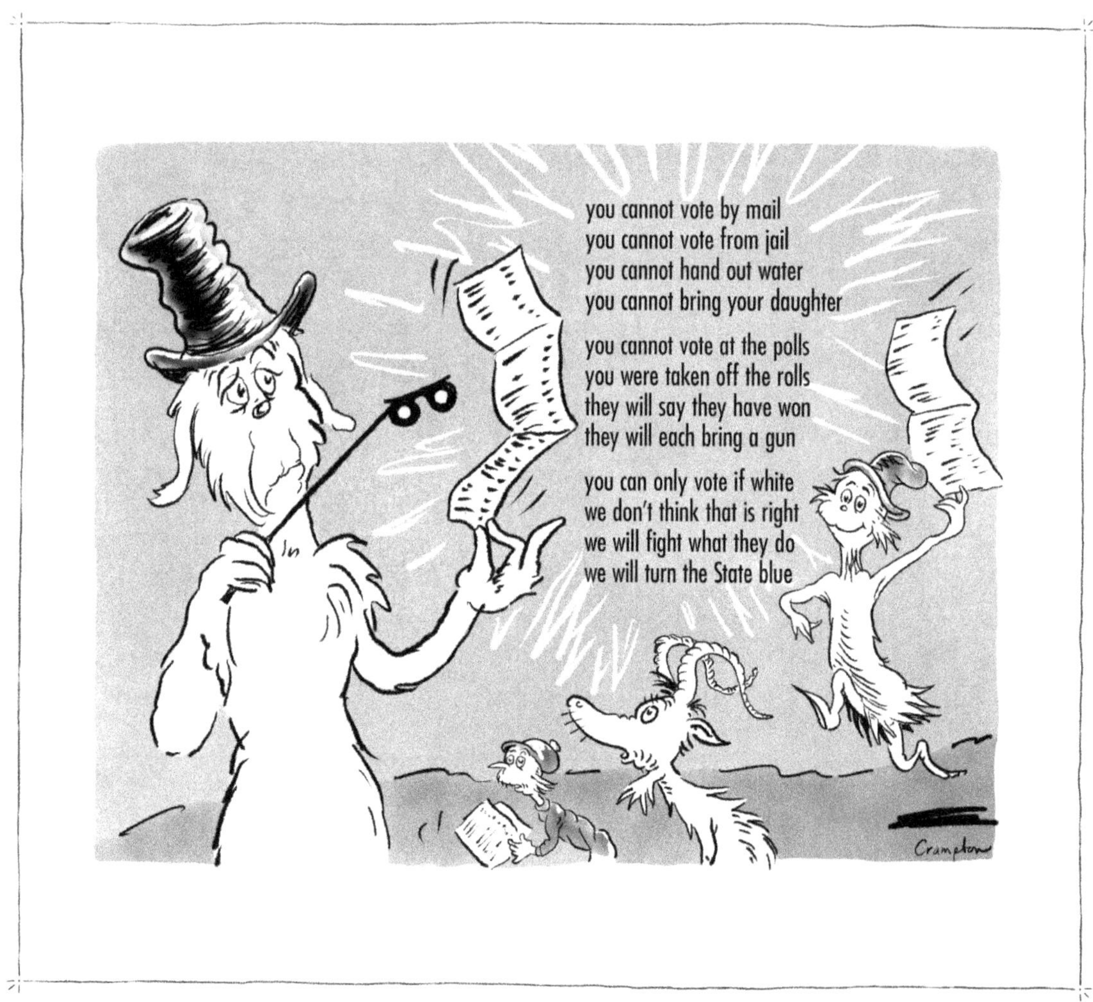

May 8, 2021
Many States intend to pass voter restriction laws–reducing poll hours and locations–which may affect working voters, and voters of color, the most. *Homage to Dr. Seuss.*

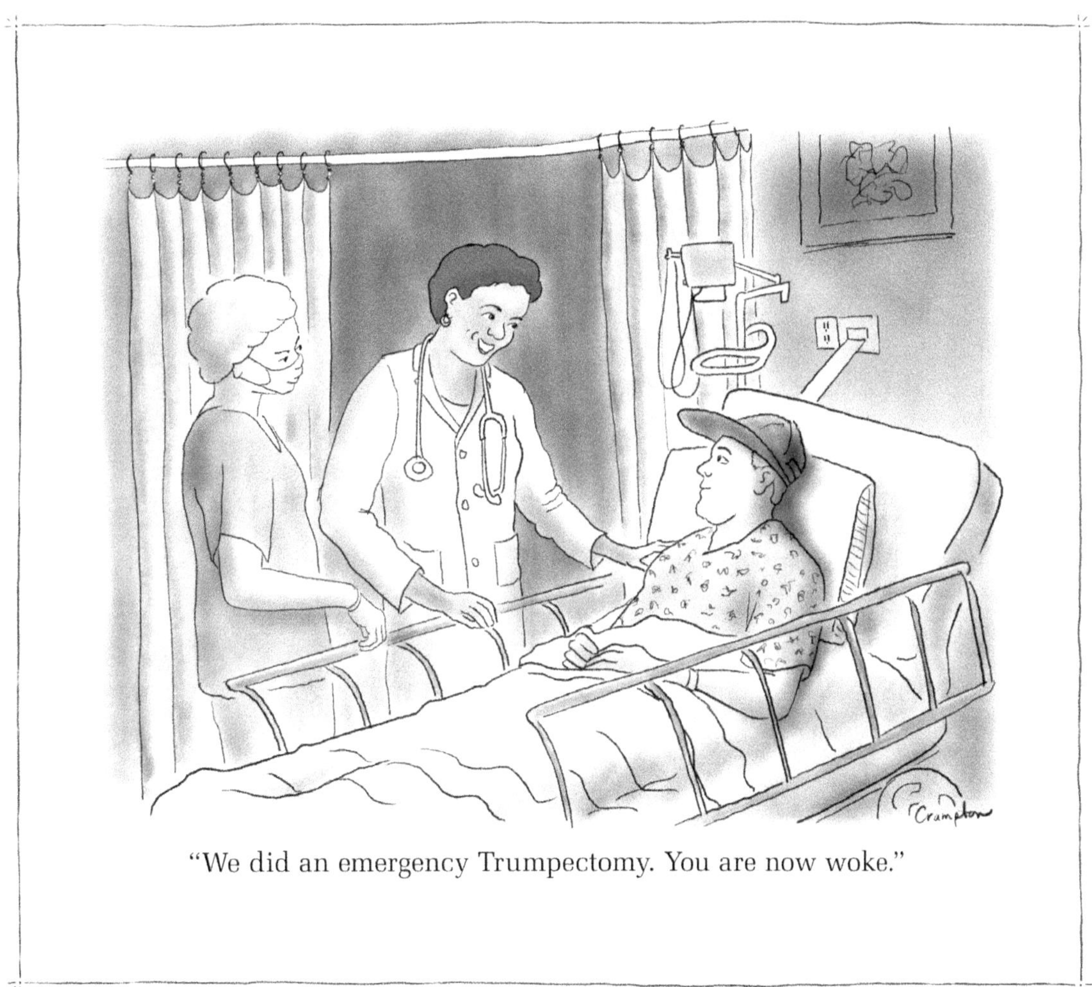

"We did an emergency Trumpectomy. You are now woke."

May 20, 2021
Lately, there are news reports that Republicans are abandoning Trump and "The Big Lie".
The FBI* is tracking down and arresting some of the Capitol rioters. **Federal Bureau of Investigation*

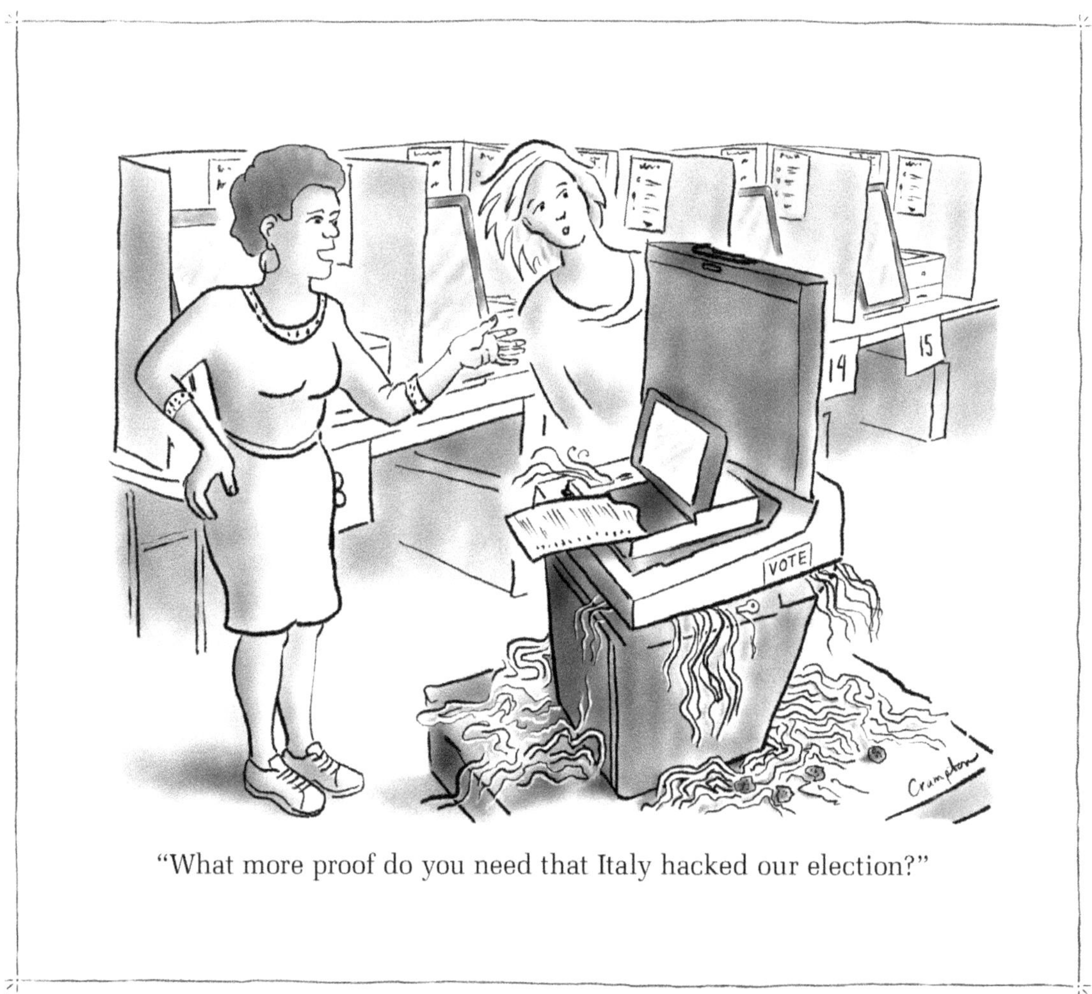

"What more proof do you need that Italy hacked our election?"

June 10, 2021
Rudy Giuliani exposes a new theory that Italy hacked the election. A man claiming to be Q* announces that he came from the future. **Whoever started QAnon is unknown*

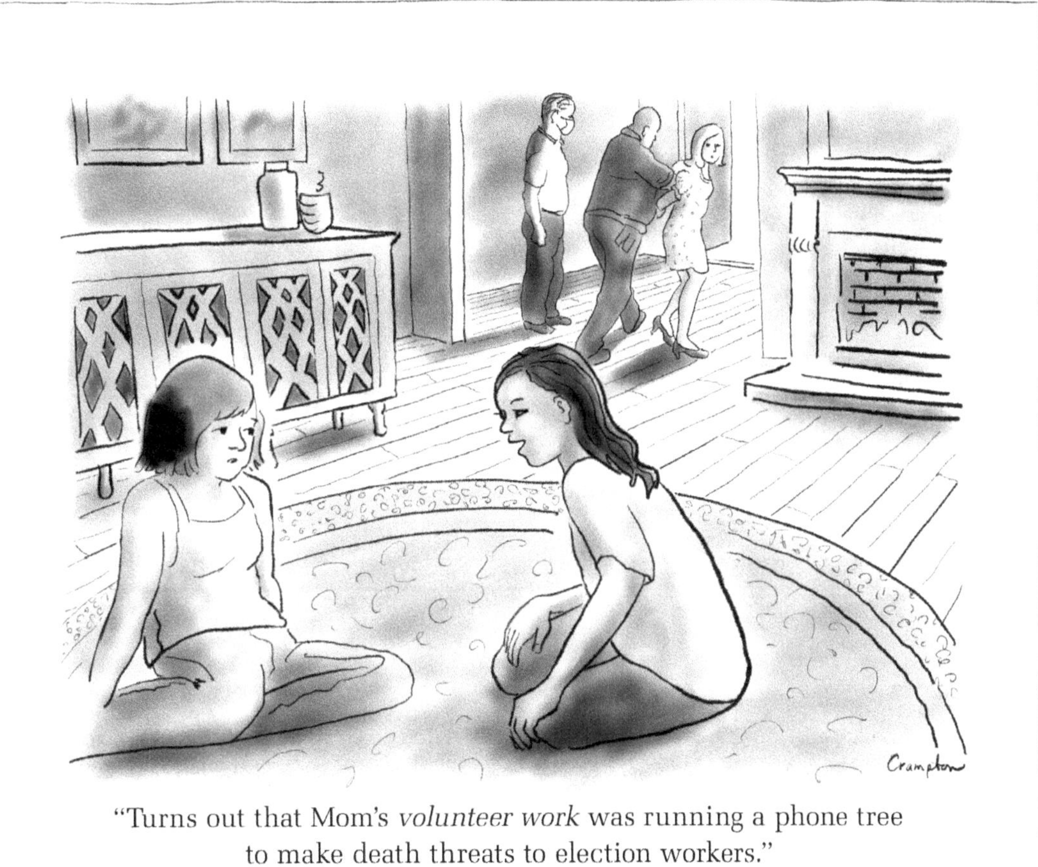

"Turns out that Mom's *volunteer work* was running a phone tree to make death threats to election workers."

June 24, 2021
Election workers in many States receive death threats and other harassment by proponents of "The Big Lie".

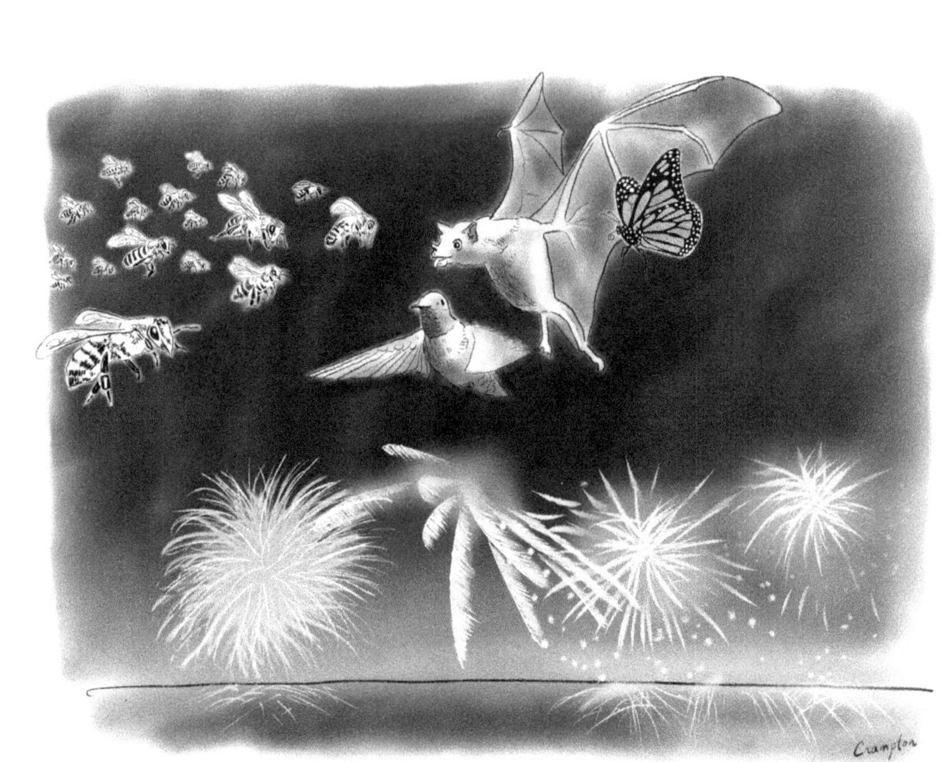

"But we make all their food—!!! Why bomb us out of existence?"

July 7, 2021
The Fourth of July holiday turned into a month of powerful fireworks going off like bombs in the cities. Very loud. People worry about veterans, the autistic, and their pets. I wonder how the wildlife fares.

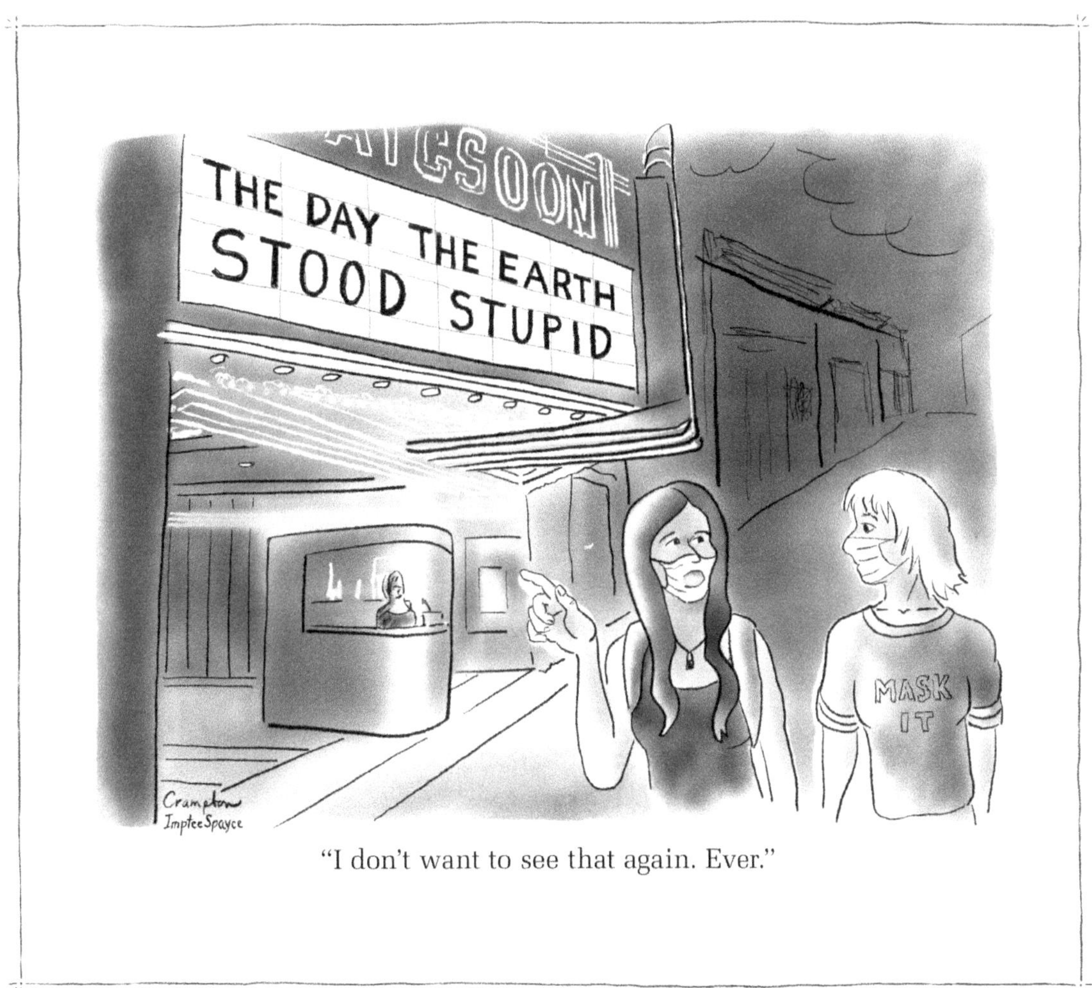

"I don't want to see that again. Ever."

August 5, 2021
The Delta variant of Covid-19 caused hospitalizations to soar worldwide, sparked by the unvaccinated. New mask mandates and restrictions ensued. *I crowd-sourced the marquee title. The winner was @ImpteeSpayce; with contributions by Michael Foster, Delia Dee Althea, David Thomasen, Will Bryne and MaryLou.*

Crampton

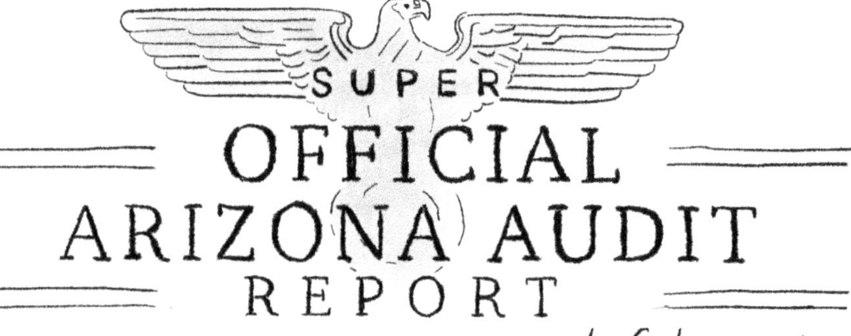

by Cyberninja's

We found too many votes cast
in these three categories:

☑ Dead people
☑ Aliens
☑ Democrats

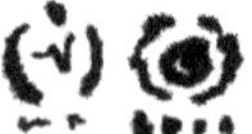

August 11, 2021
The Arizona GQP* Audit Report is finally about to be released. Here is my preview of the results.
The report was delayed because three of the Cyber Ninja's ballot-counters caught Covid-19.
Stands for Republicans who support QAnon fascist conspiracy theories

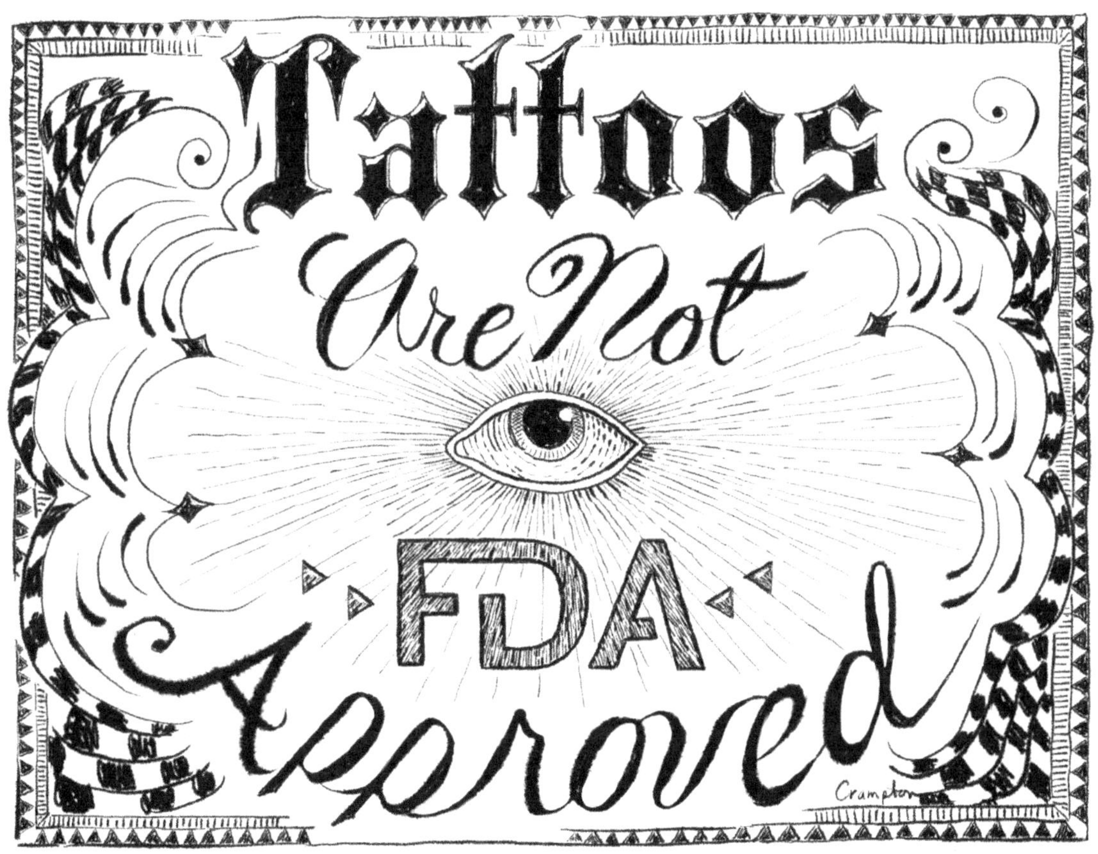

August 24, 2021
The Right complains that Covid-19 vaccinations are not officially approved by the FDA*.
The FDA hasn't approved tattoo inks and tattoos either.
*Thanks to Lyle Hunter Sorrell. *Food and Drug Administration*

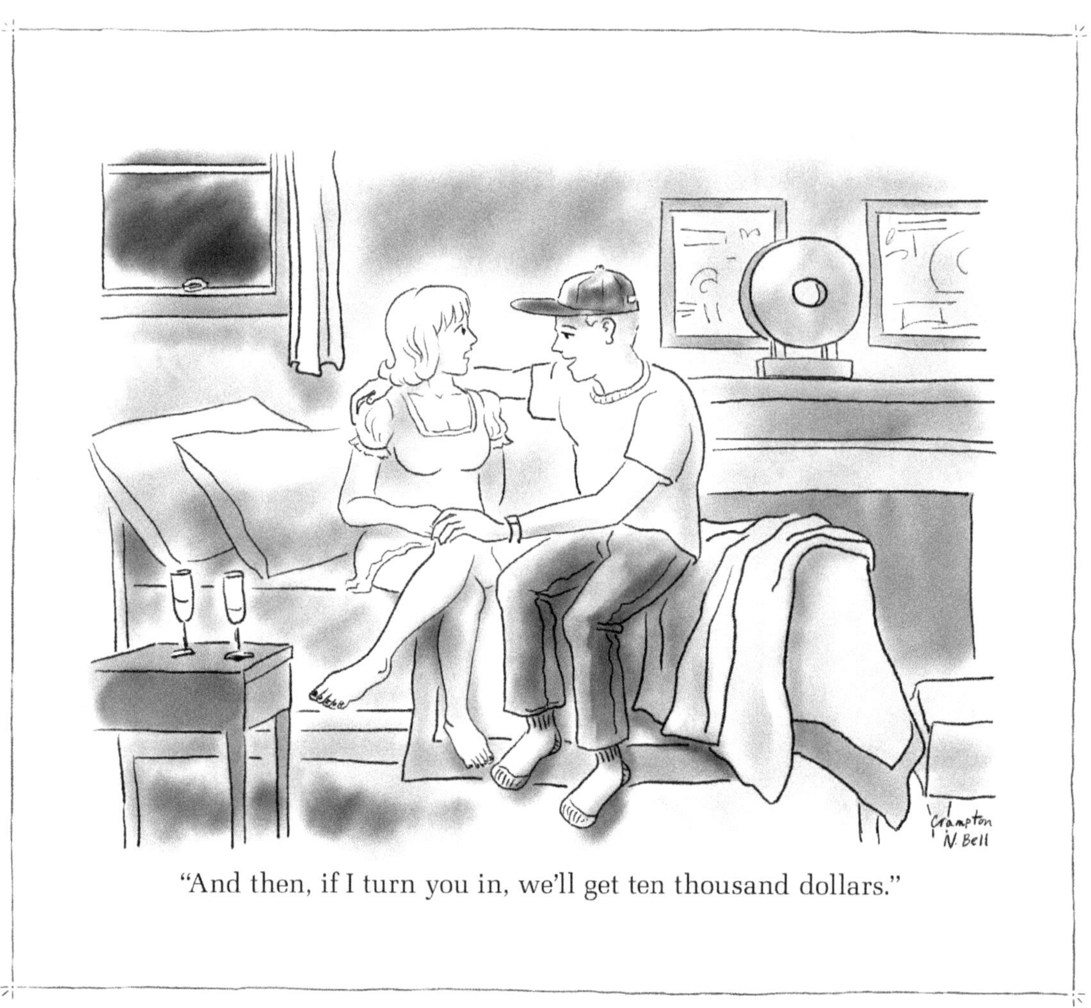

"And then, if I turn you in, we'll get ten thousand dollars."

September 2, 2021
Texas passed a law where any citizen can take a woman, who may have had an illegal abortion, to court and win $10,000.
Thanks to N. Bell.

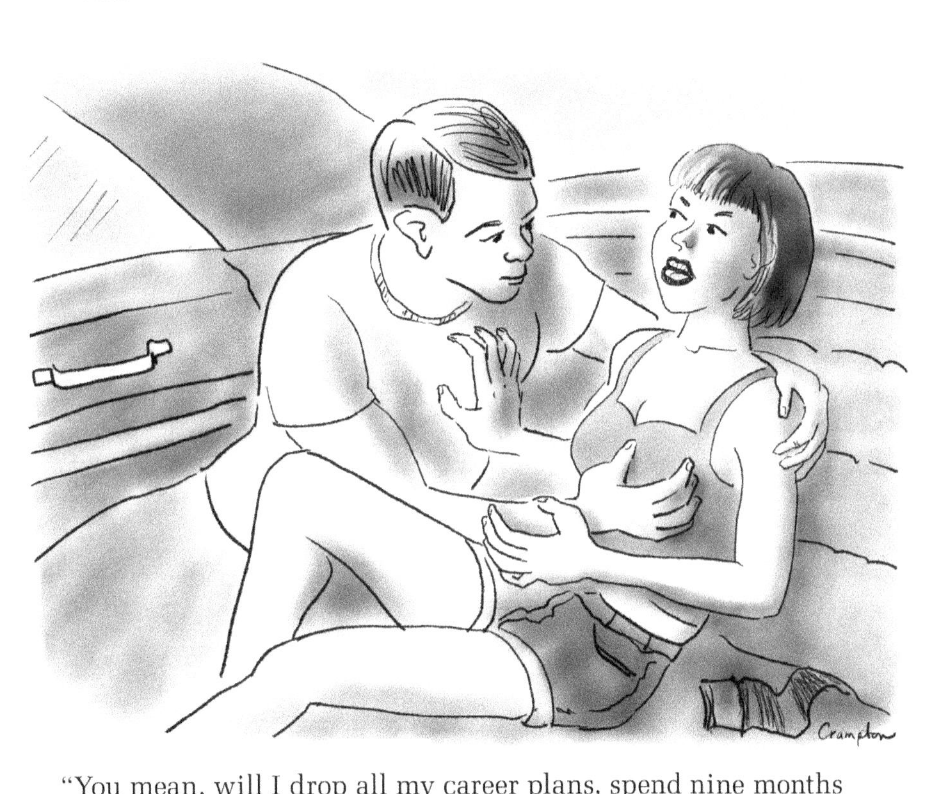

"You mean, will I drop all my career plans, spend nine months pregnant, be forced to move back home, have midnight diaper runs, a lifetime of crappy part-time jobs, never go clubbing again, and raise your spawn for, like, twenty years?"

September 4, 2021
Inspired by the debate about the Texas law: I want to point out that women don't get pregnant by themselves.

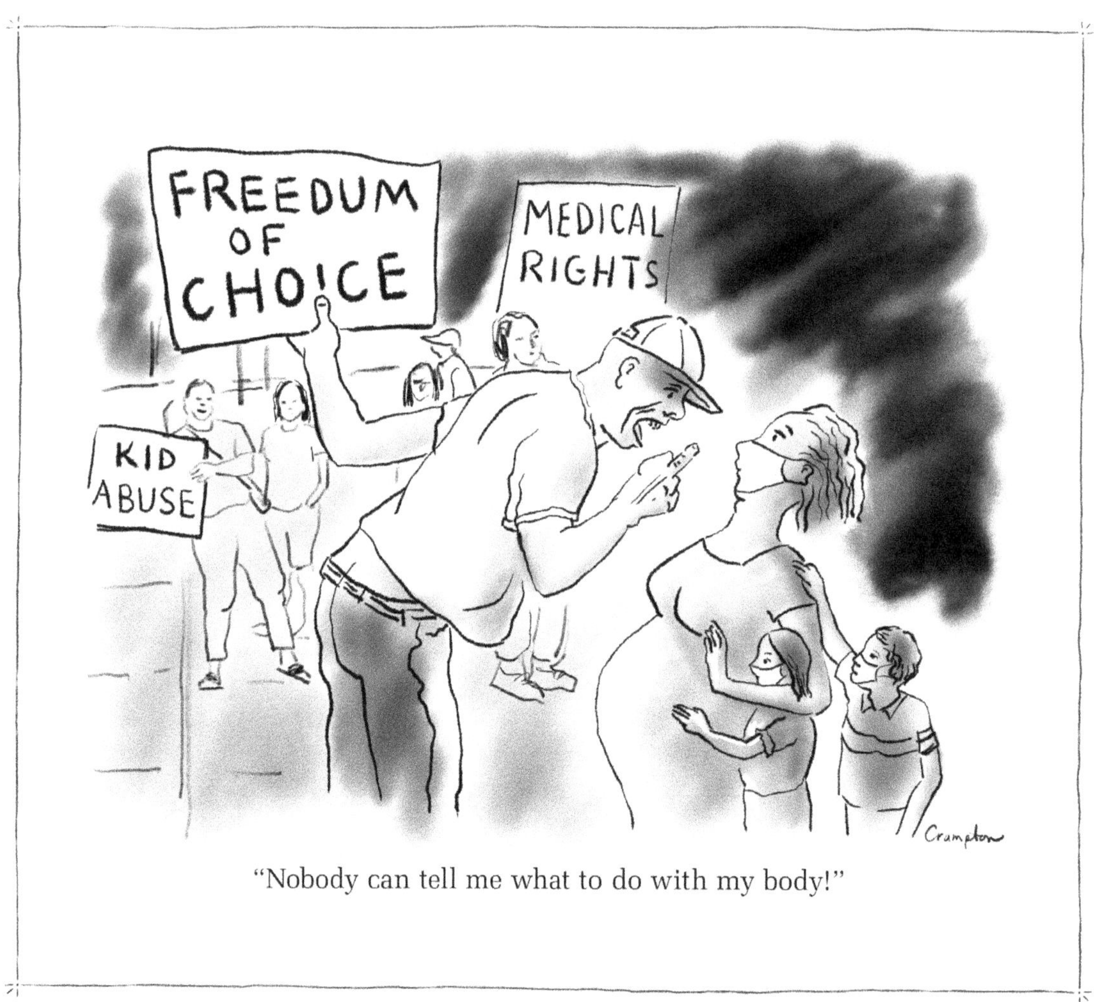

"Nobody can tell me what to do with my body!"

September 10, 2021
During all the debate about abortion, there are more news accounts complaining about Covid-19 mask mandates, and laments about the loss of freedom for jailed January 6th violent rioters.

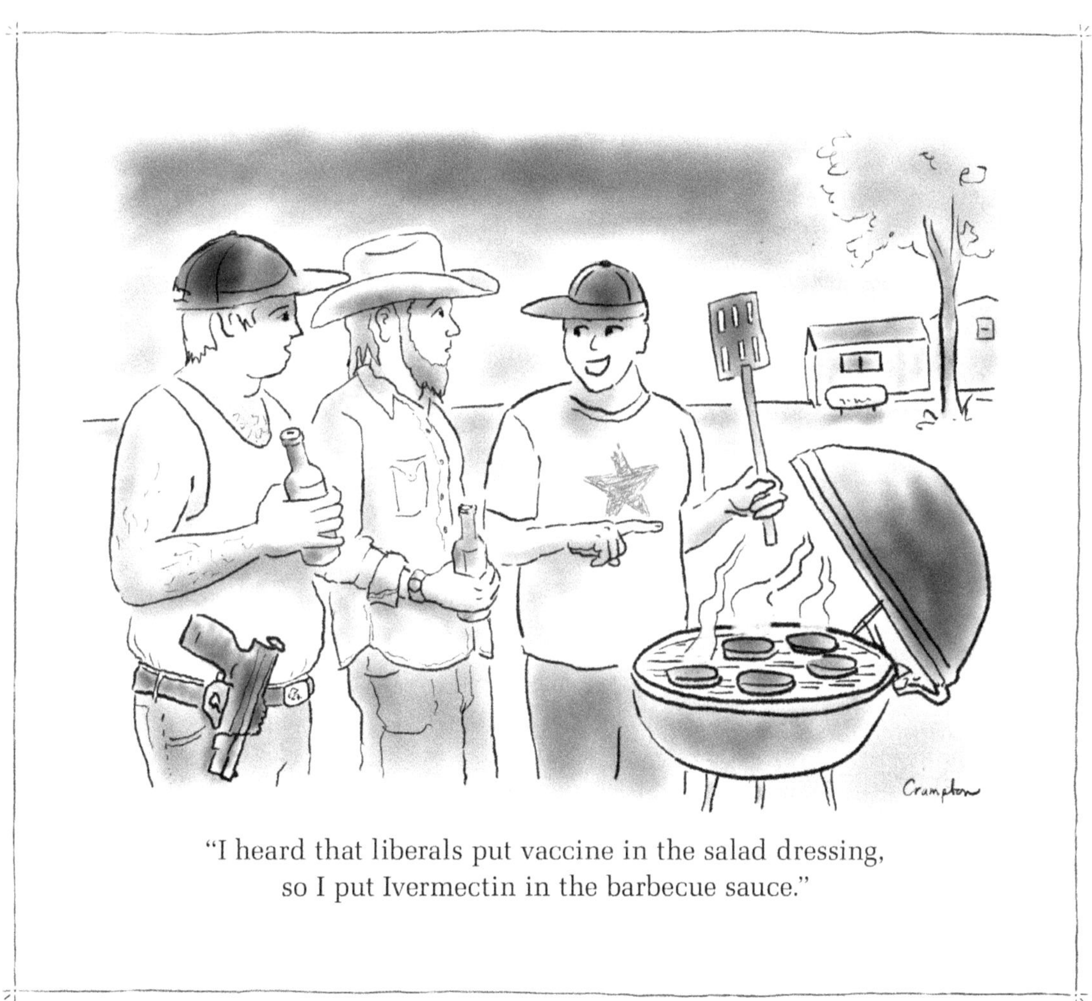

"I heard that liberals put vaccine in the salad dressing, so I put Ivermectin in the barbecue sauce."

September 23, 2021
Ivermectin or horse suppositories are a Covid-19 cure touted in right-wing media as an alternative to vaccines.

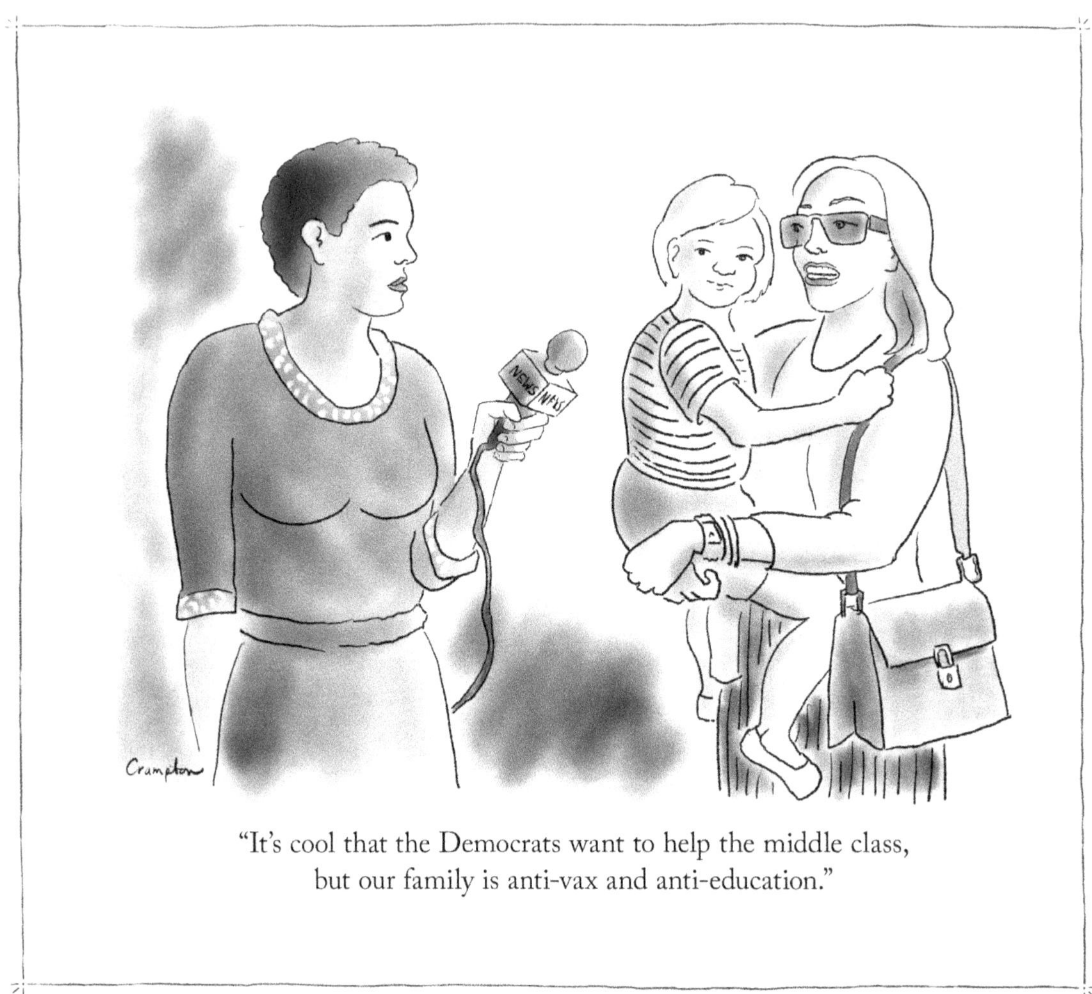

"It's cool that the Democrats want to help the middle class, but our family is anti-vax and anti-education."

October 17, 2021
A large percentage of Republic voters believe that vaccines are some kind of deep-State plot.
Covid-19 continues to rage in the red States.

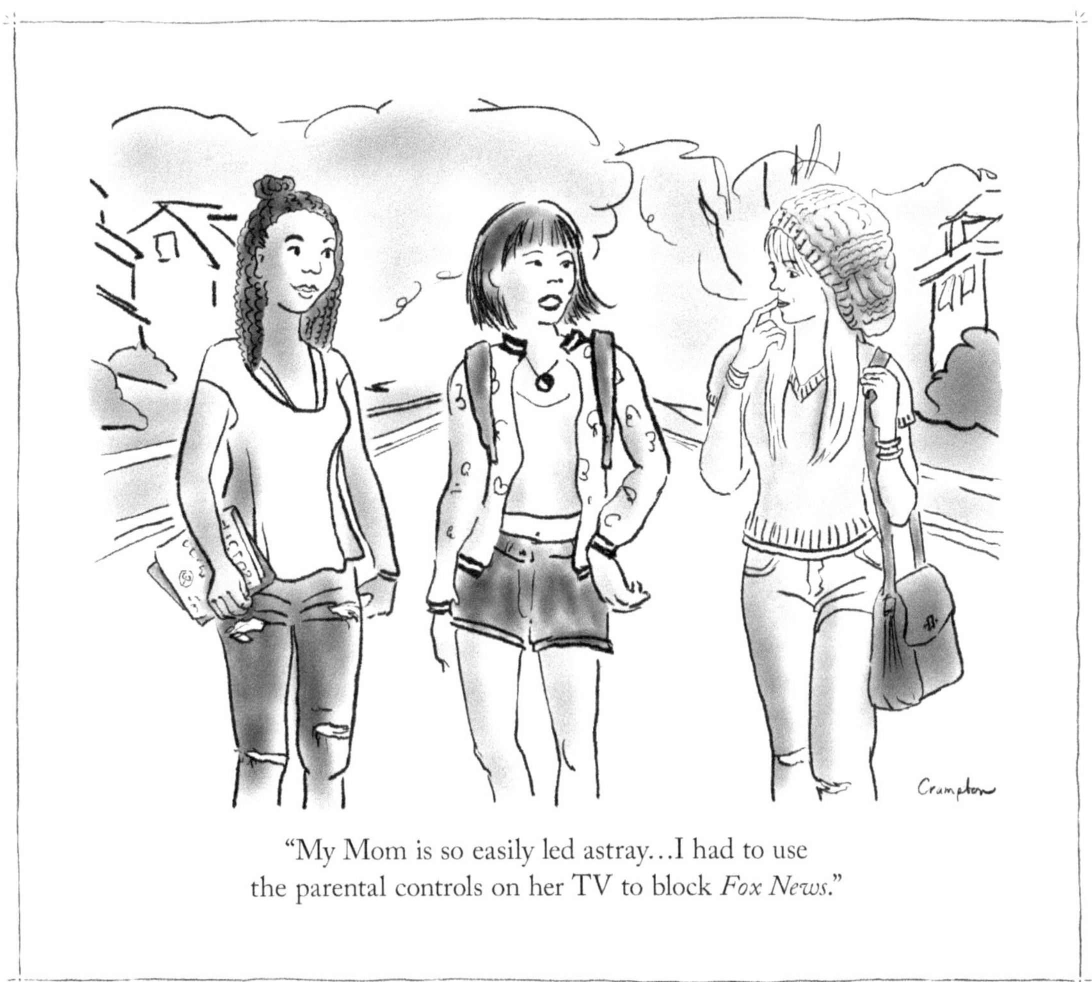

"My Mom is so easily led astray…I had to use the parental controls on her TV to block *Fox News*."

November 5, 2021
Hundreds of QAnon supporters gathered to witness the rebirth of John F. Kennedy, and JFK Junior, at Dealey Plaza, in Dallas, where JFK was assassinated in 1963. *(Note: They waited there for a month.)*

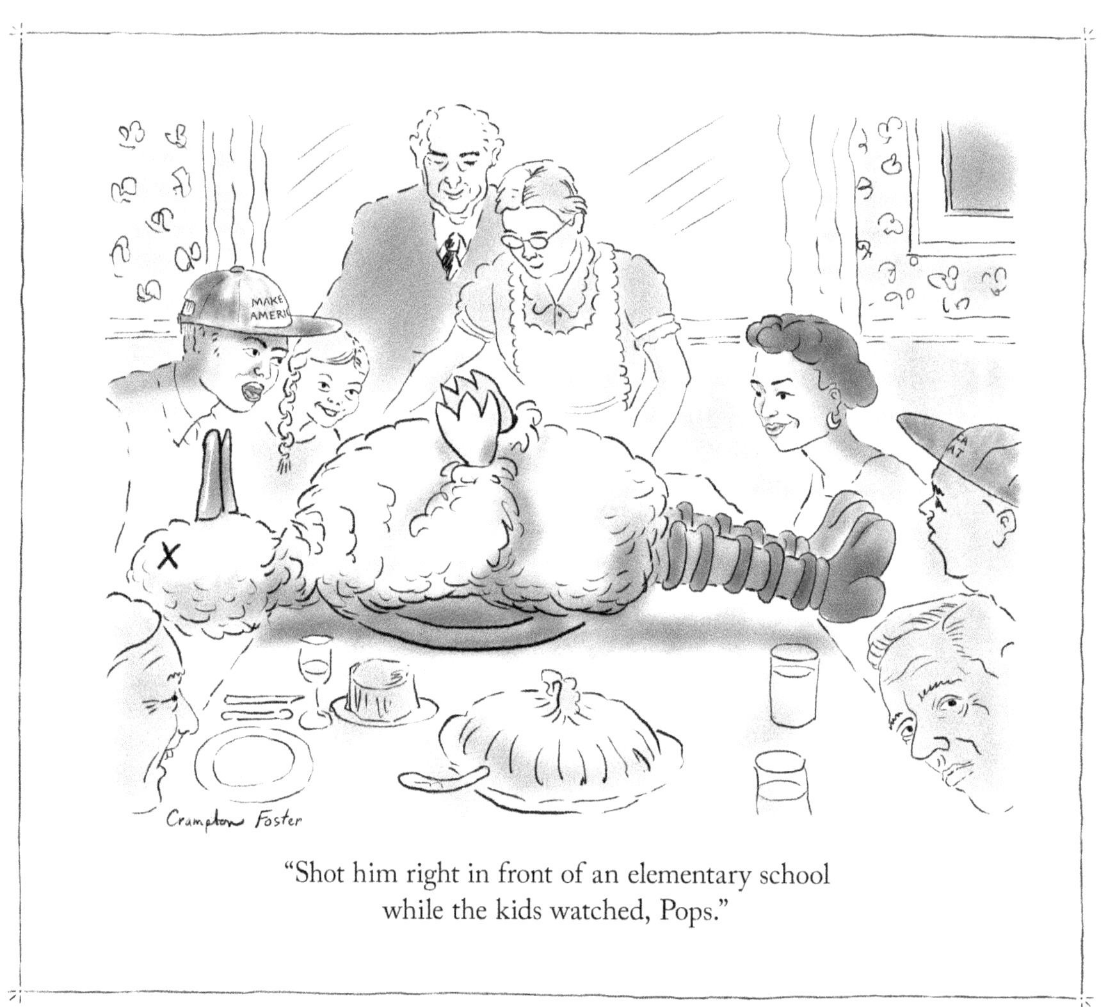

"Shot him right in front of an elementary school while the kids watched, Pops."

November 10, 2021
Thanksgiving again. Big Bird is deployed as a spokesperson to roll out vaccines for children. Senater Ted Cruz and right-wing media accuse the government of propaganda. *Thanks to Michael Foster. Homage to Norman Rockwell.*

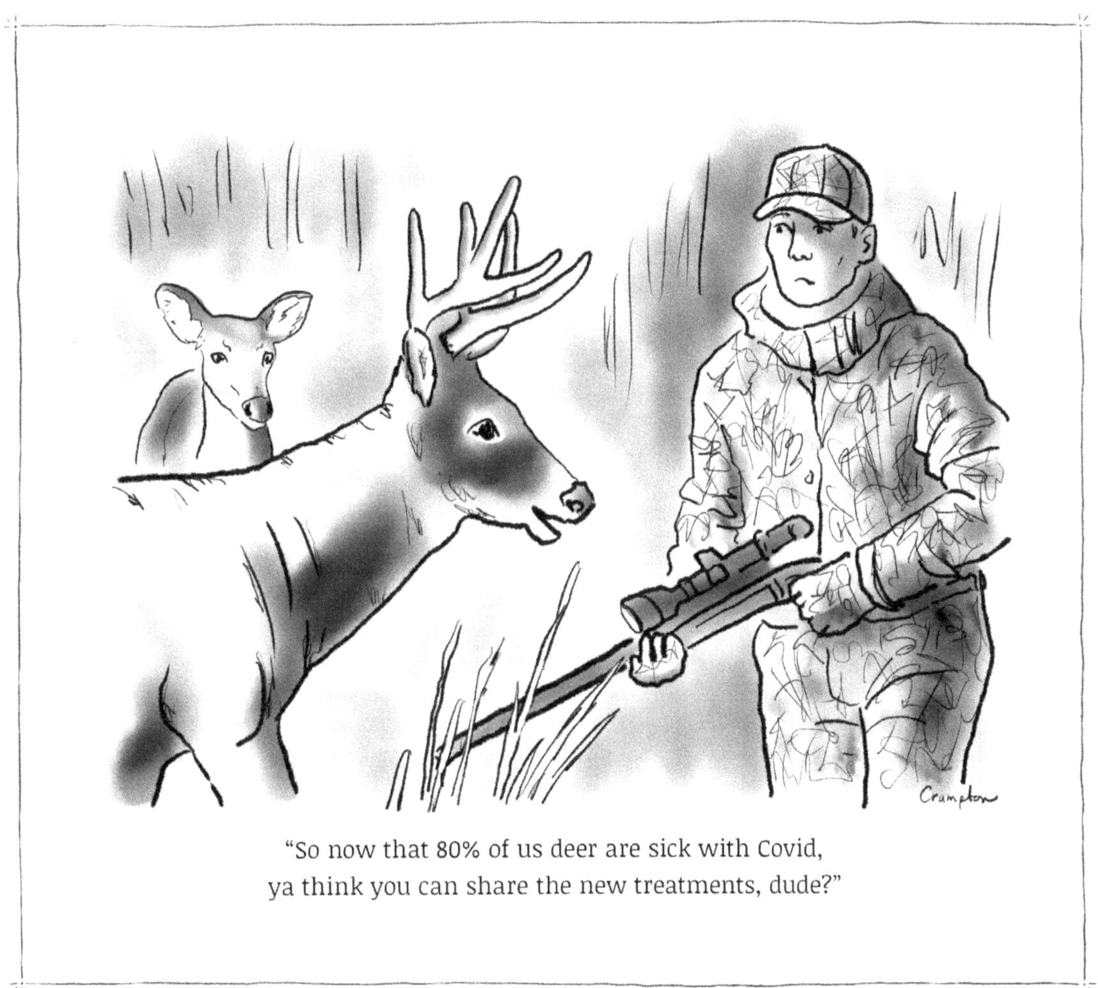

"So now that 80% of us deer are sick with Covid,
ya think you can share the new treatments, dude?"

November 21, 2021
80% of the wild, white-tailed deer tested in scientific studies in Iowa, tested positive for same strains of Covid-19 as in humans, but in higher rates than in humans. This coincided with the dates of the hunting season. Odd.

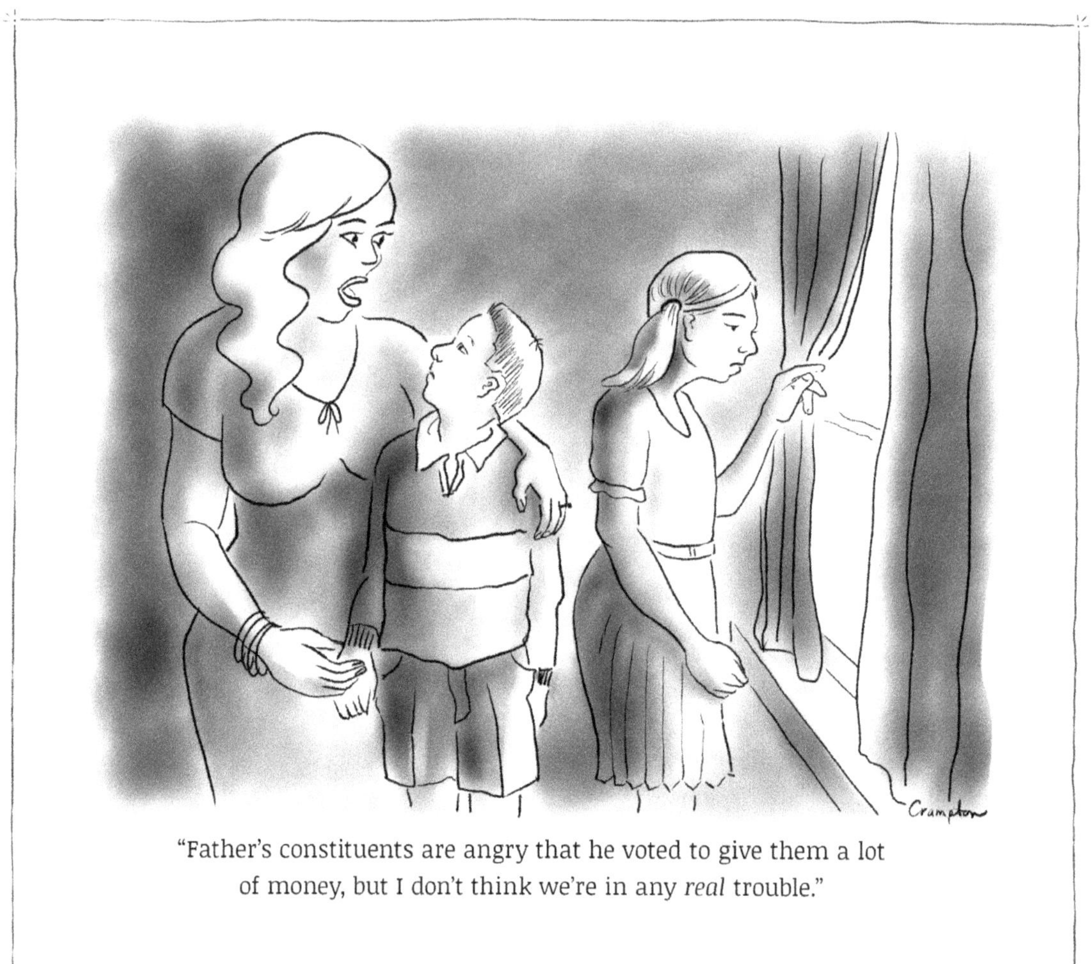

"Father's constituents are angry that he voted to give them a lot of money, but I don't think we're in any *real* trouble."

November 21, 2021
Democrats pass a large Infrastructure bill because 19 Republicans voted for it.
On social media, there are immediate calls for retaliatory violence against these Republicans.

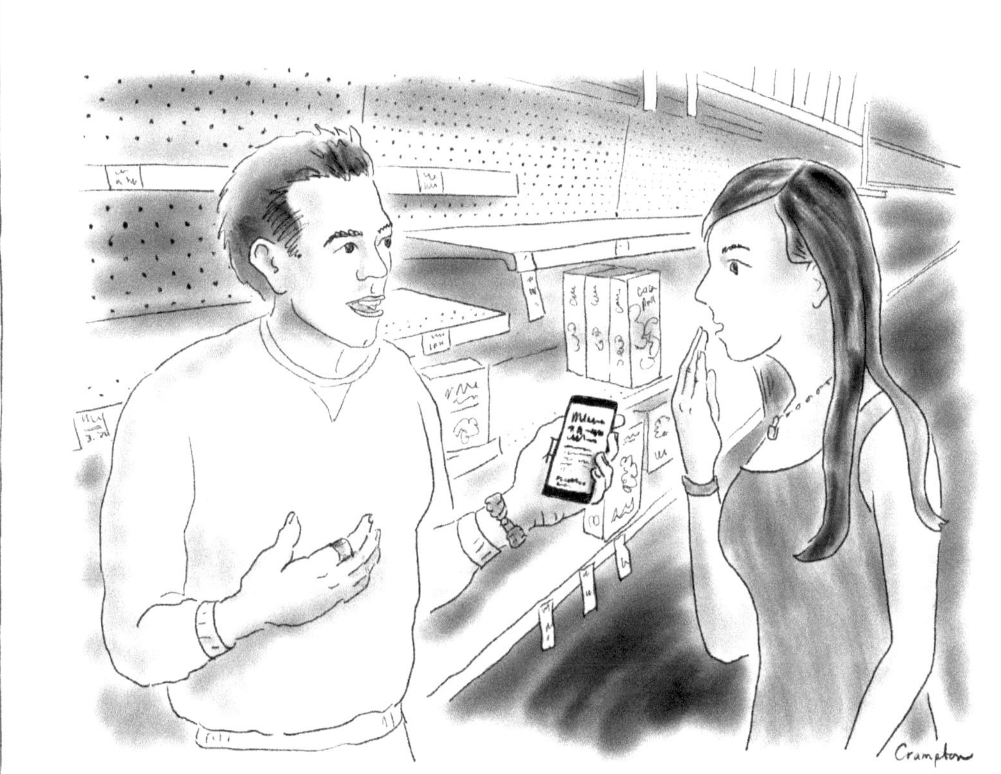

"Yes, Biden's gonna solve everything. But I *love* the JFK Jr. rallies, the horse pills, the numerology, and, *ohmygod*, those AR-15 Christmas cards!!"

December 10, 2021
While Democrats attempt to pass a second large bill to combat Covid variants and supply chain issues, Republicans on the far right supposedly drink hydrogen peroxide and eat "magic" dirt, rather than get vaccines. Christmas cards feature families posing with automatic rifles and other guns.

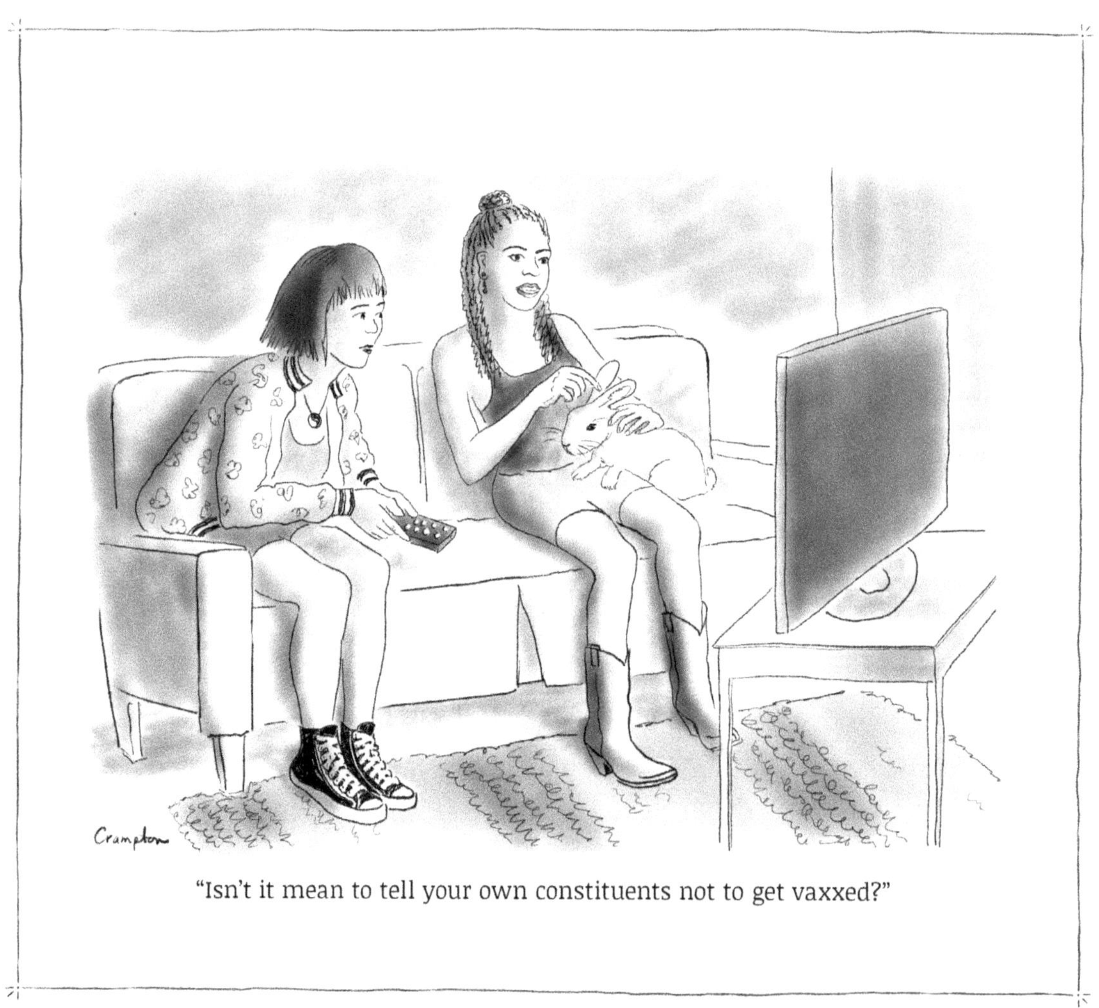

"Isn't it mean to tell your own constituents not to get vaxxed?"

December 22, 2021
A huge Covid-19 spike puts the unvaccinated in danger most. Plenty of people are dying.
Originally, this was meant to be a Republicans-suppress-voting-while-killing-off-their-own-voters cartoon, but I settled on something simpler.

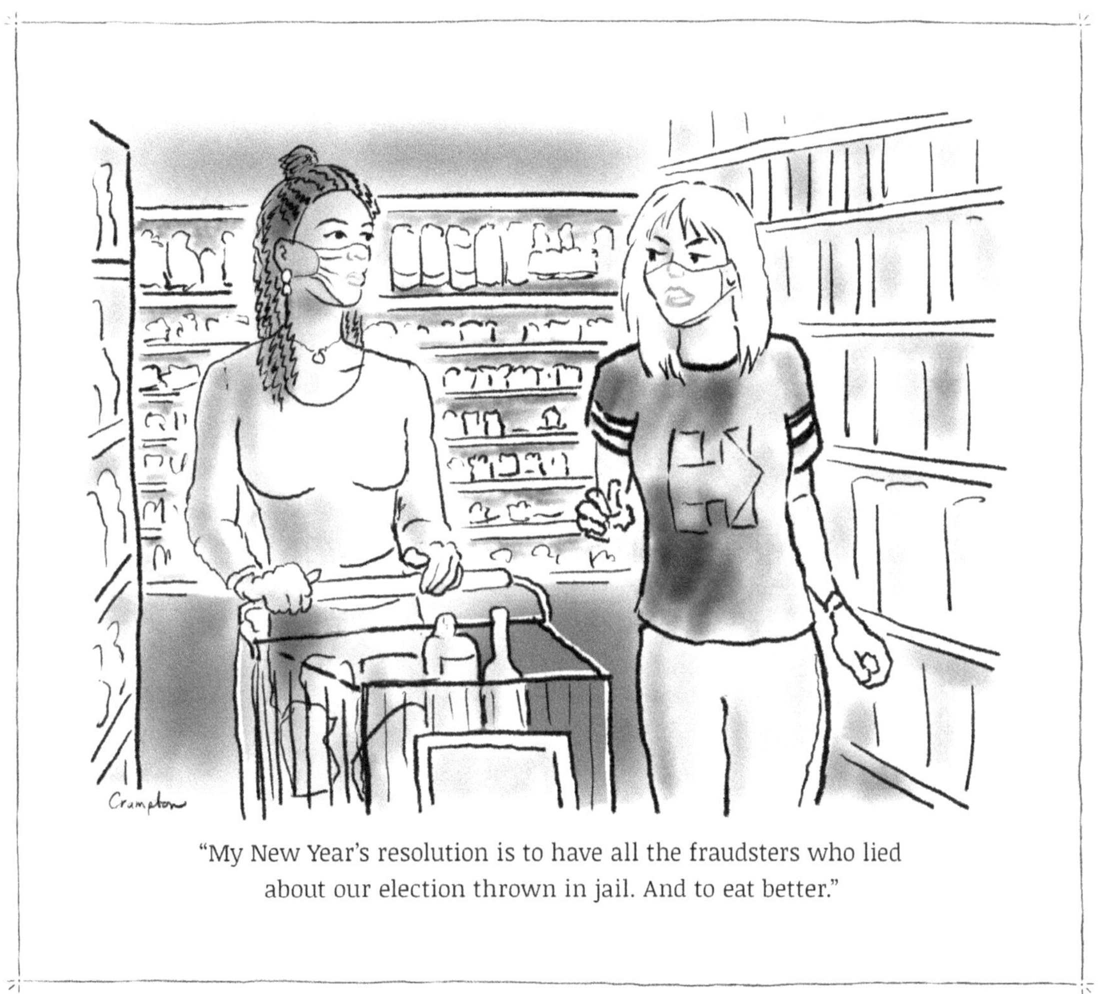

"My New Year's resolution is to have all the fraudsters who lied about our election thrown in jail. And to eat better."

January 4, 2022
The January 6th House Select committee and reporters uncover new information about the Capitol invasion, but so far, only misdemeanors have been charged. They have not caught the pipe-bomber.

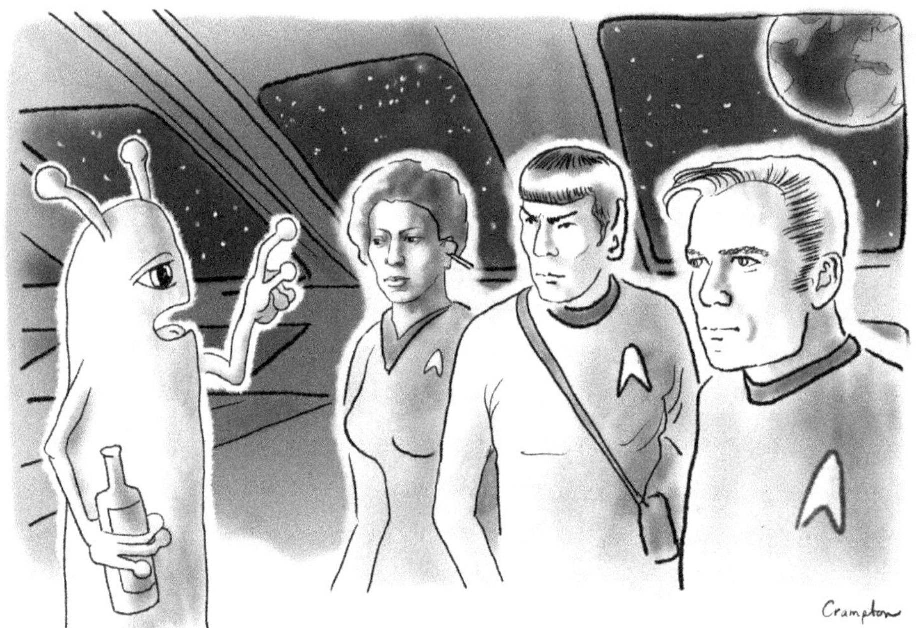

"To save the earth, you must time travel back to 12.11.2000, convince the Supreme Court to allow Florida to count all its ballots, ensuring that the 43rd President is Al Gore—the one who tried to warn us about global warming."

January 10, 2022
A new film called "Don't Look Up" has people talking about the climate crisis. Right-wing extremists still mention "Jewish space lasers". *You may notice that I'll use any excuse to draw an homage to "Star Trek".*

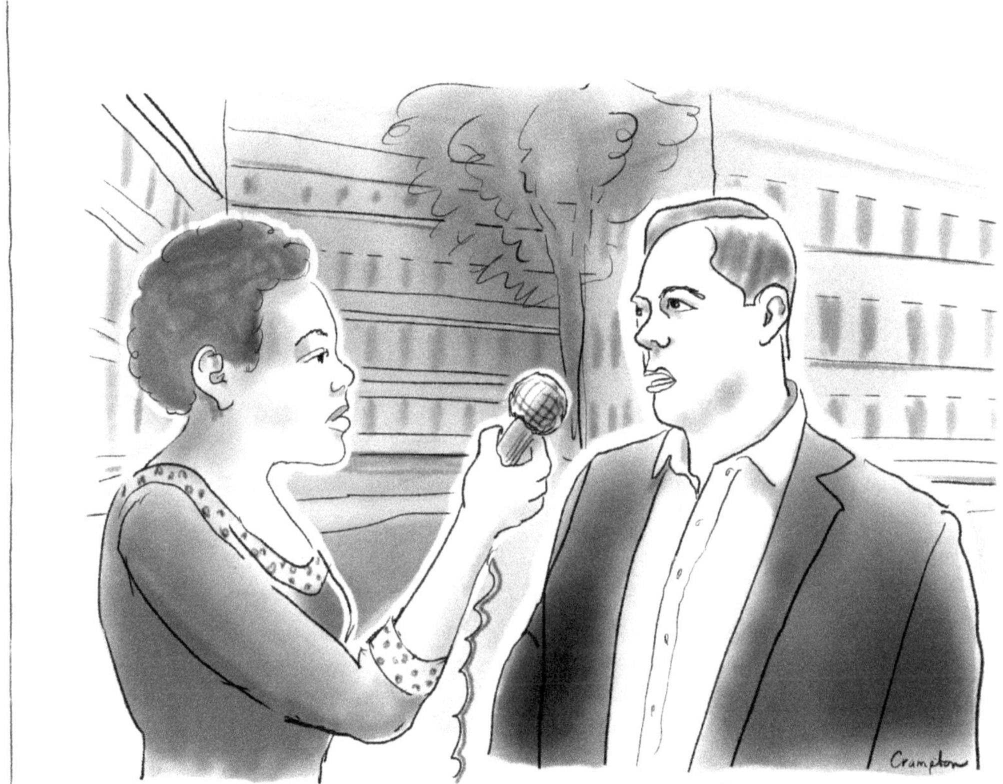

"Hey, if my guy loses an election and then asks me to sign some forged official certificate and take horse de-wormer, of course I'm gonna do it."

January 13, 2022
Arizona, Nevada, Michigan, Wisconsin and Georgia forged 2020 Electoral College certificates declaring Trump the winner, and sent them to the National Archives for Congress, as if they were real. Radio host, Glenn Beck, said yesterday that he treated a second serious bout of Covid-19 with ivermectin and hydroxychloroquine. "This is basic science, this is basic medicine."

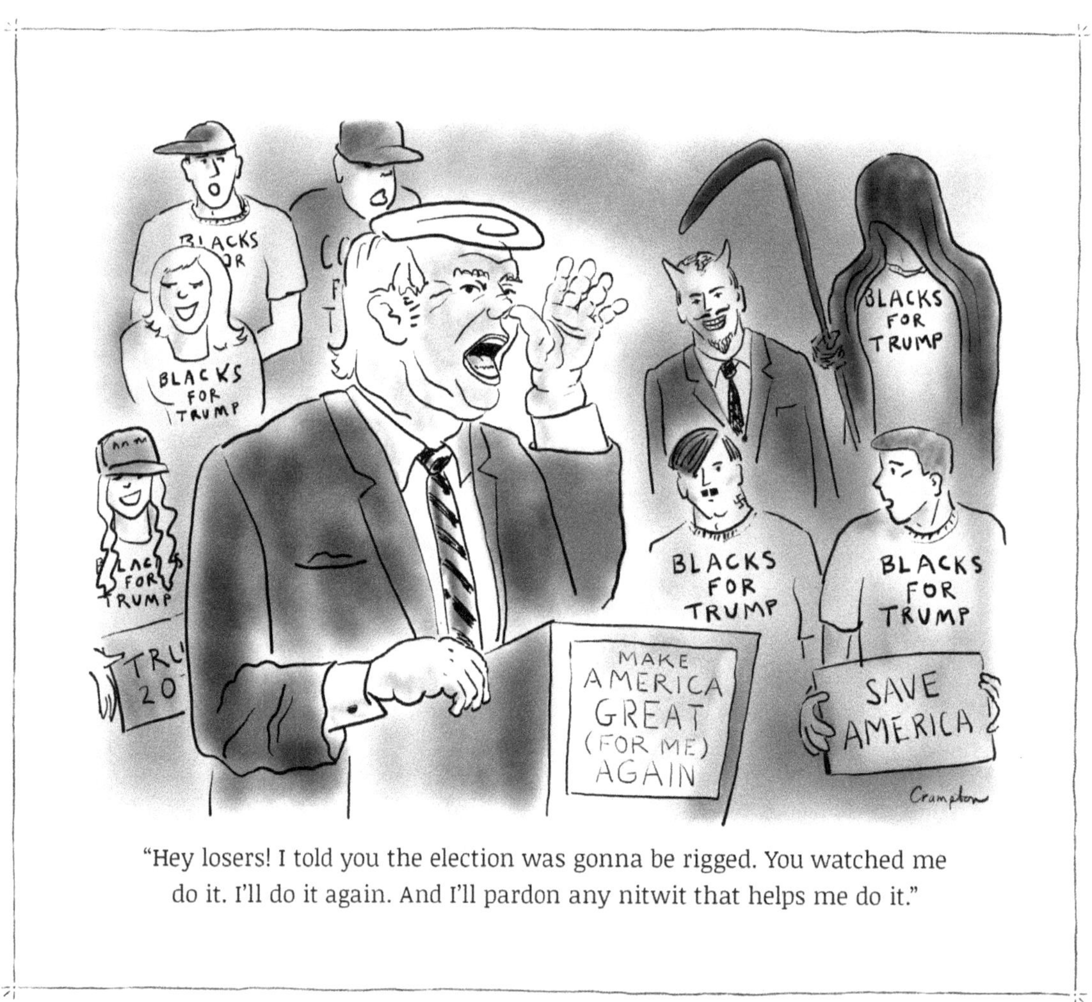

"Hey losers! I told you the election was gonna be rigged. You watched me do it. I'll do it again. And I'll pardon any nitwit that helps me do it."

February 3, 2022
Trump holds rallies again to raise money—or maybe, to distract from the House's January 6th Commission, which released information about fake electors, attempts to commandeer voting machines, and other election plots.

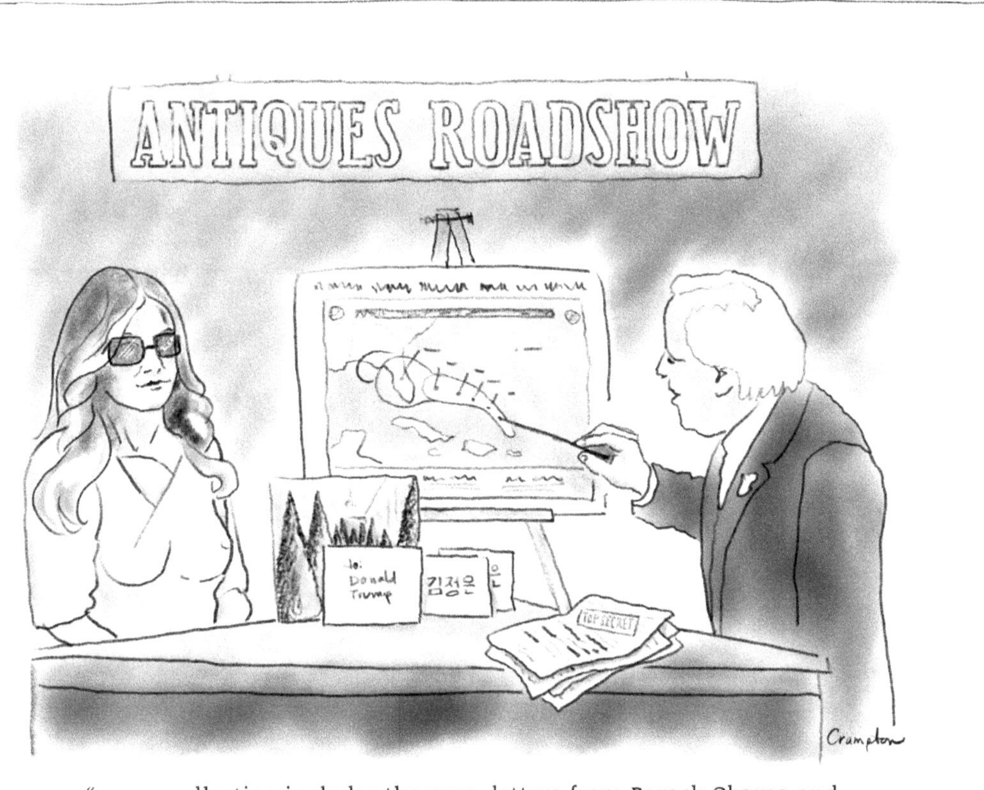

"...your collection includes the map, letters from Barack Obama and Kim Jung-un, 12 blood-red Christmas trees; all with impeccable provenance, but at auction, the most valuable may be the top secret documents."

February 20, 2022
Trump took a bunch of secret documents to Mar-a-Lago when he vacated the White House.

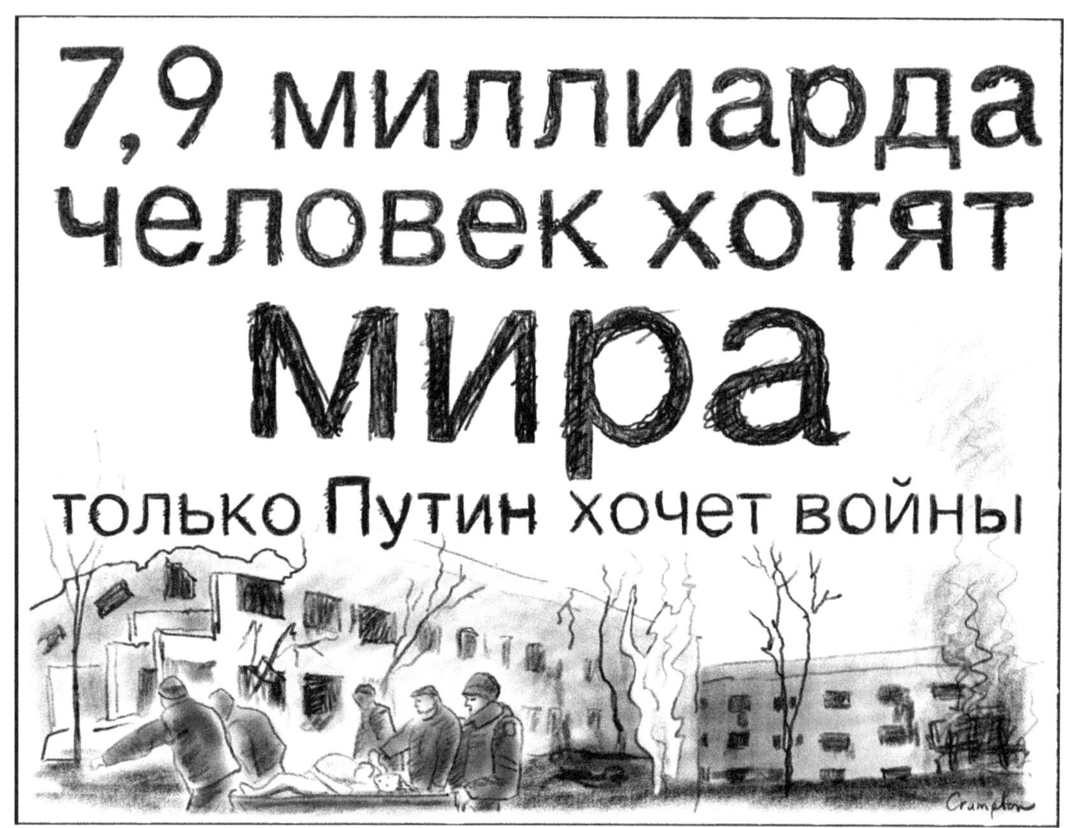

March 31, 2022
"7.9 million people want peace, only Putin wants war." Putin misled the Russian people about the invasion of Ukraine on February 24, saying it was just a small operation against Nazis. *I thought it might help to do a cartoon in Russian.*

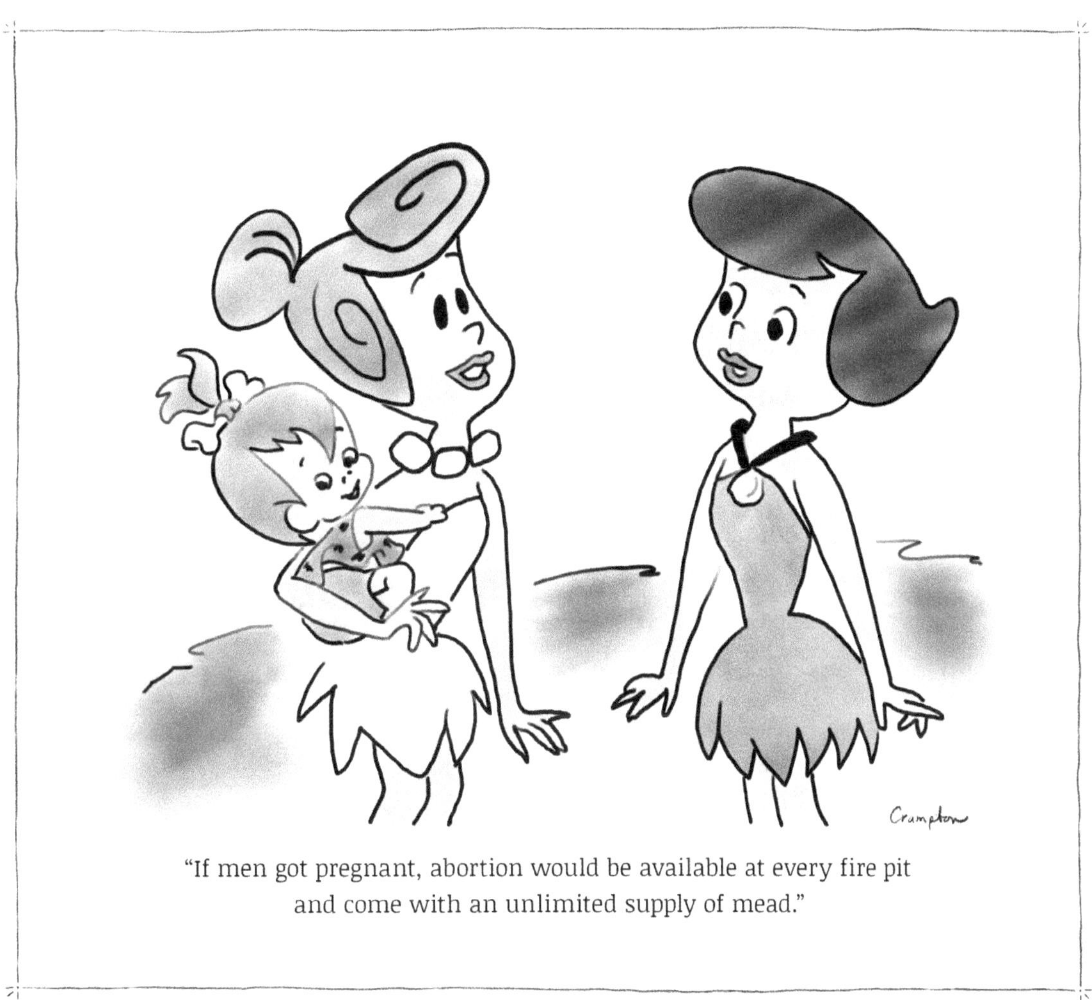

"If men got pregnant, abortion would be available at every fire pit and come with an unlimited supply of mead."

May 4, 2022
A leaked Supreme Court brief reveals a decision that threatens to overturn Roe v Wade.

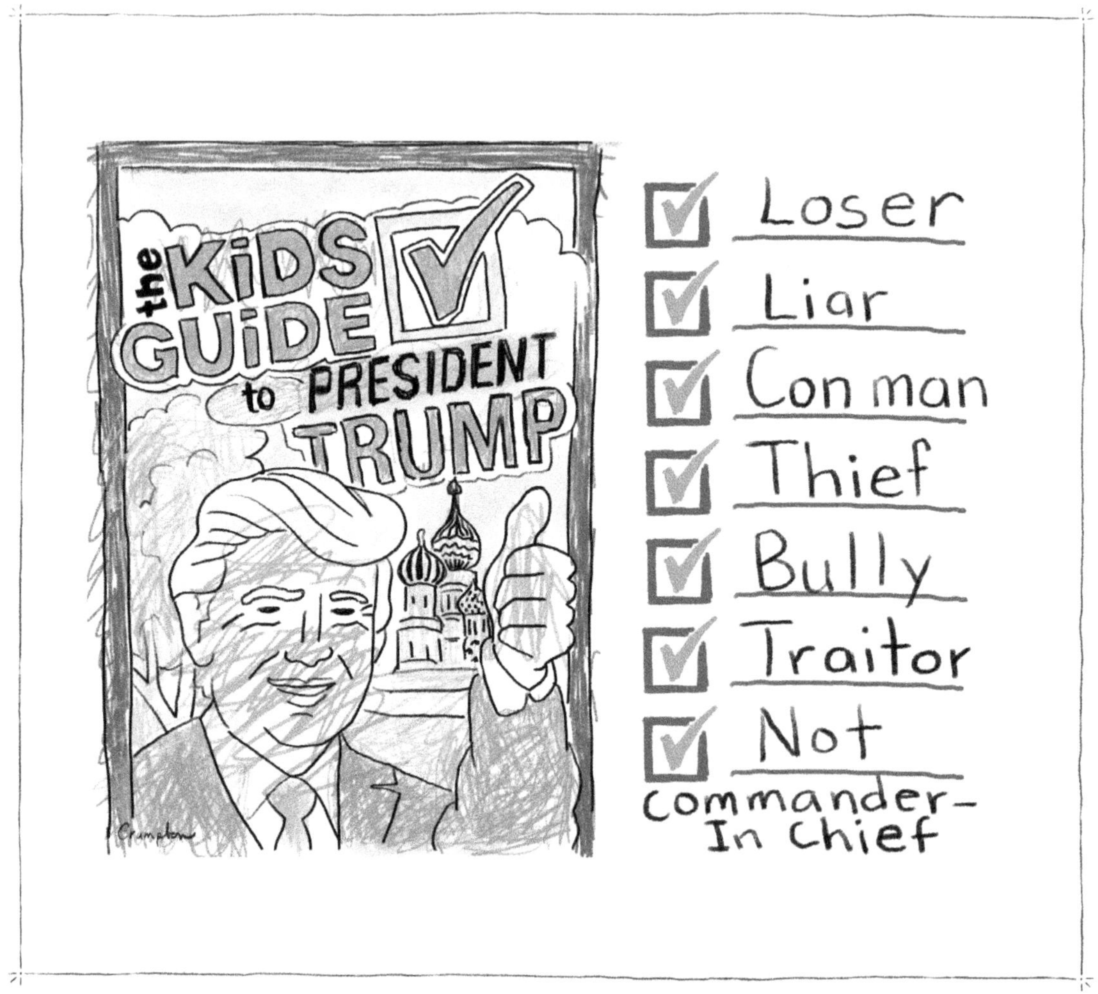

May 5, 2022
I'm making fun here of a real brochure about Trump for kids.

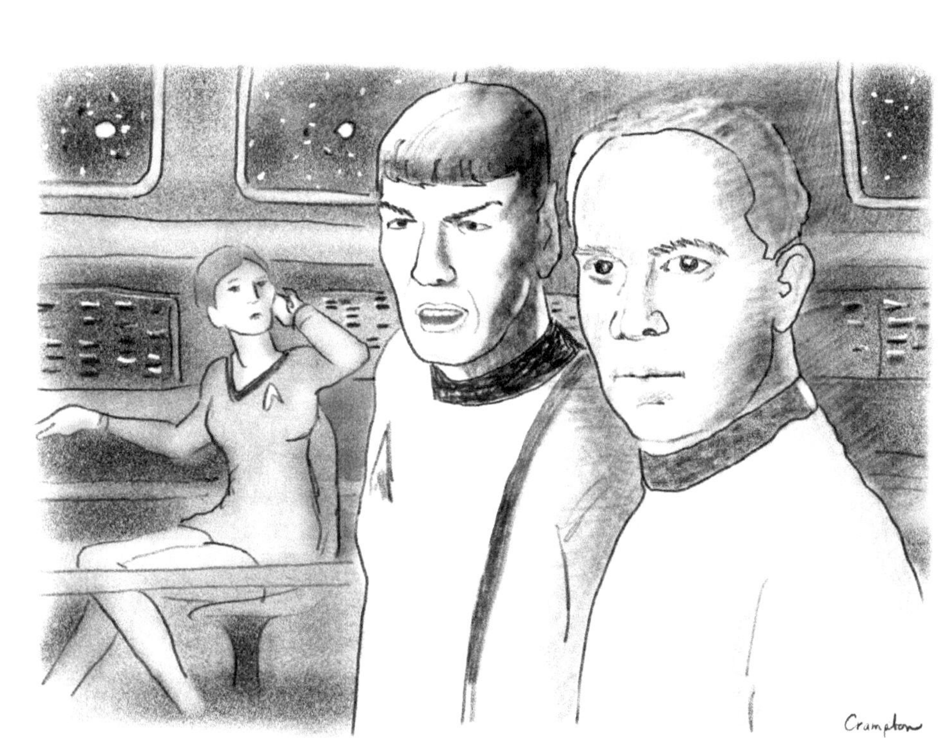

"Captain, we have arrived at Earth, Stardate 2022. Shall we proceed with our mission to wake humanity using the Jewish Space Laser?"

May 23, 2022
"Fox News" talks about "woke", grooming centers, sexual brainwashing, and calls President Biden "groomer-in-chief". This echoes QAnon theories that Democrats and Hollywood elites are a secret ring of Satanic pedophiles and that there is a Jewish space laser which caused 9/11 and the Californian wildfires.

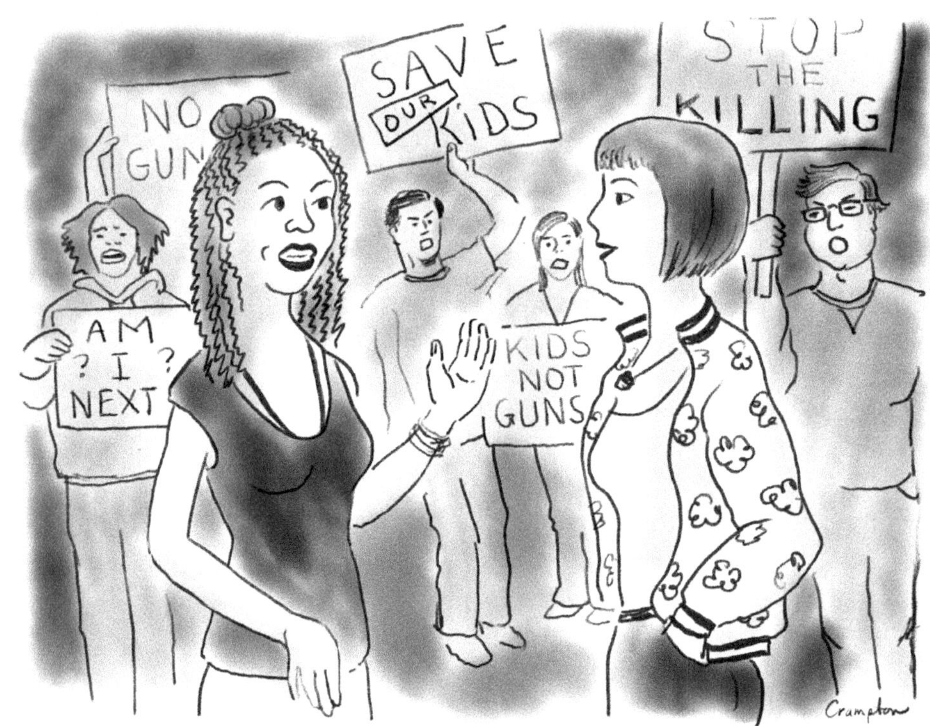

"So perfect that the NRA offers its *deepest sympathies* while actively selling the leading cause of childhood death in the U.S.A."

May 28, 2022
Mass shootings happen all over the U.S.A. culminating in a horrific school shooting on May 24 in Uvalde, Texas. Trump and Senator Ted Cruz brazenly spoke at an NRA* rally and gun show, in Houston, a few days later.
**National Rifle Association*

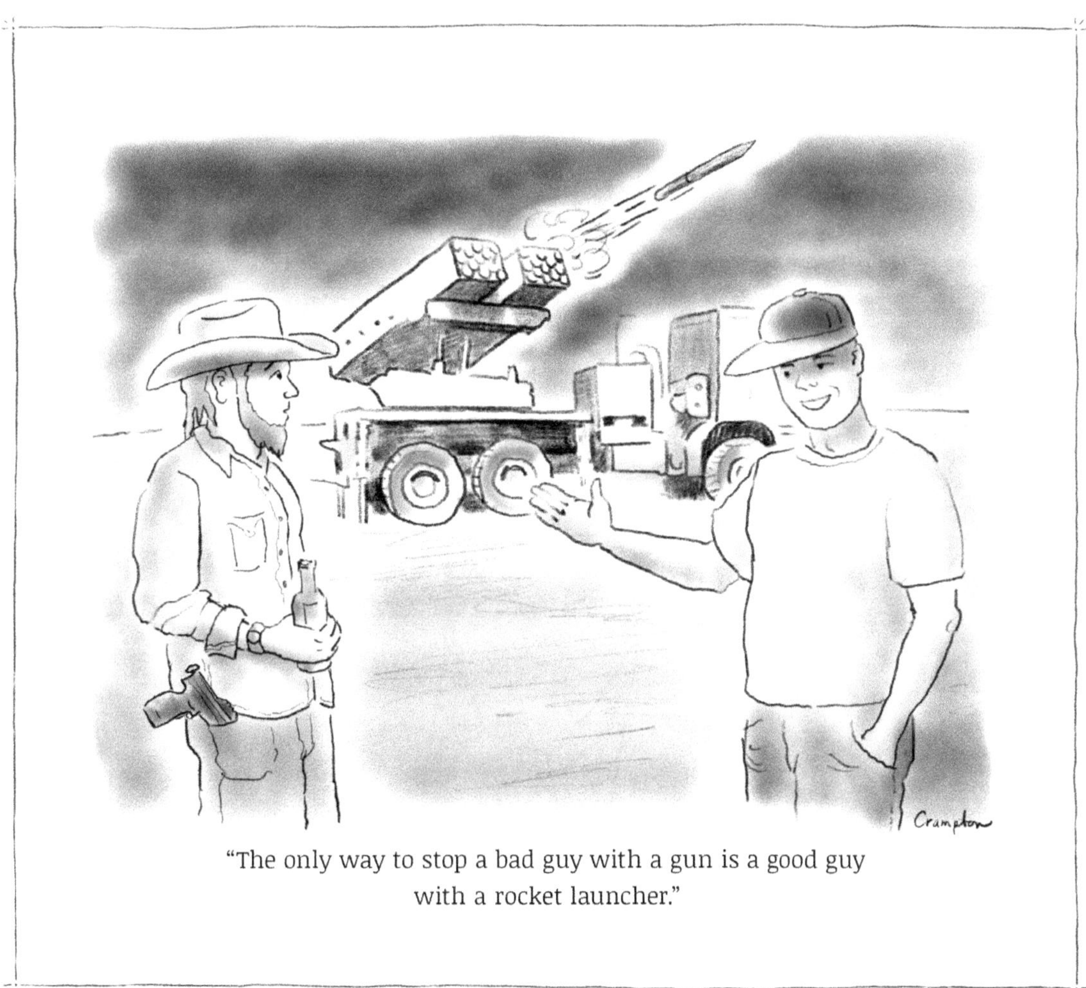

"The only way to stop a bad guy with a gun is a good guy with a rocket launcher."

June 3, 2022
Nineteen kids and two teachers were shot with an AR-15. Police, cowed by the fire power, waited more than an hour for a SWAT* team. Republican politicians say that we not only need more guns in schools but better doors.
**Special Weapons and Tactics police*

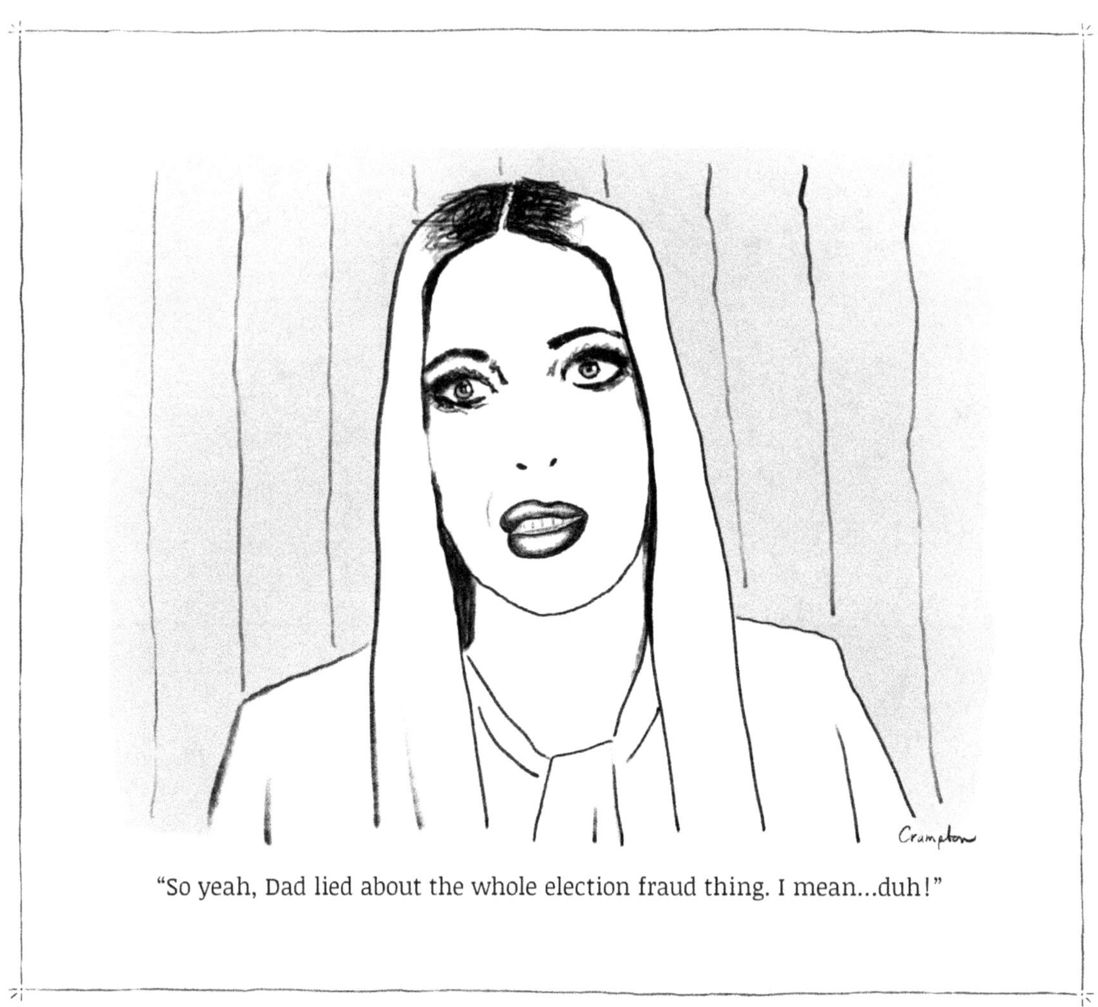

"So yeah, Dad lied about the whole election fraud thing. I mean...duh!"

June 10, 2022
Ivanka Trump appears in the January 6th Committee Hearings and says that election fraud claims were "a big lie". Trump quickly states that she was not involved and doesn't know much.

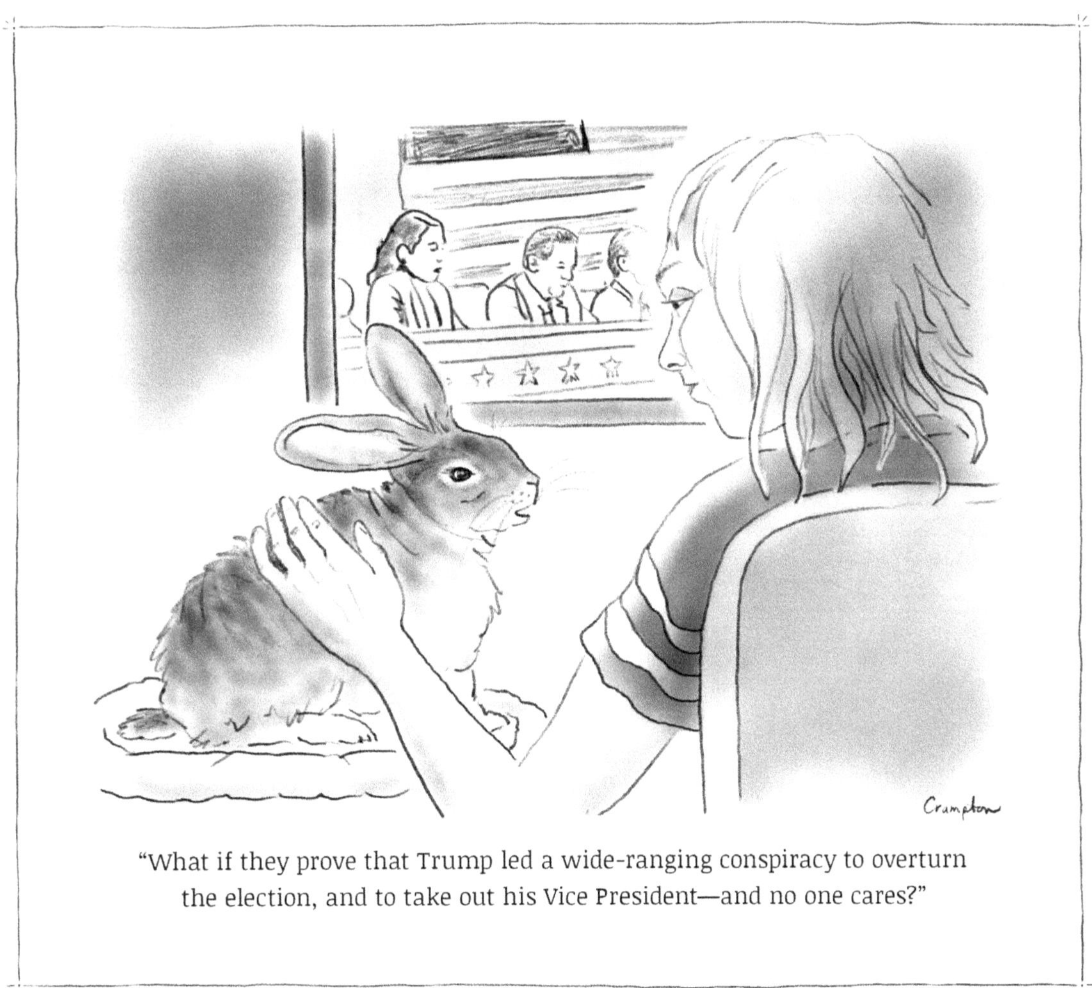

“What if they prove that Trump led a wide-ranging conspiracy to overturn the election, and to take out his Vice President—and no one cares?”

June 21, 2022
The January 6th Congressional Committee has a second hearing. No one I know bothered to watch it. The first hearing was completely ignored by "Fox News".

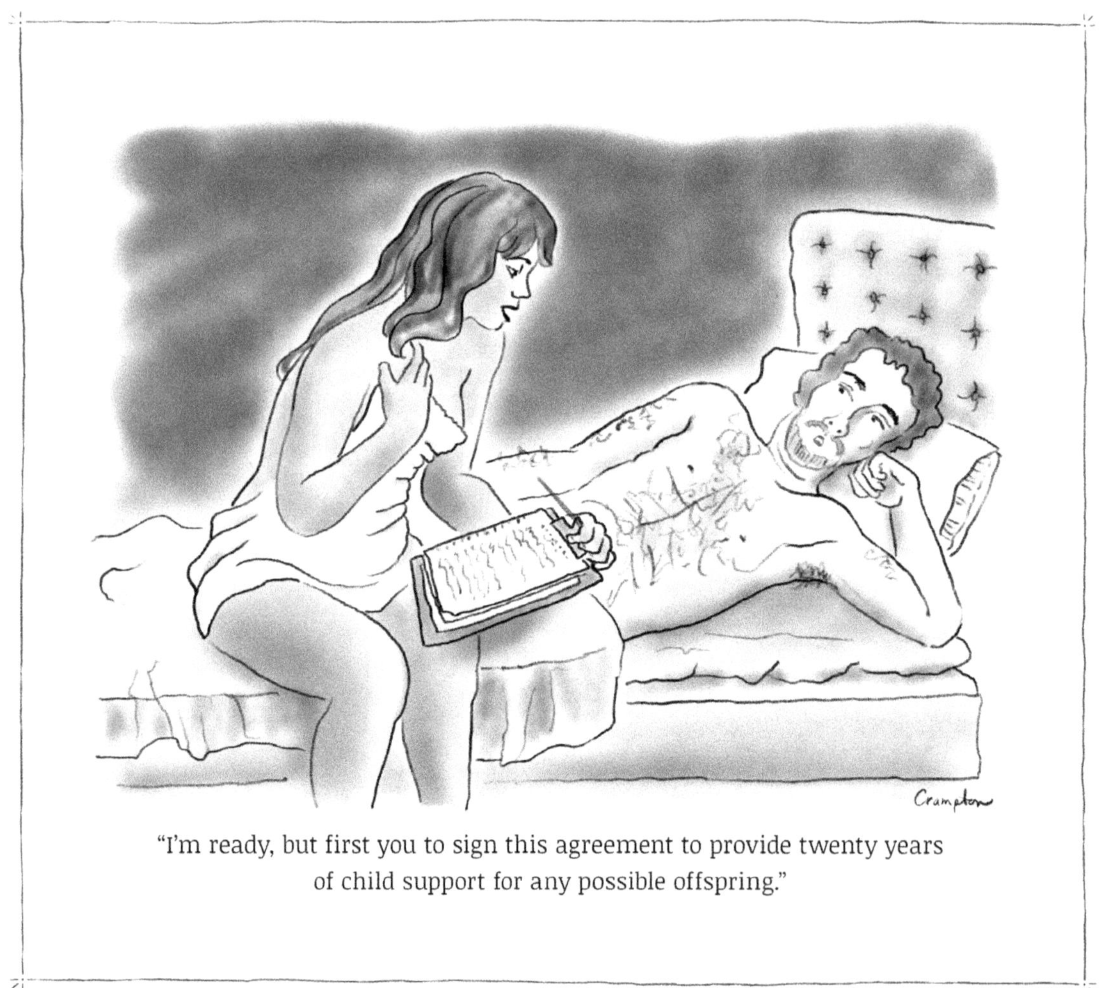

"I'm ready, but first you to sign this agreement to provide twenty years of child support for any possible offspring."

June 28, 2022
The Supreme Court overturns Roe v Wade which makes abortion illegal in many States.
Judge Thomas muses about going after birth control and gay marriage next. *Homage to Renoir and Alice Neel.*

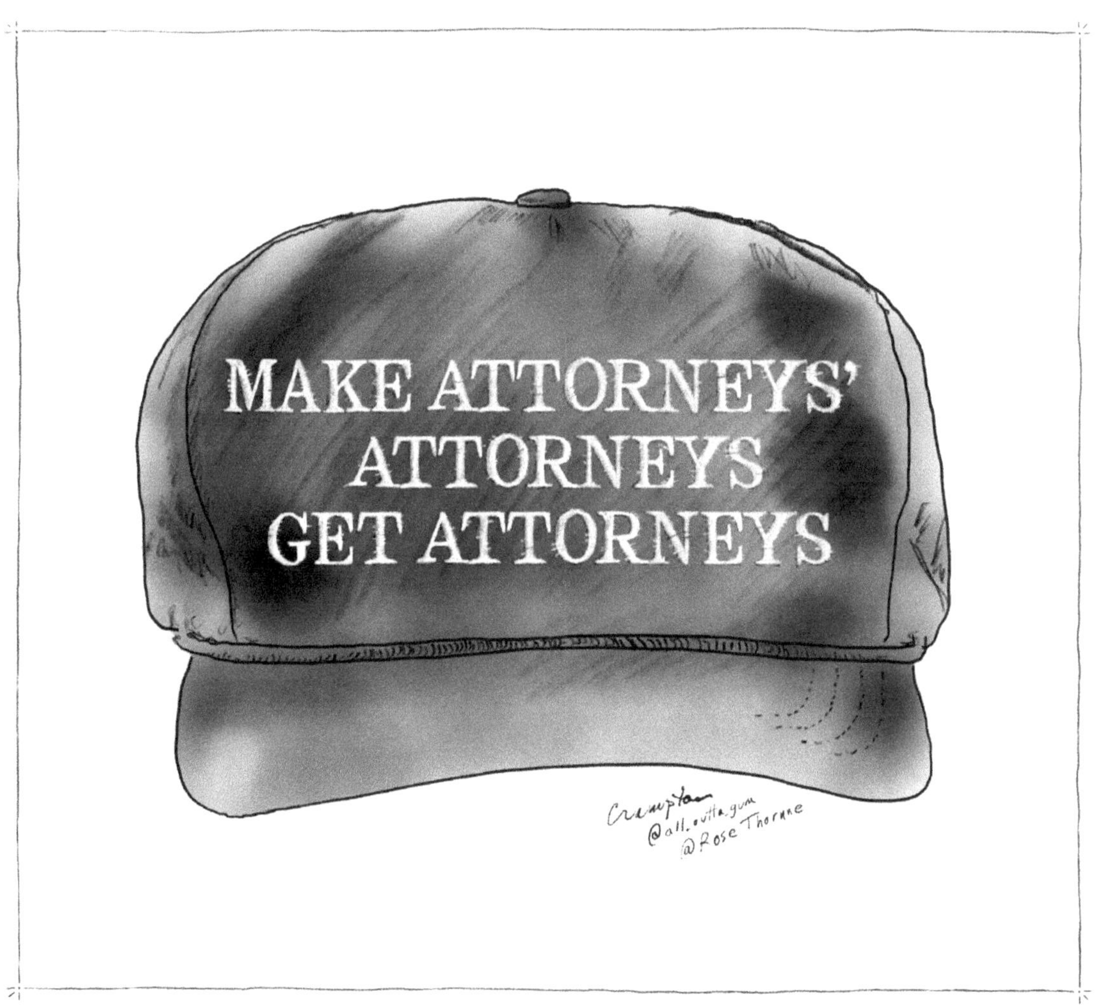

July 10, 2022
The January 6th Committee causes many Trump-associated attorneys to hire their own defense attorneys.
Thanks to @RoseThornne and @all_outta_gum.

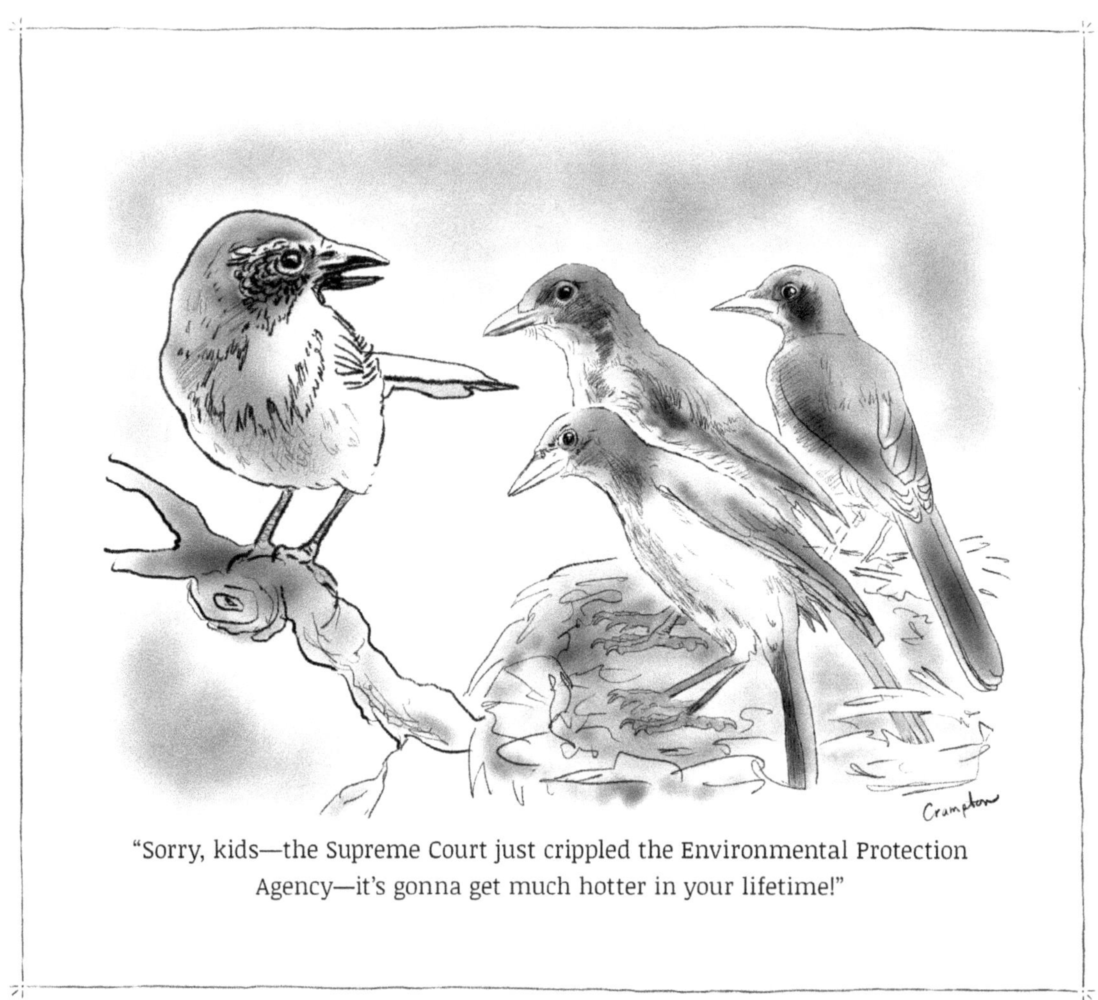

"Sorry, kids—the Supreme Court just crippled the Environmental Protection Agency—it's gonna get much hotter in your lifetime!"

July 12, 2022
The Conservative judges on the Supreme Court reduce the power of the Environmental Protection Agency, making it more difficult to mitigate climate change. My local scrub jays have fledglings.

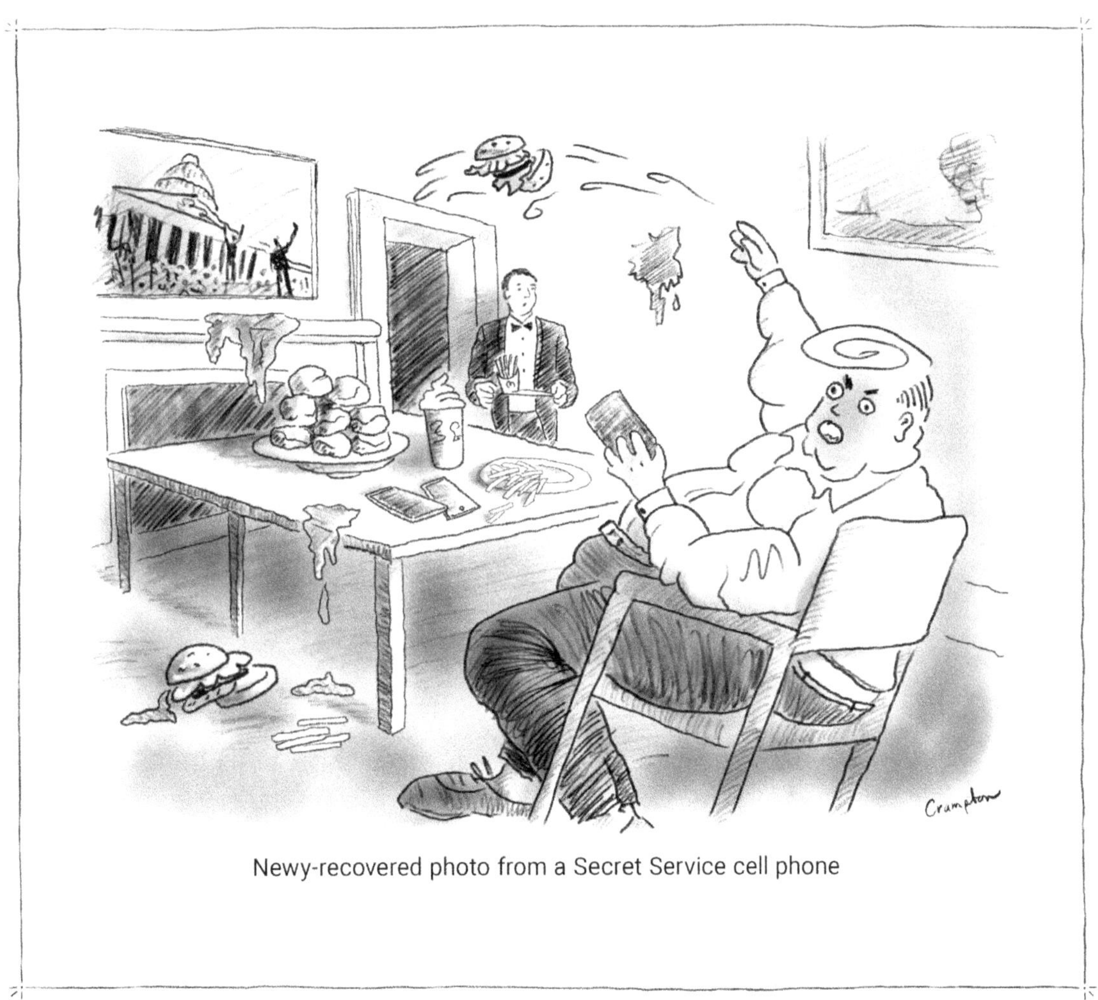

Newy-recovered photo from a Secret Service cell phone

August 4, 2022
Another scandal breaks about the Secret Service's phone data—requested by the January 6th Committee—but which was deleted and not backed up. This is a behind-the-scenes on January 6th drawing.

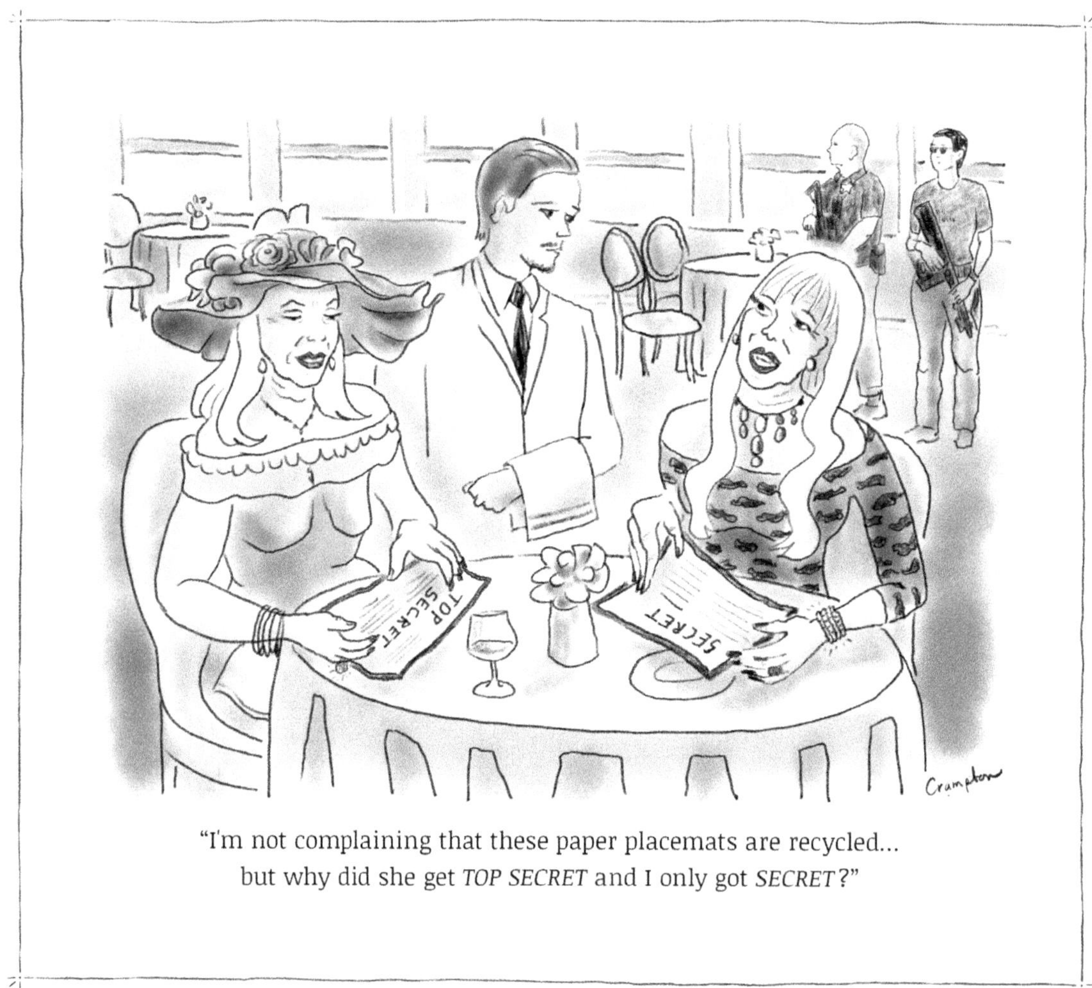

"I'm not complaining that these paper placemats are recycled...
but why did she get *TOP SECRET* and I only got *SECRET*?"

August 9, 2022
After many ignored requests, FBI agents raid Trump's Mar-a-Lago club, to retrieve classified and top secret documents. Some are so secret, they cannot be described.

You are cordially invited
to our
Exclusive Photography Club
Basement, Mar-a-Lago

Donation: $1,000,000 cash
Ladies in Bikinis Always Free
Burgers and Patriotic Cocktails
RSVP: WhatsApp

All you can Shoot
Classified Nuclear Data
Hot Procedural Documents
Tour of Melania's Closet

It Will Be Wild!

Crampton

August 13, 2022
The FBI finds documents in the basement, office and closets–areas which are visited routinely by Hotel staff.

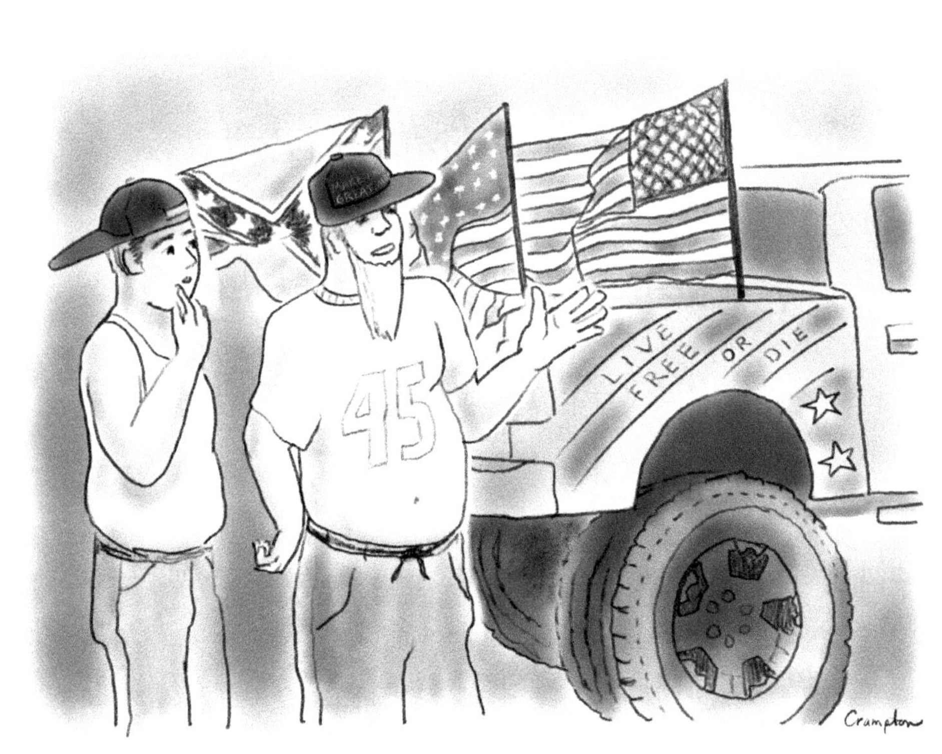

"This beaut? Bought her for $300. Told the bank she was worth $300,000.
Got a home loan. Now I'm selling her for $3,000,000.
If she don't sell, I'll drive her into the lake and claim insurance."

September 23, 2022
Inspired by news of Trump's alleged tax and insurance practices.

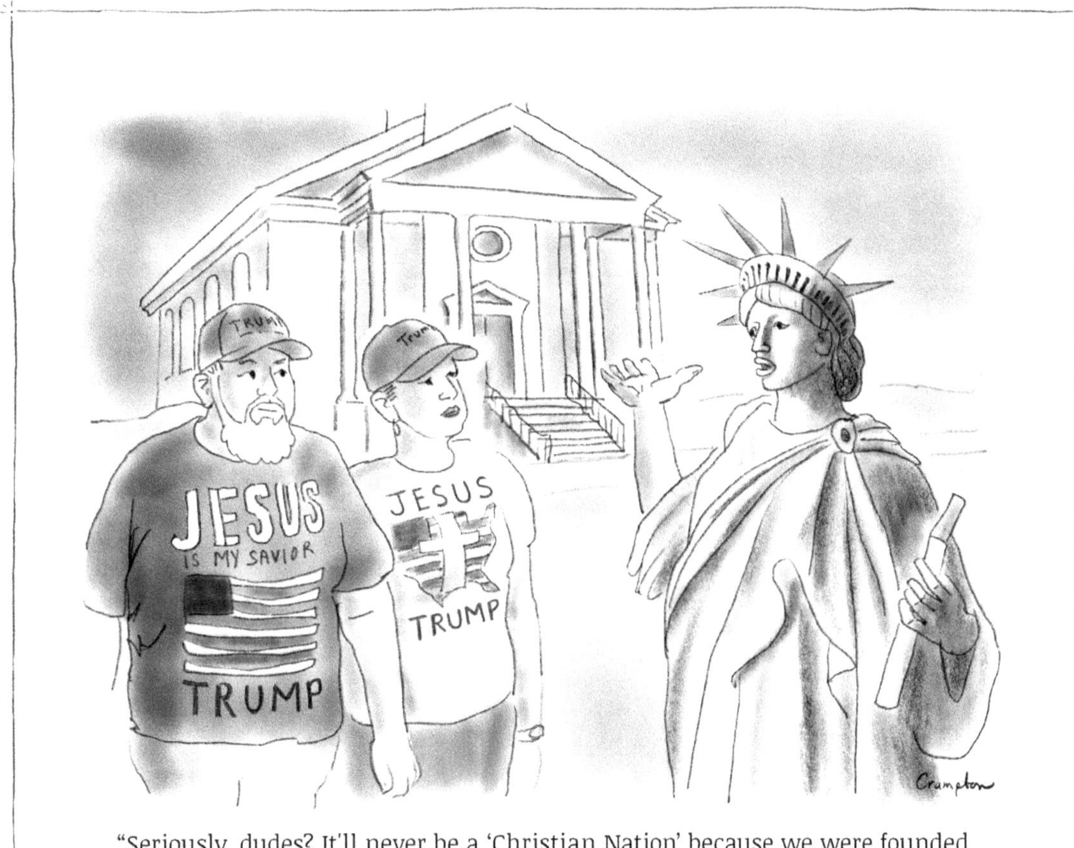

"Seriously, dudes? It'll never be a 'Christian Nation' because we were founded for religious liberty. And separation of church and state. I mean...duh!"

October 8, 2022
Republican leaders and candidates tout the idea of Christian Nation as part policy platform, especially in outreach to the LatinX population. In a Pew Research study, 45% of adults asked said that the U.S.A. was a Christian Nation. Have anyone read the First Amendment to the Constitution?

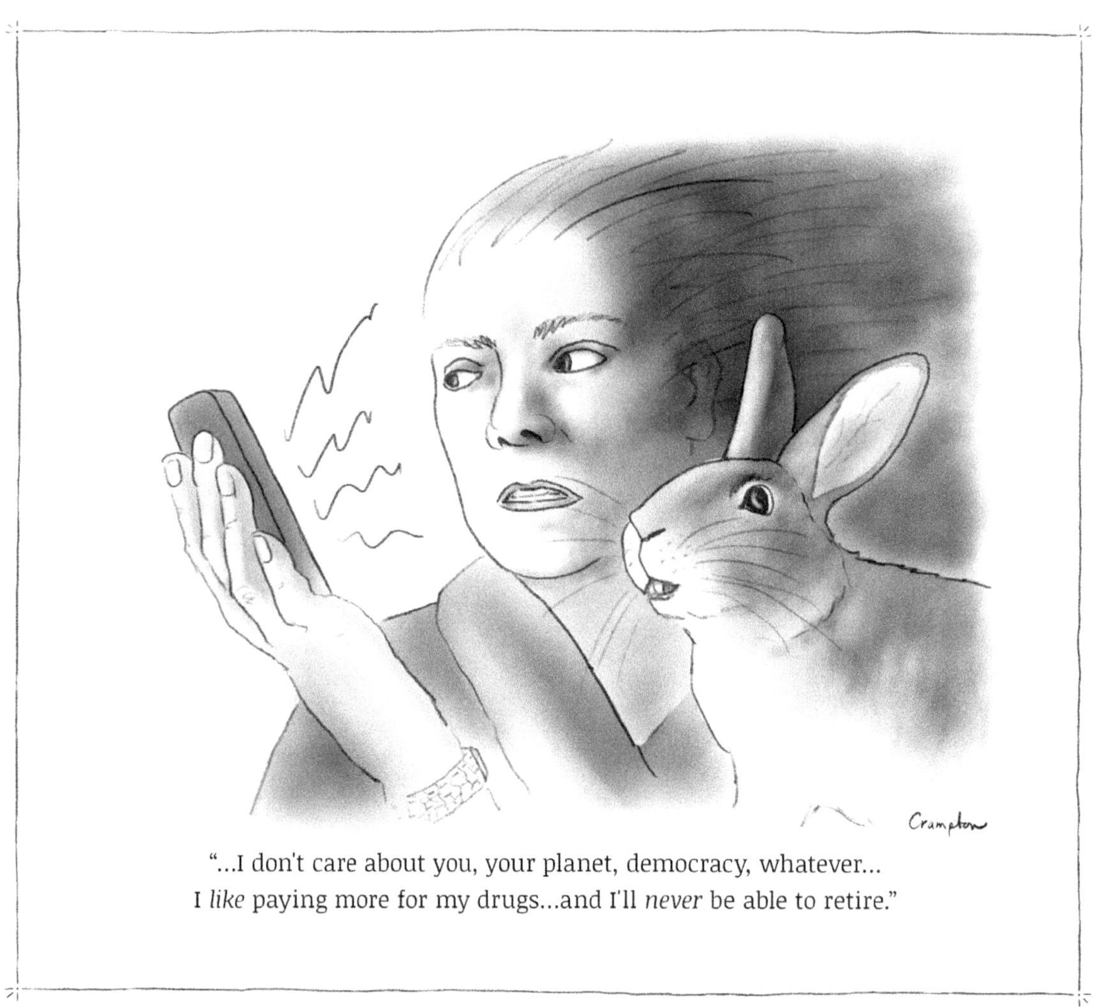

"...I don't care about you, your planet, democracy, whatever...
I *like* paying more for my drugs...and I'll *never* be able to retire."

November 3, 2022
I read similar comments from Republicans on "Truth Social" about how they would vote.
This represents an imaginary phone conversation.

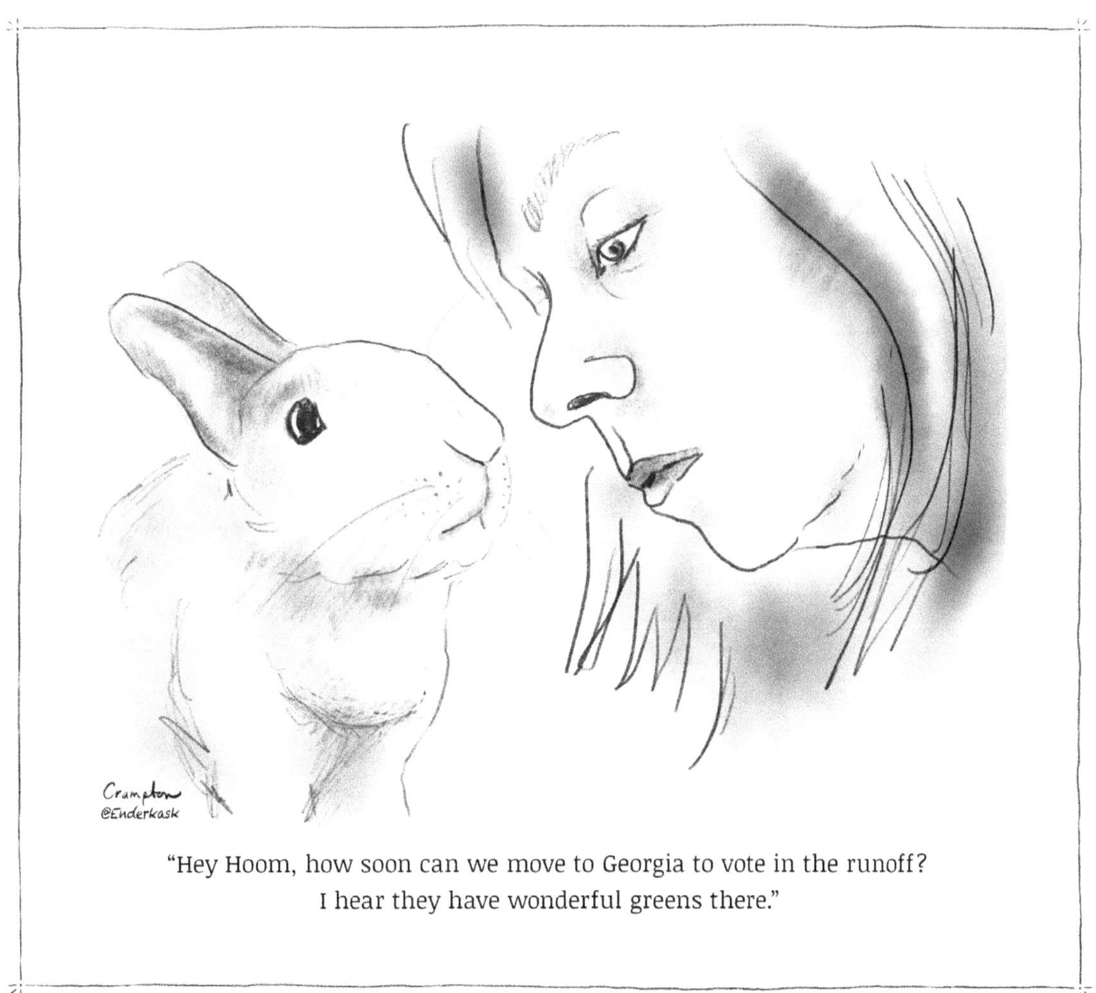

"Hey Hoom, how soon can we move to Georgia to vote in the runoff?
I hear they have wonderful greens there."

November 9, 2022
After the mid-term election on November 8th, Representative Rev. Raphael Warnock defeated Herschel Walker by less than a full point triggering a new run-off election. This election may decide which party controls the Senate. *Thanks to @Enderkask. Am I drawing too many rabbits now?*

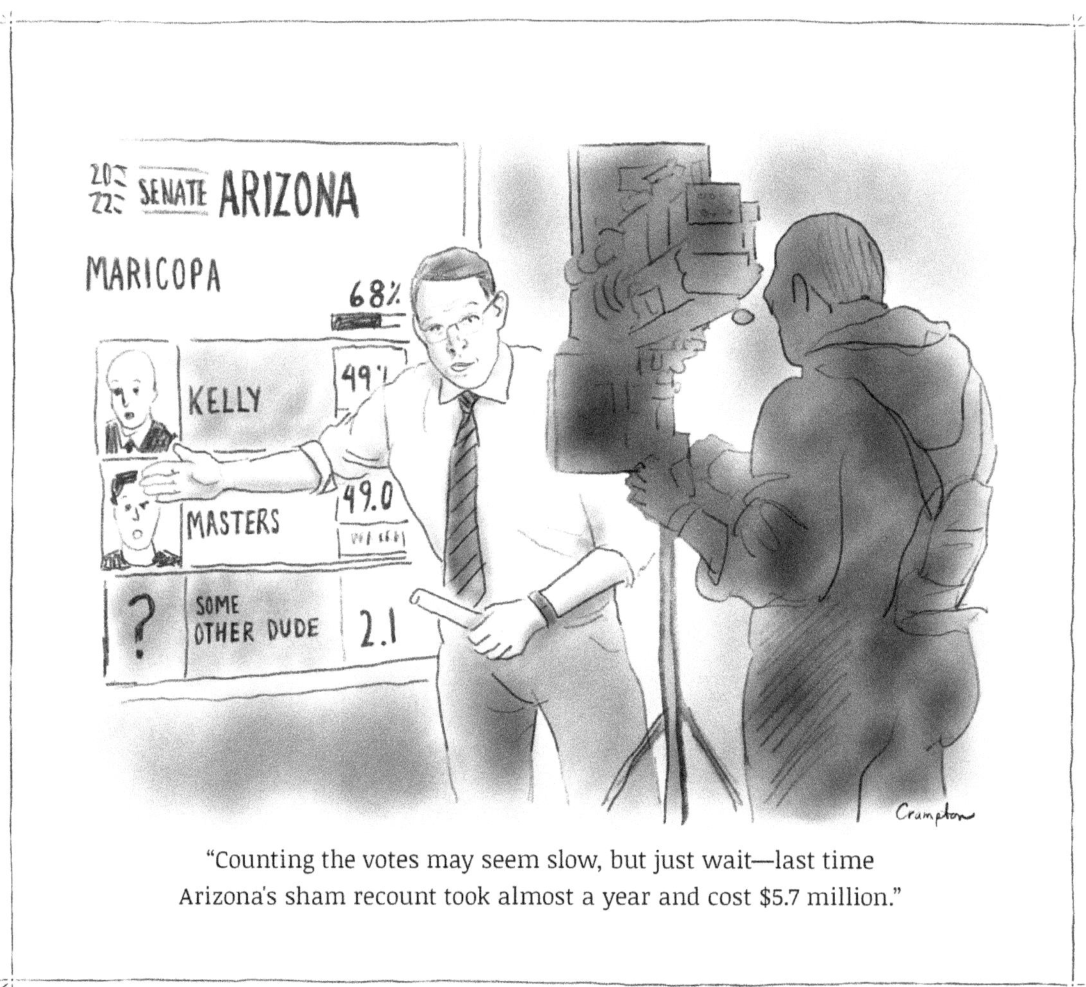

"Counting the votes may seem slow, but just wait—last time Arizona's sham recount took almost a year and cost $5.7 million."

December 12, 2022
After the mid-term elections, Kari Lake refuses to concede in the race for Governor of Arizona and sues the County. The race for Attorney General, decided by 511 votes, triggered a mandatory statewide recount.
(Note: Lake didn't concede but decided to run for Senate in 2024.)

B	I	N	G	O
Trump Organization tax fraud case	Defying supoena from Jan. 6 Committee	SDNY civil bank/ insurance fraud	Mar-a-Lago classified documents	E. Jean Carroll rape case
Ordering IRS audit on enemies	Georgia State election interference	Inciting an insurrection	Lying about Covid	Lying about path of hurricane
NY State insurance/ tax case	Burying your ex-wife on golf course	GO DIRECTLY TO JAIL	Dangling pardons to avoid explosure	Lying about Melania's kidneys
Fake electors scheme	Attempt to assassinate VPOTUS	Emoluments	Filing bogus briefs to SCOTUS	Passing data to foreign adversary
Trying to write off My Pillow	Withholding funds to Ukraine	Using personal iphone	Flushing secret docs down toilet	Eating top secret documents

December 1, 2022
There are so many ongoing investigations of Trump or the Trump organization that one wonders which will hit first. On December 6th the Trump Organization was found guilty on all counts in the NY State criminal insurance/tax case.

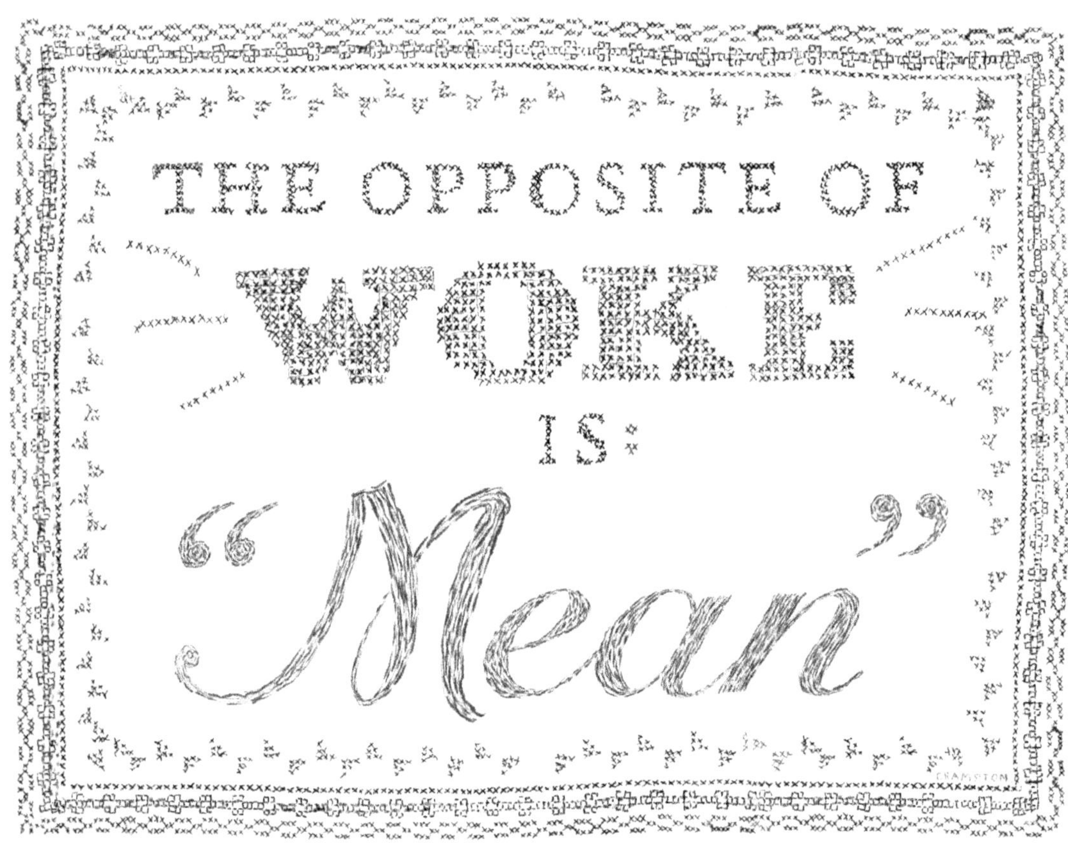

December 17, 2022
Republicans, in traditional and social media, throw the word "Woke" around as way to insult Liberals.

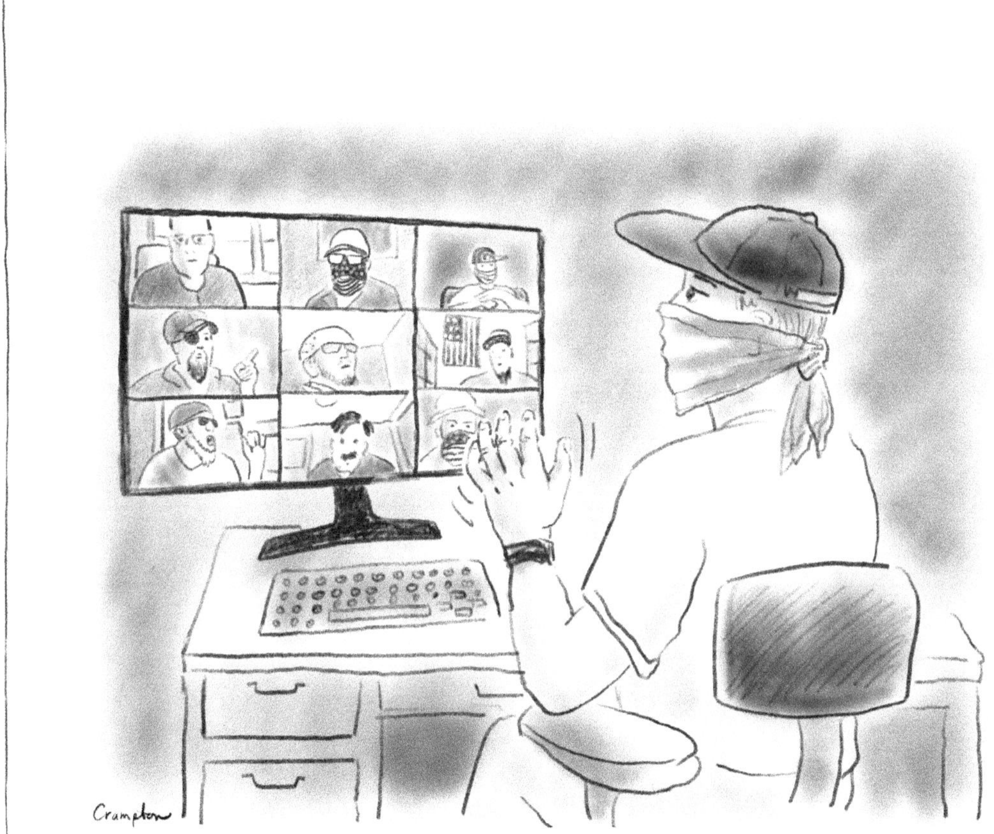

"Just so you know, they both come in "Coyote", but the Voodoo Entry Assault tactical vest is $91 dollars less than the Valkyrie Plate carrier."

December 21, 2022
The full January 6th Congressional Committee Report was just issued.
I haven't read it yet, but I decided to do some behind-the-scenes illustrations.

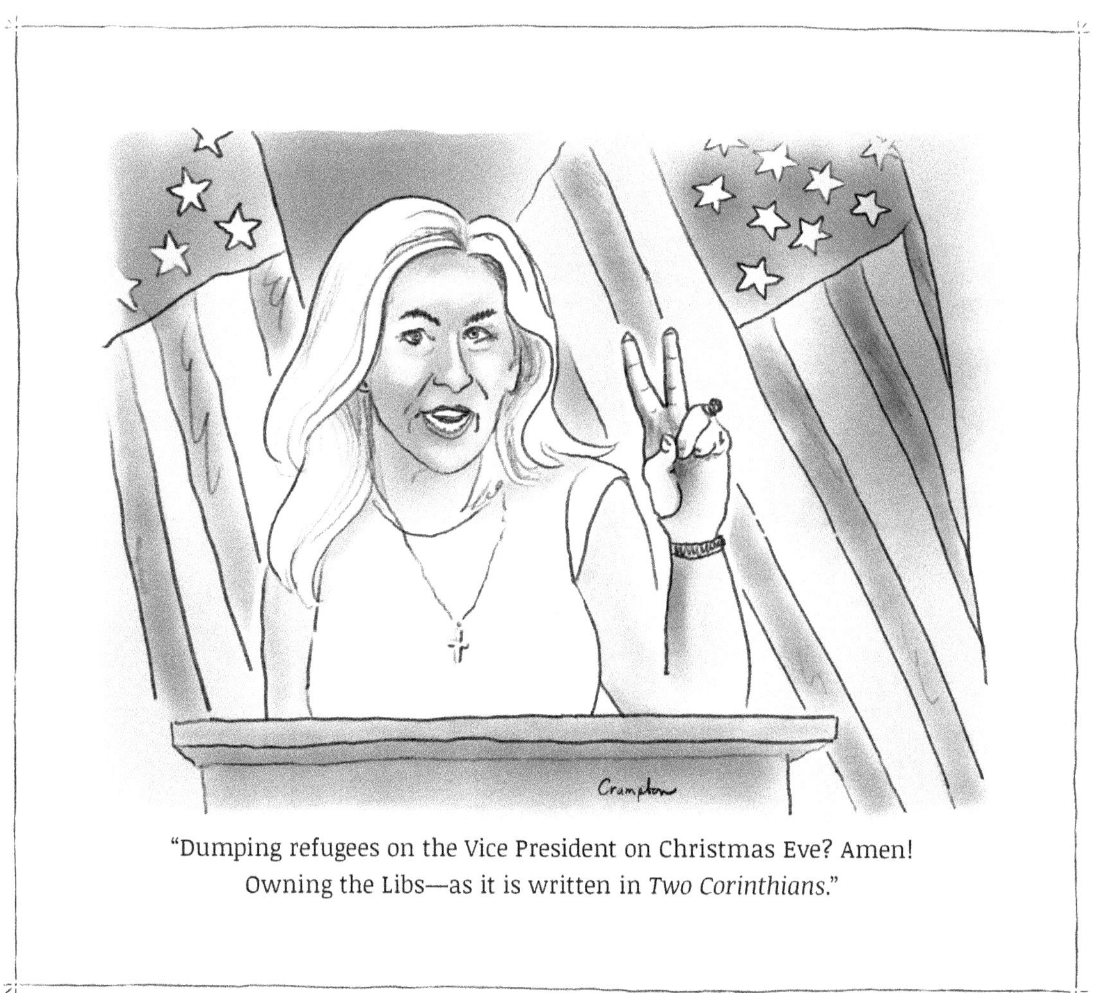

"Dumping refugees on the Vice President on Christmas Eve? Amen! Owning the Libs—as it is written in *Two Corinthians*."

December 28, 2022
Texas Governor Greg Abbott shipped over 100 migrants to VP Kamala Harris' Washington home on Christmas Eve; as a surprise. Trump-sycophant Rep. Marjorie Taylor Greene may force concessions from wannabe House Speaker Kevin McCarthy. Trump can't name a favorite Bible verse, or his preference for the Old or the New Testament. He said his favorite part was "2 Corinthians".

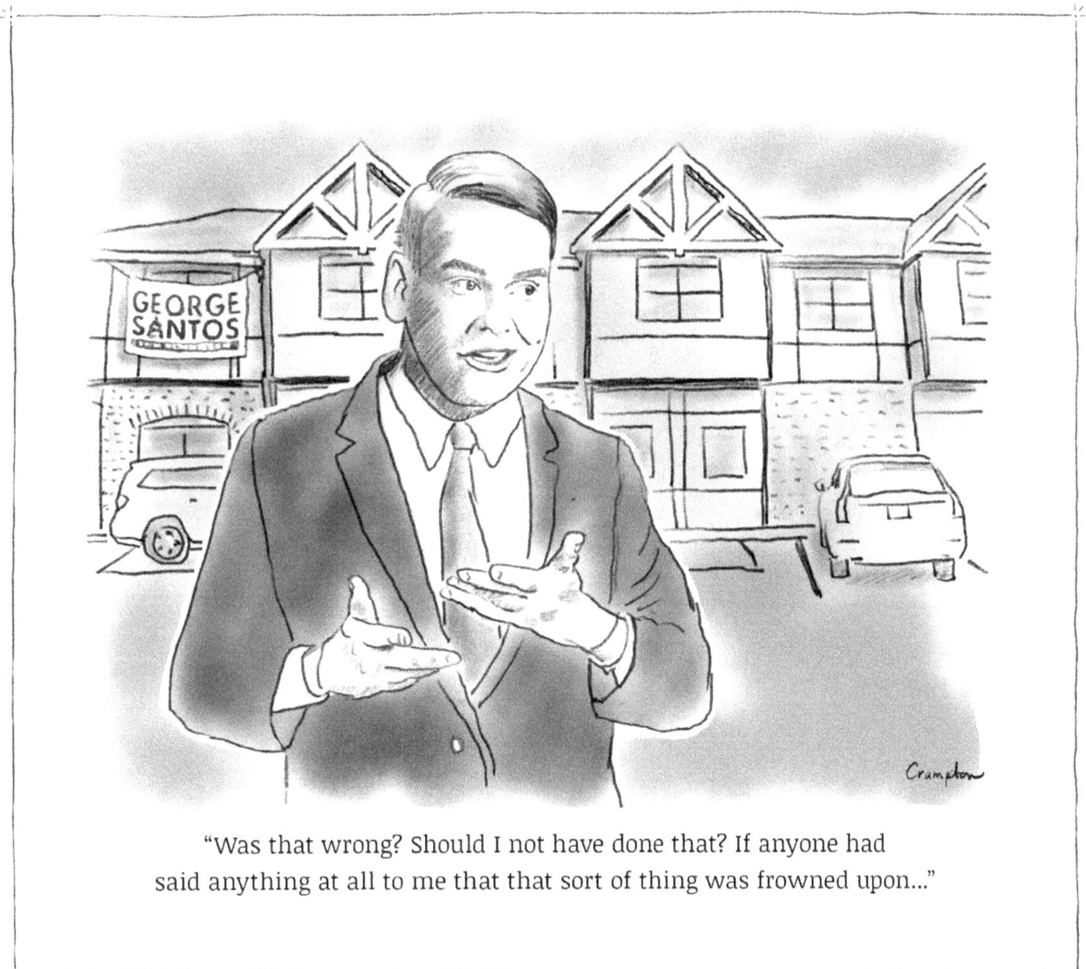

"Was that wrong? Should I not have done that? If anyone had said anything at all to me that that sort of thing was frowned upon..."

December 29, 2022
George Santos was elected to the House of Representatives using a fake resume and possibly with funds from a cousin of a Russian Oligarch. *This tagline is from a "Seinfeld" episode where George gets caught having sex on his office desk with the cleaning lady.*

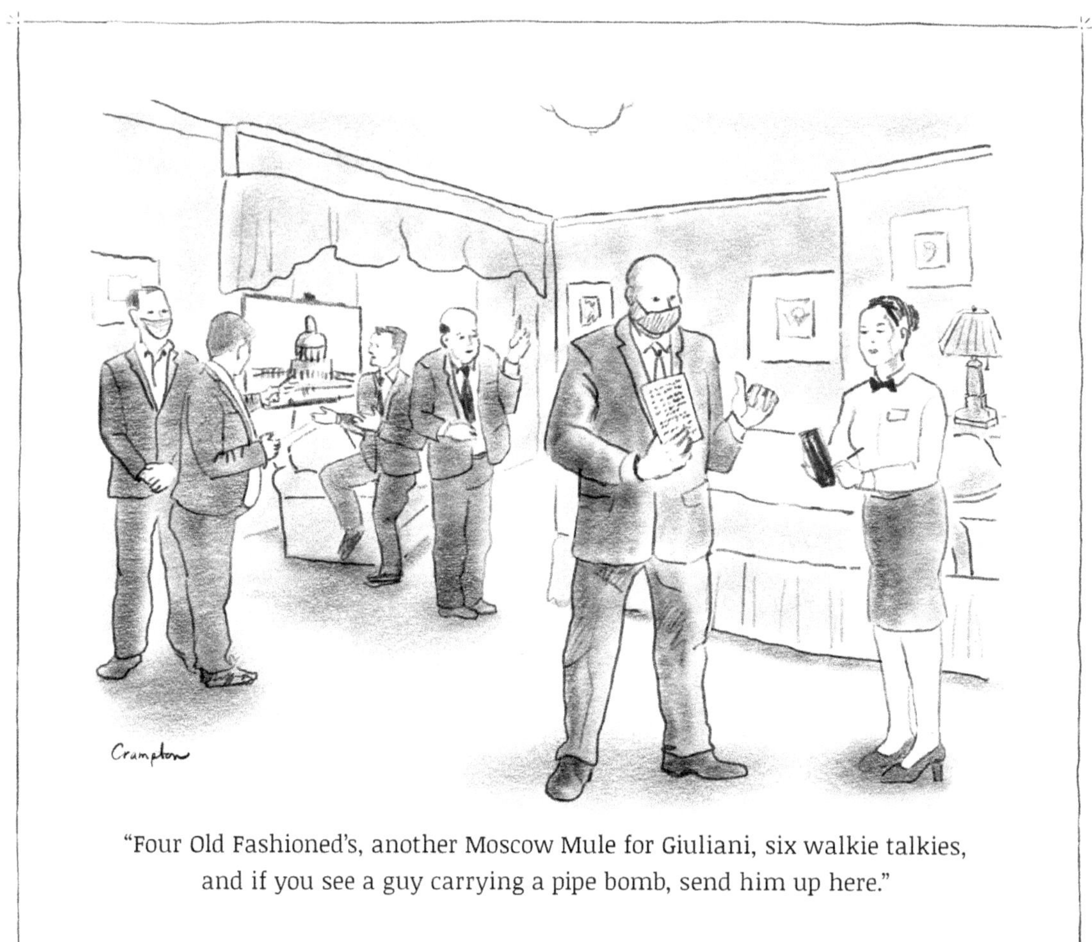

"Four Old Fashioned's, another Moscow Mule for Giuliani, six walkie talkies, and if you see a guy carrying a pipe bomb, send him up here."

January 11, 2023
More imagined behind-the-scenes of the January 6th Congressional Committee Report.

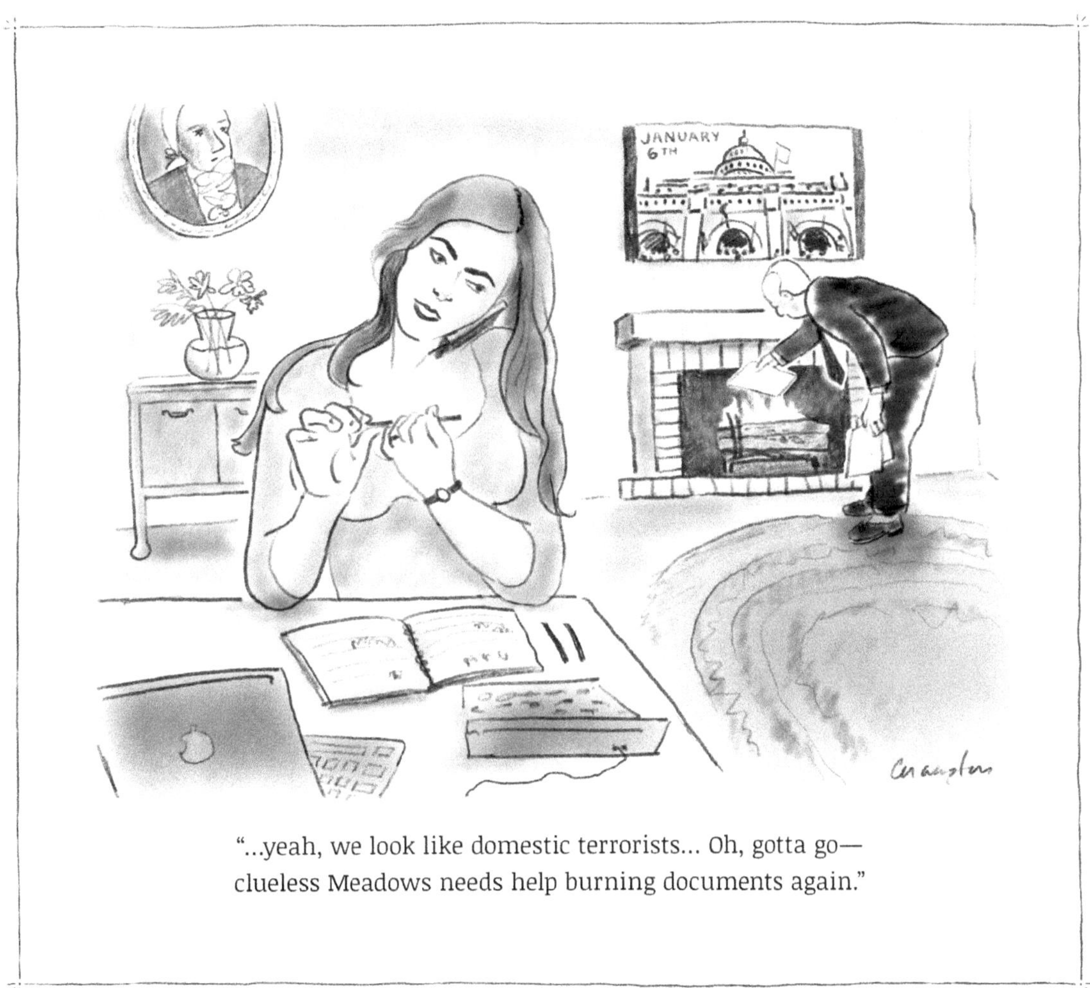

"...yeah, we look like domestic terrorists... Oh, gotta go—
clueless Meadows needs help burning documents again."

January 18, 2023
Another behind-the-scenes of the January 6th Congressional Committee Report.

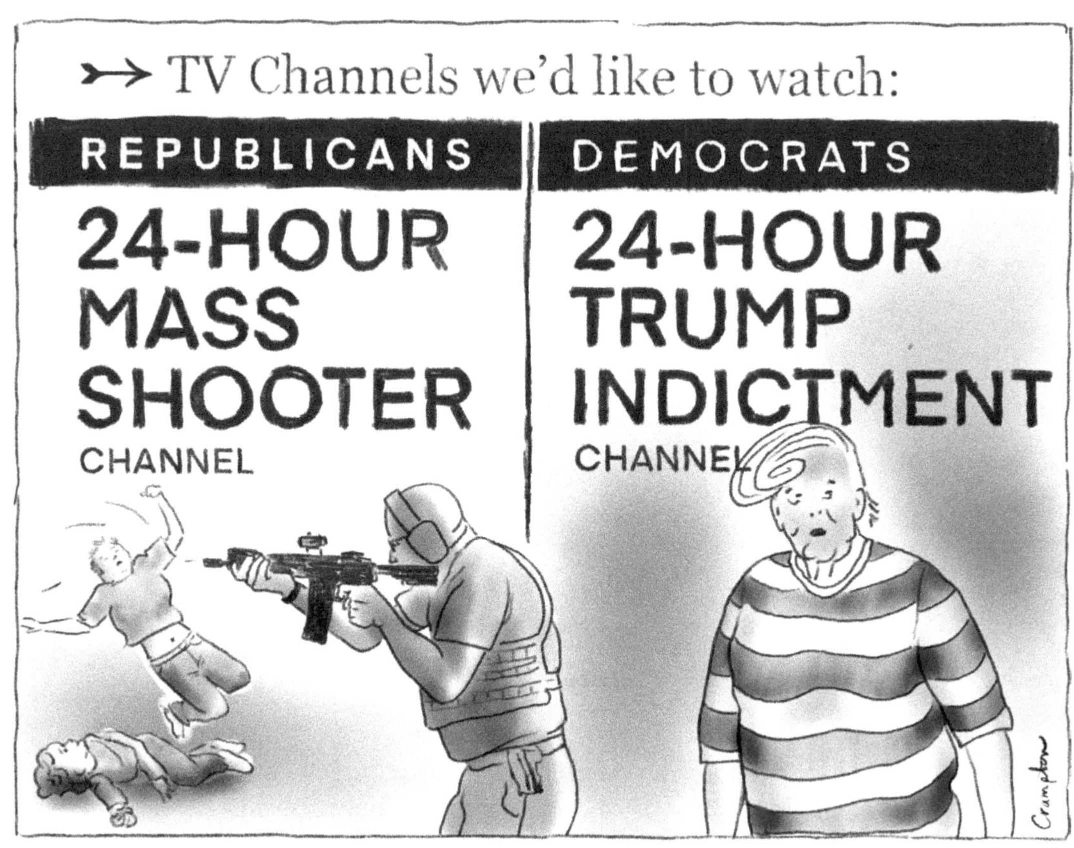

February 14, 2023
More mass shootings and indictment news than you can shake a stick at.

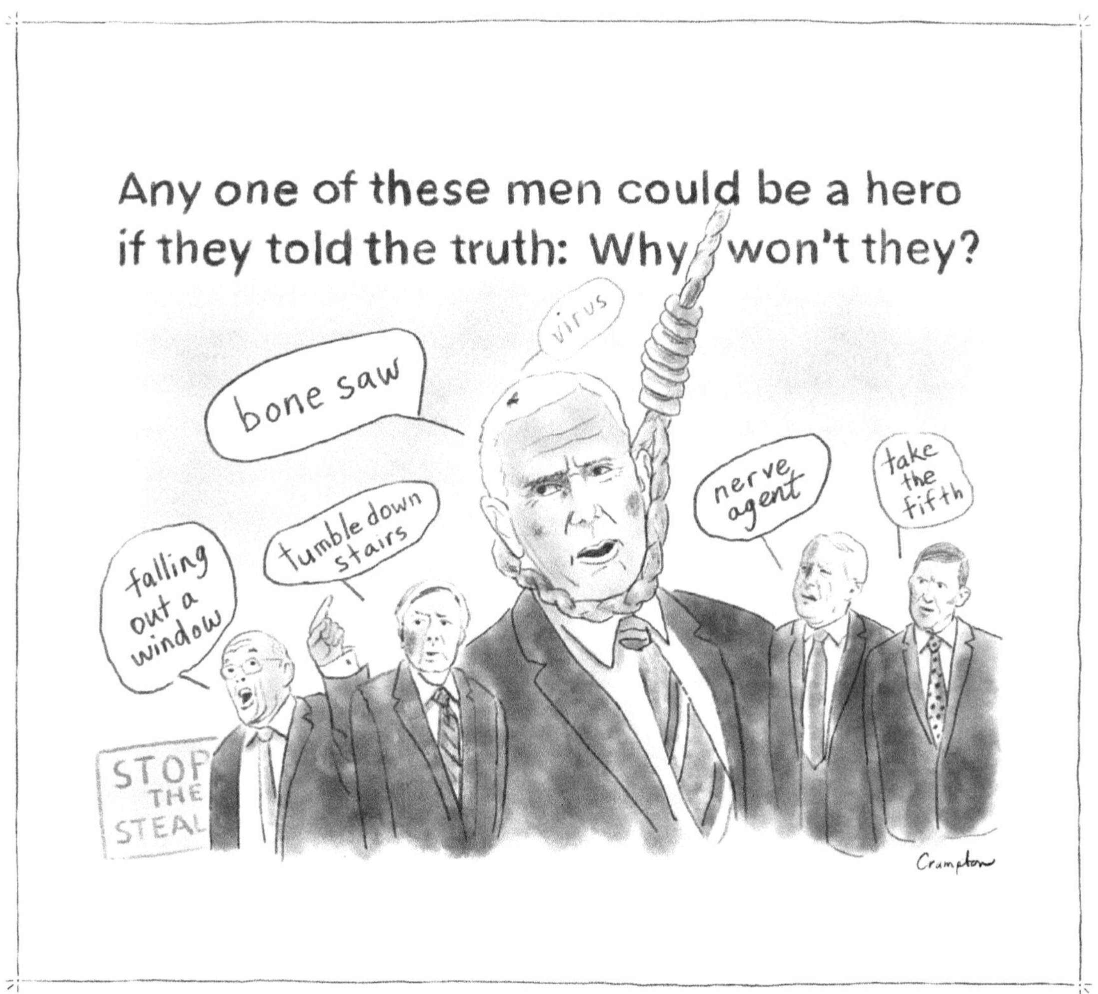

February 18, 2023
Reporters say that Republicans grumble off-the-record but won't criticize Trump in public–and this includes former Vice President Mike Pence. Trump's wanted Pence not to certify the election. Why they are so silent?

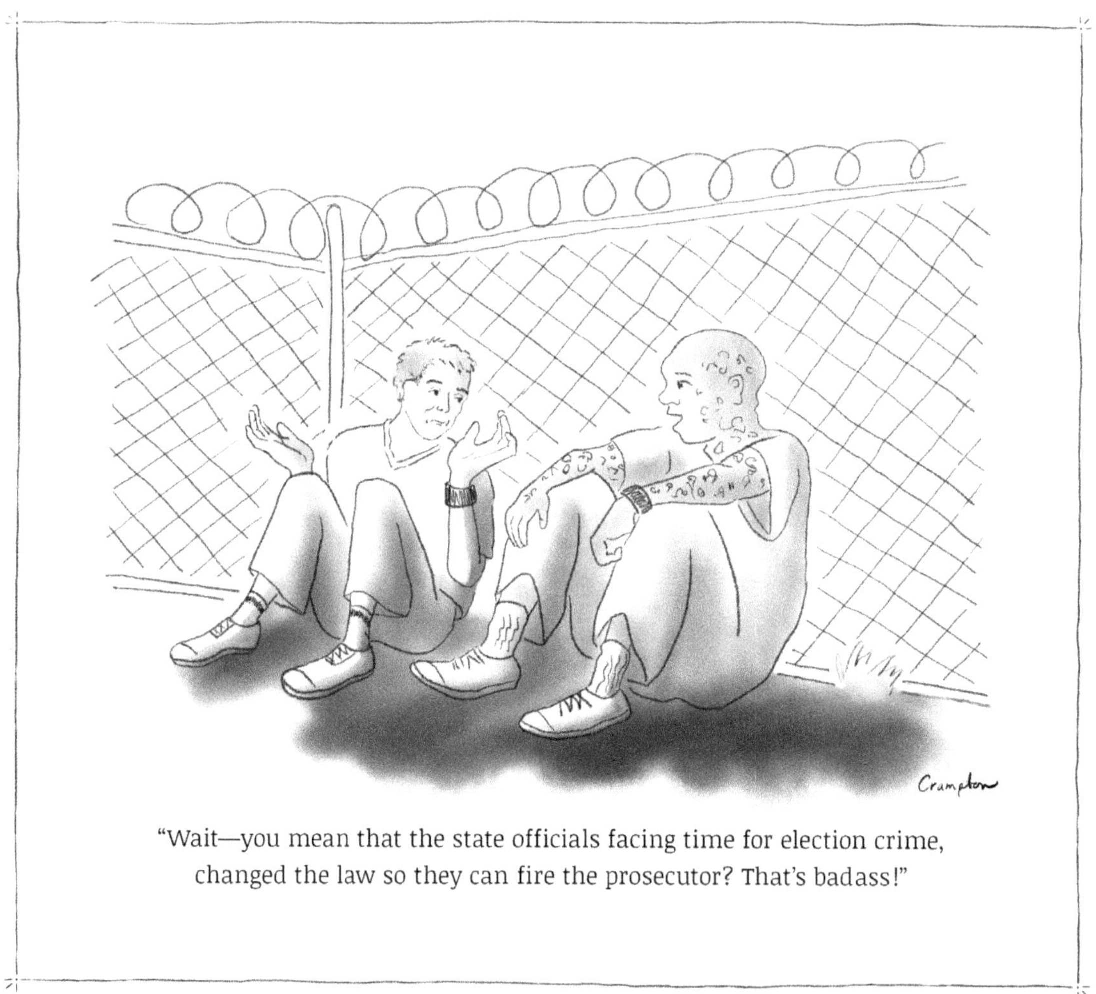

"Wait—you mean that the state officials facing time for election crime, changed the law so they can fire the prosecutor? That's badass!"

March 14, 2023
Republican State officials in Georgia try to remove Fani Willis, the Fulton County District Attorney, from her role as lead prosecutor in the case of Trump's efforts to overturn the 2020 election.

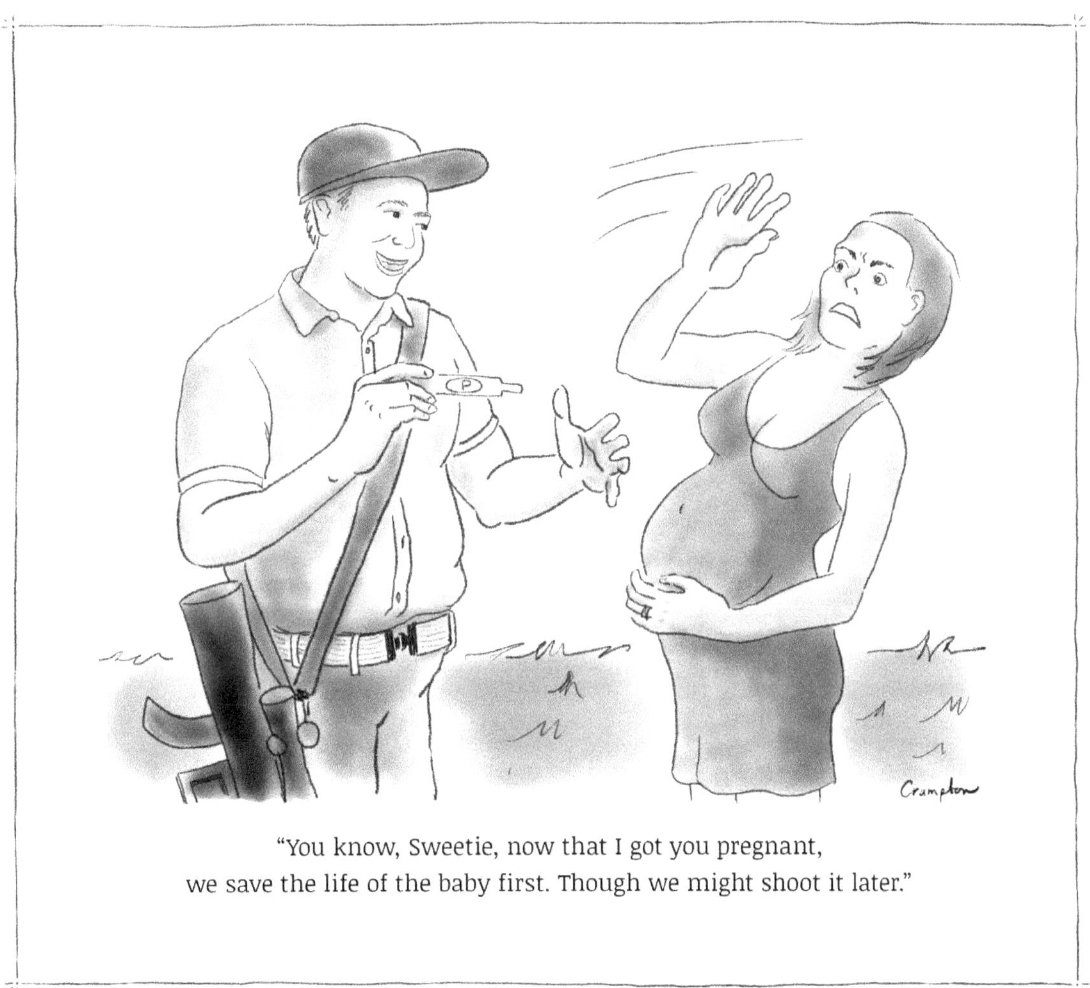

"You know, Sweetie, now that I got you pregnant,
we save the life of the baby first. Though we might shoot it later."

April 12, 2023
More child mass-shooting victims. The Supreme Court hears a case to uphold a Texas ban on Mifepristone, an FDA-approved drug, widely-used for abortions and miscarriages. *Yes, this is not funny.*

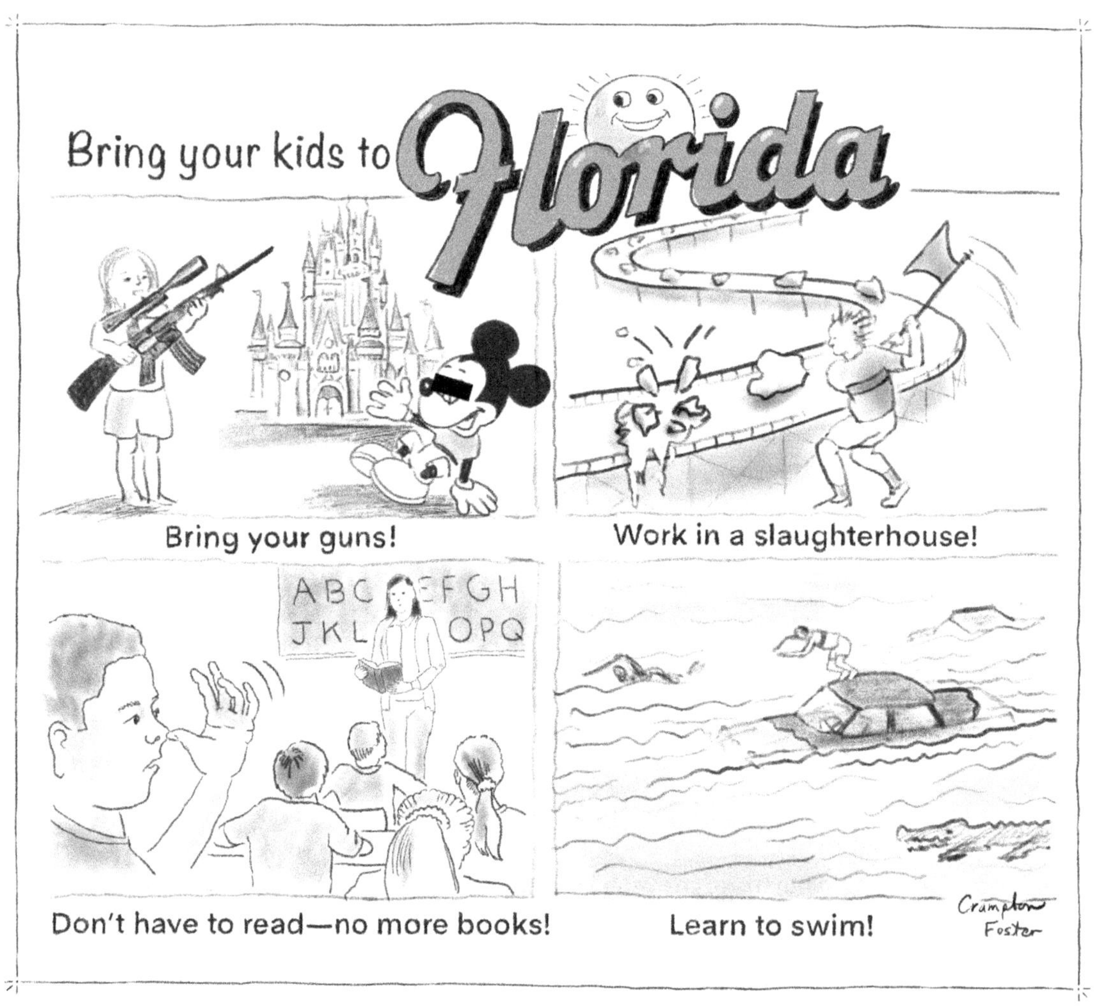

April 17, 2023
Florida Governor Ron DeSantis made changes to ease child labor laws and ban books. Florida is an open carry state.* There was an historic flash flood in the Fort Lauderdale area.
*Concept by Michael Foster. *You can't really bring guns to the amusement parks*

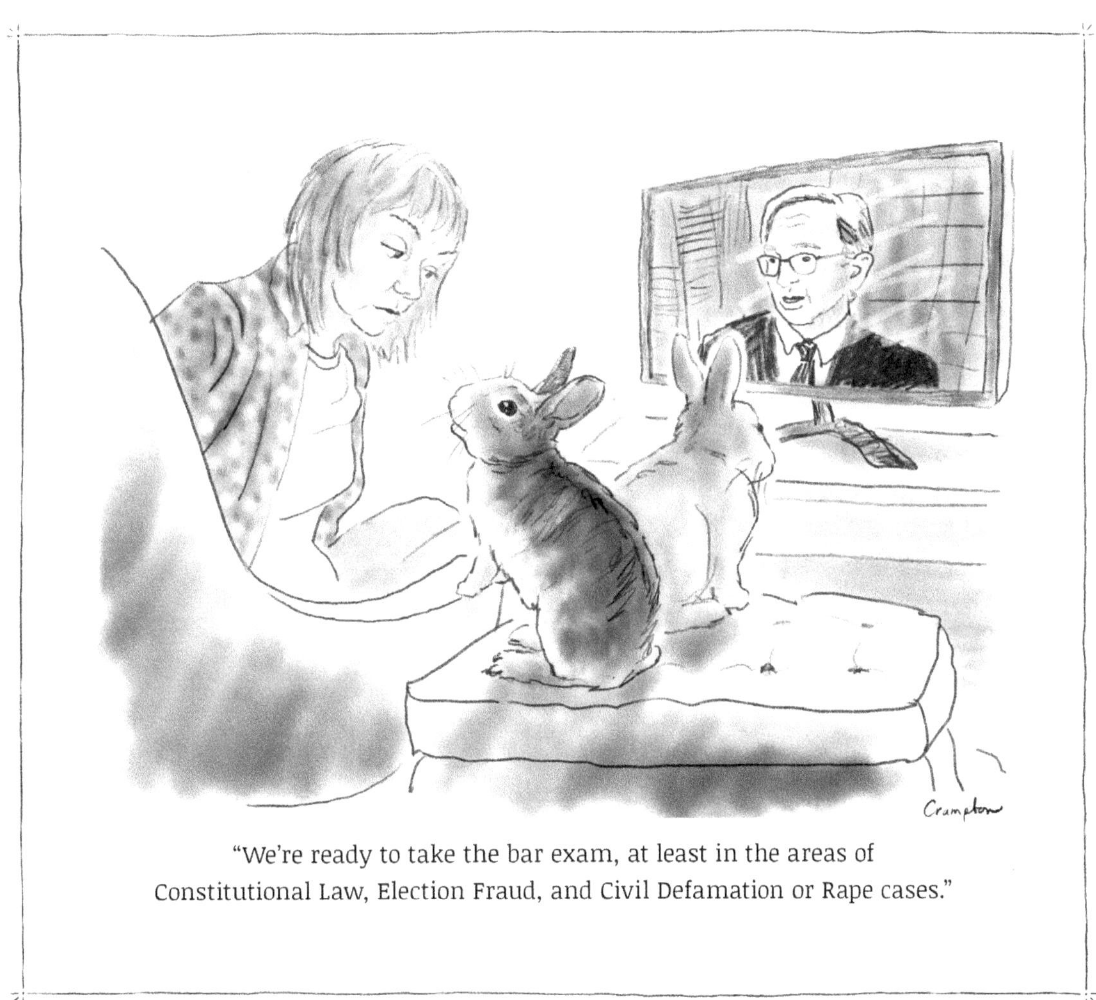

"We're ready to take the bar exam, at least in the areas of Constitutional Law, Election Fraud, and Civil Defamation or Rape cases."

May 2, 2023
Inspired by the defamation suit of E. Jean Carroll versus Donald Trump.

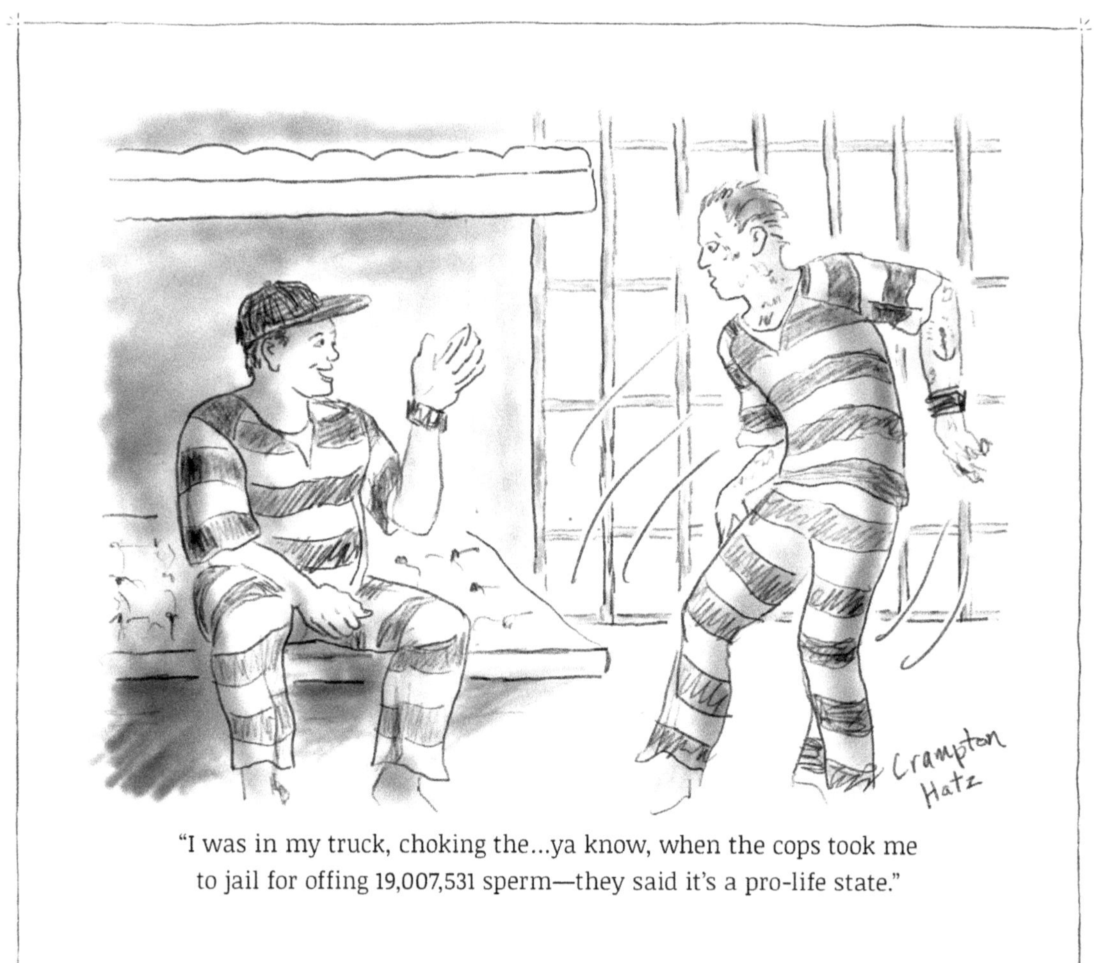

"I was in my truck, choking the…ya know, when the cops took me to jail for offing 19,007,531 sperm—they said it's a pro-life state."

May 28, 2023
A pro-life-related cartoon. I am not picking on Mississippi but apparently they still wear stripes in some jails there. *Idea and tagline by Kat Hatz.*

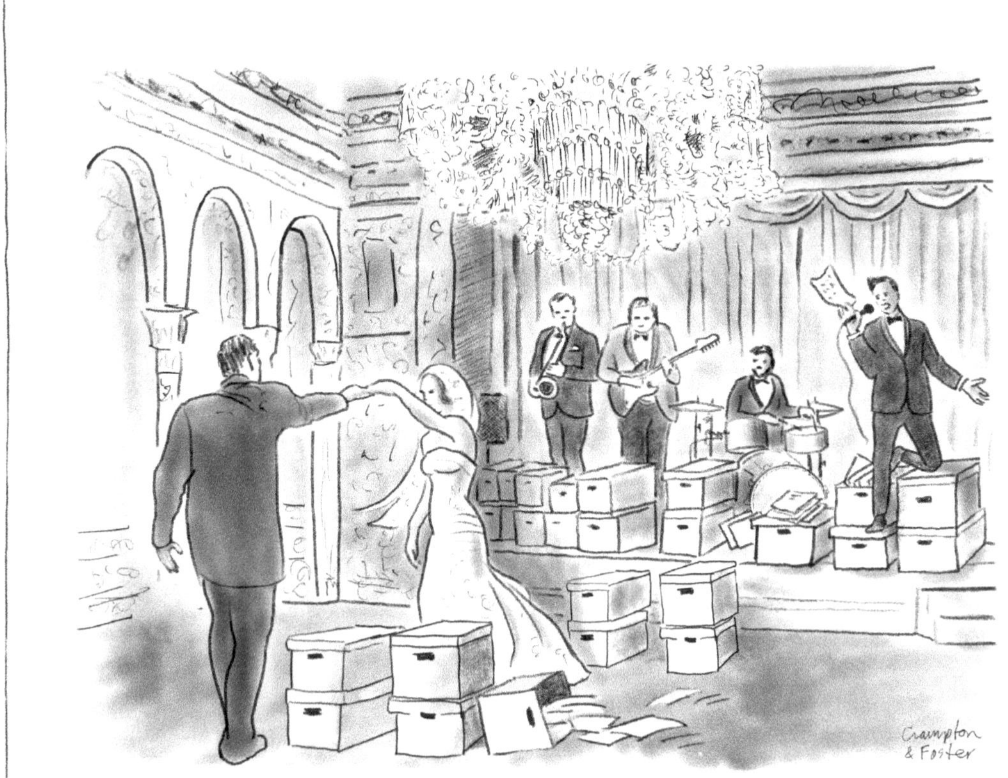

♫♫"...and I ain't seen the sunshine, since I don't know when. I'm stuck in Folsom prison, and time keeps draggin' on, but that train keeps a rollin'..."

June 9, 2023
I started drawing this as soon as I saw the photos of Trump's classified documents boxes at Mar-a-Lago.
Thanks to Michael Foster.

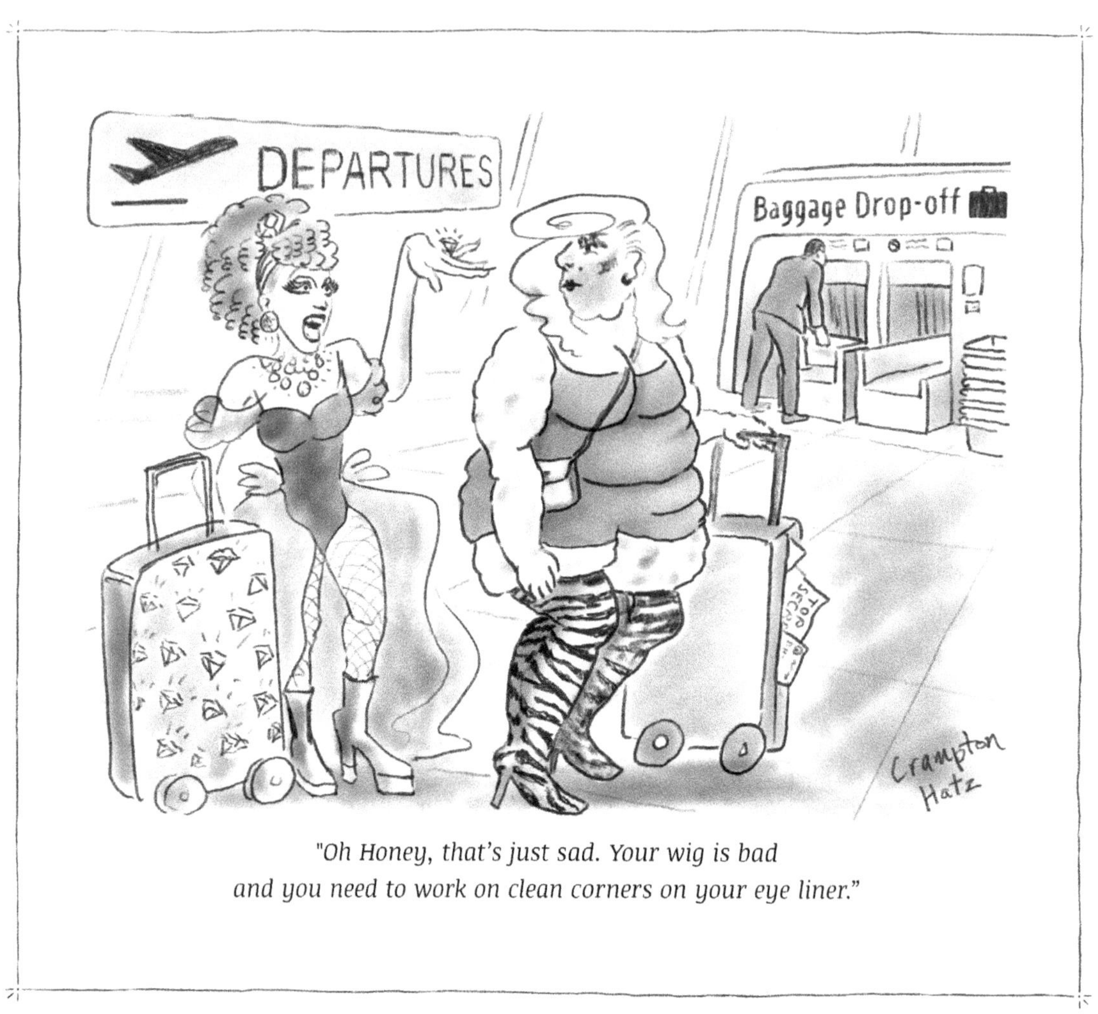

"Oh Honey, that's just sad. Your wig is bad and you need to work on clean corners on your eye liner."

June 14, 2023
Imagining Trump trying to flee to another country* because the Feds didn't take his passport at the arraignment.
*Idea and tagline by Kat Hatz. *Homage to the film "La Cage aux Folles"*

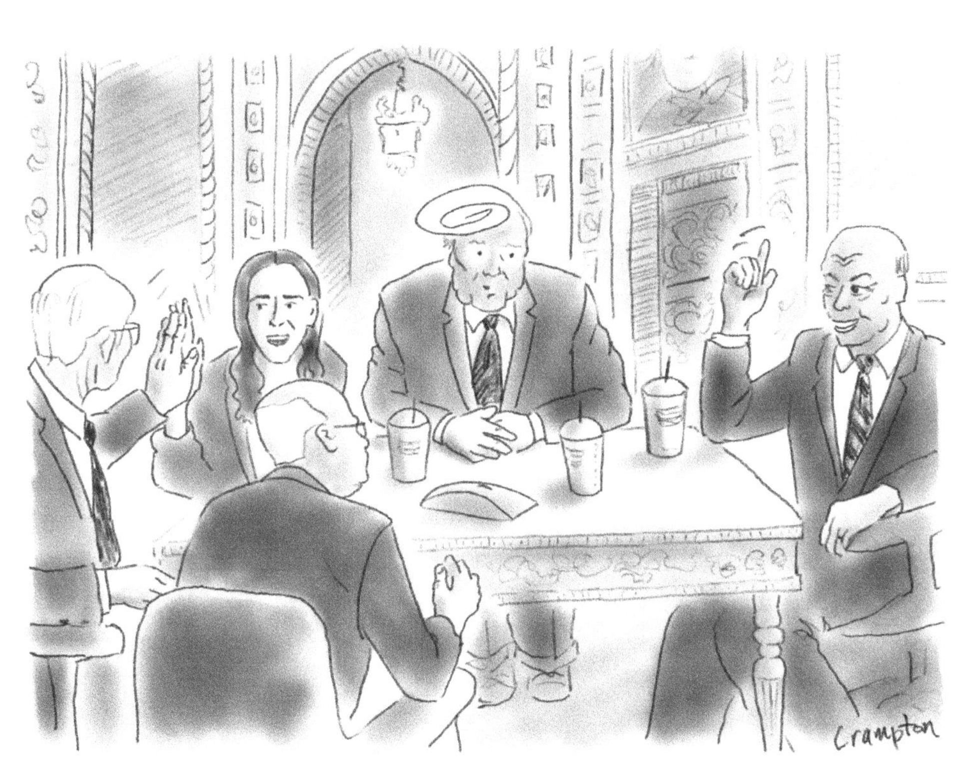

"What if President Trump testifies that he and Walt were starting a Movers & Storage company, and were just practicing moving boxes?"

July 10, 2023
A behind-the-scenes of attorneys brainstorming a defense for the Mar-a-Lago classified documents trial.
(Note: Videos show boxes being off-loaded from a plane in New Jersey. Ivana Trump was cremated but had a heavy casket. She was buried on the golf course. My Twitter followers agreed on the location of the missing documents.)

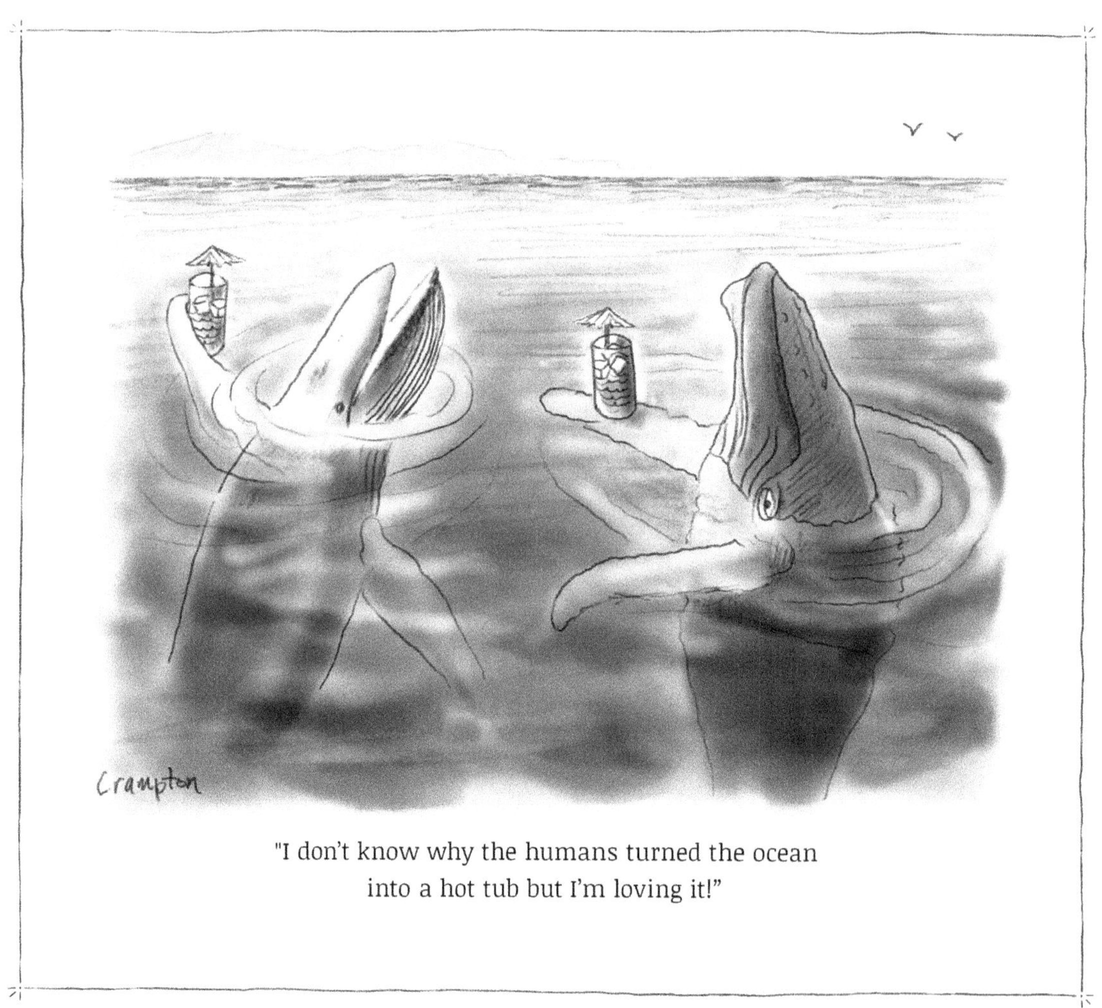

"I don't know why the humans turned the ocean
into a hot tub but I'm loving it!"

July 20, 2023
A buoy off South Florida records ocean temperatures surpassing 100 degrees Fahrenheit.

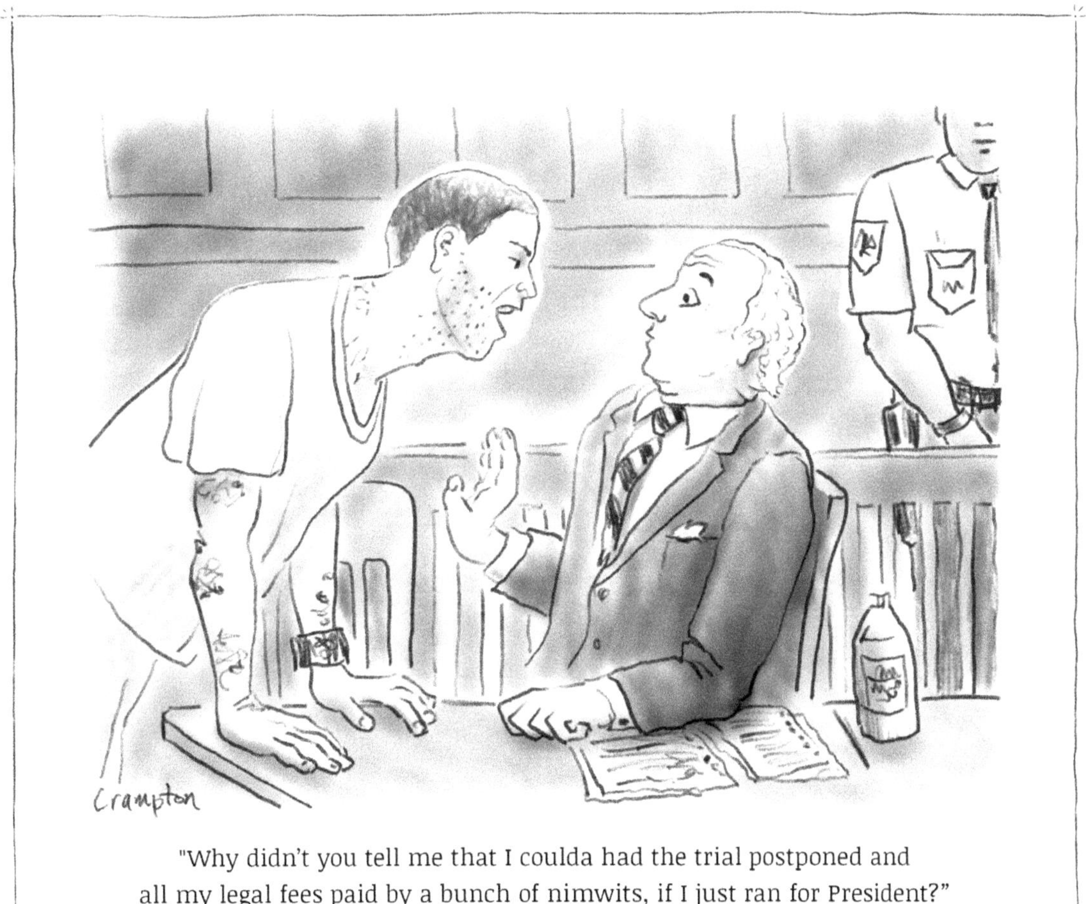

"Why didn't you tell me that I coulda had the trial postponed and all my legal fees paid by a bunch of nimwits, if I just ran for President?"

August 2, 2023
Donald Trump uses his many court cases to fundraise on "Truth Social" and elsewhere.

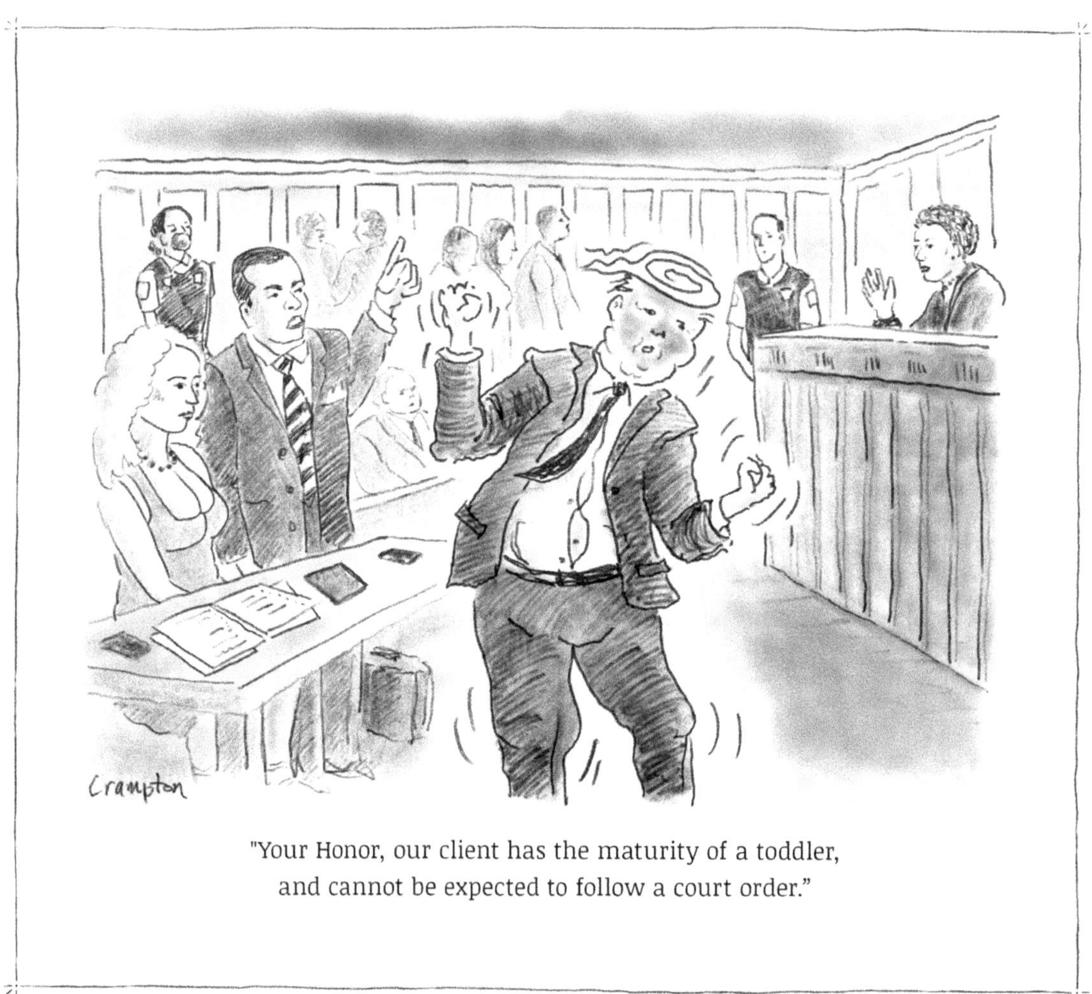

"Your Honor, our client has the maturity of a toddler, and cannot be expected to follow a court order."

August 9, 2023
Judge Lewis Kaplan, in the E. Jean Carroll defamation trial, clears the way for Trump to testify in court, after defense lawyers raised concerns that he would 'sow chaos'.

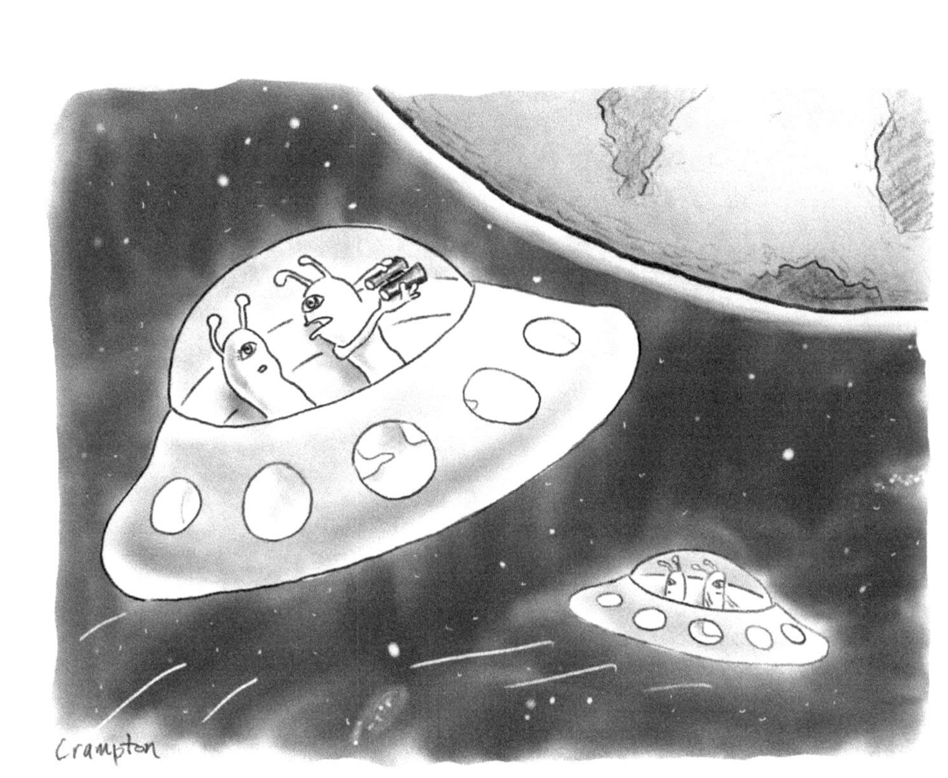

"Even *I* am surprised that they asked a question about UFO's at the Republican Presidential Debate."

October 3, 2023
During the first Republican Presidential Candidate debate, Governor Chris Christie was asked if, as president, he would share information about UFO encounters. Trump did not participate in the debate.

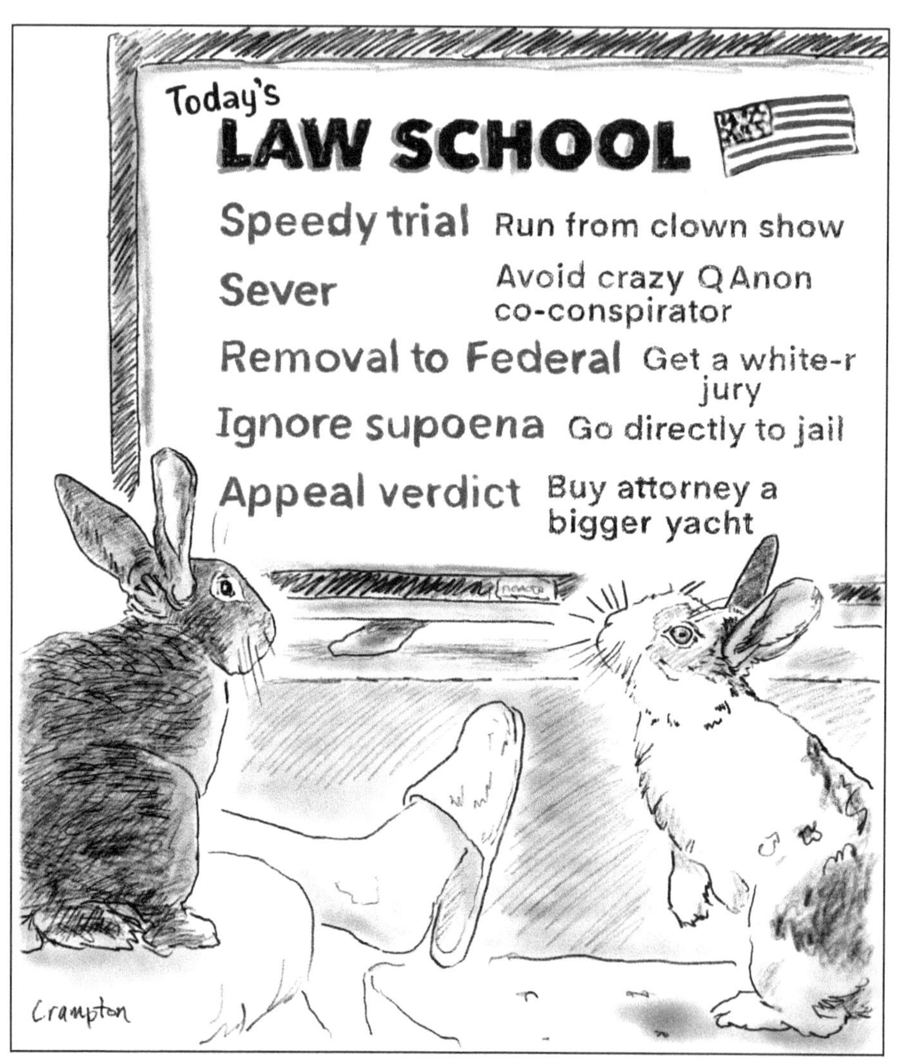

September 8, 2023
Two defendants in the Georgia Election Interference case (Kenneth Chesebro and Sidney Powell), ask for a speedy trial. Trump asked to sever his trial from theirs. So many legal terms to learn.

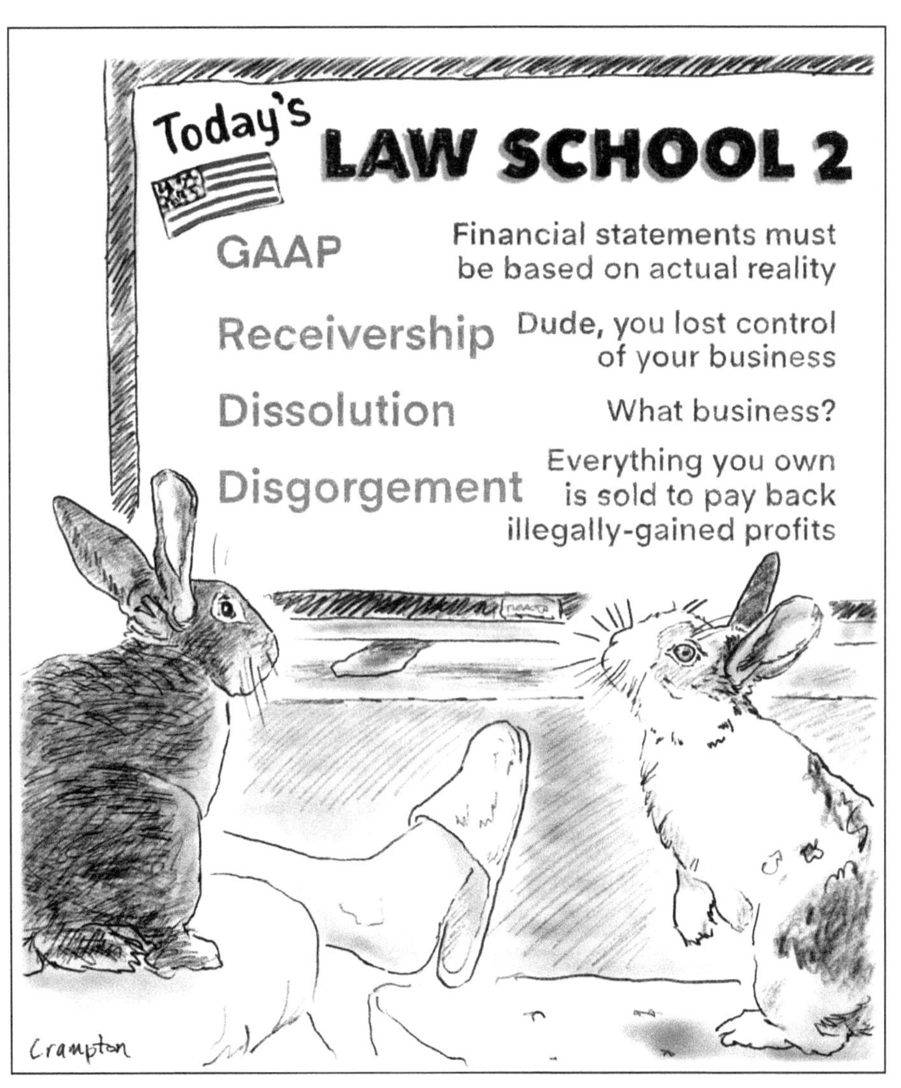

October 3, 2023
More legal terms in the news. Judge Arthur Engoron rules that Donald Trump committed fraud for years in a civil trial brought by New York Attorney General Letitia James.

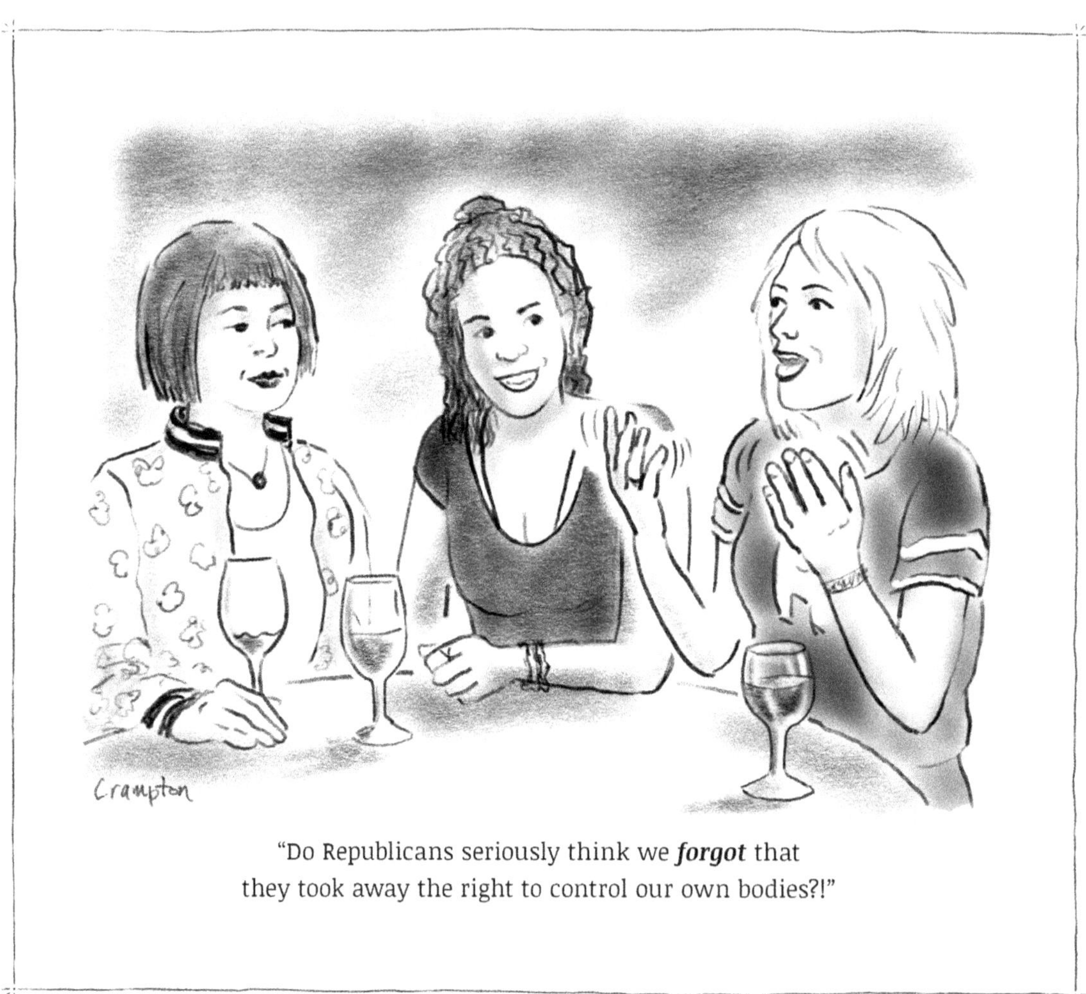

"Do Republicans seriously think we ***forgot*** that they took away the right to control our own bodies?!"

November 8, 2023
Since the Supreme Court overturned Roe v. Wade, Republican legislatures in more than twenty States have restricted abortion, and banned it outright in 14 States. But Democrats won ballot measures in Ohio, Virginia, Kentucky, Montana, and Kansas.

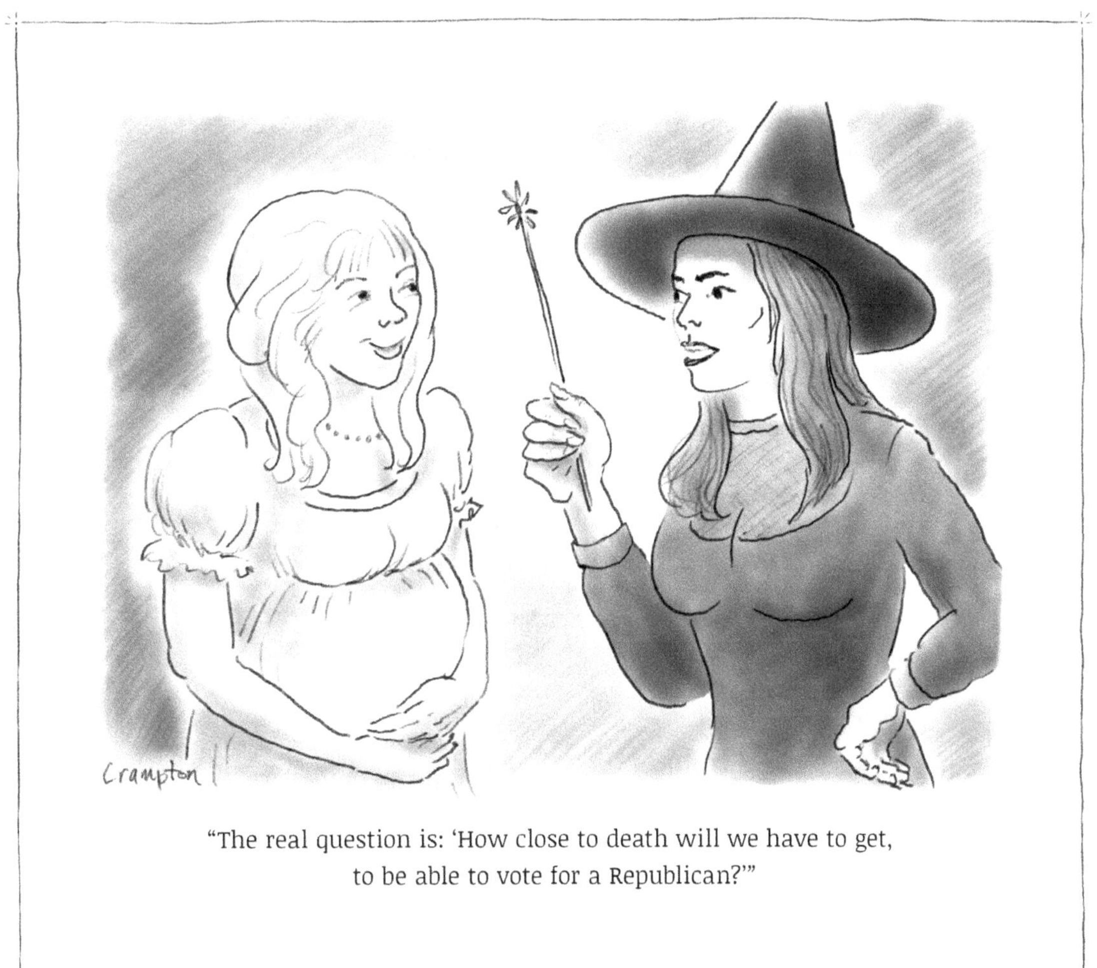

"The real question is: 'How close to death will we have to get, to be able to vote for a Republican?'"

December 13, 2023
18 women from ten States say that abortion bans brought some of them to the brink of death before they were allowed to get needed health care.

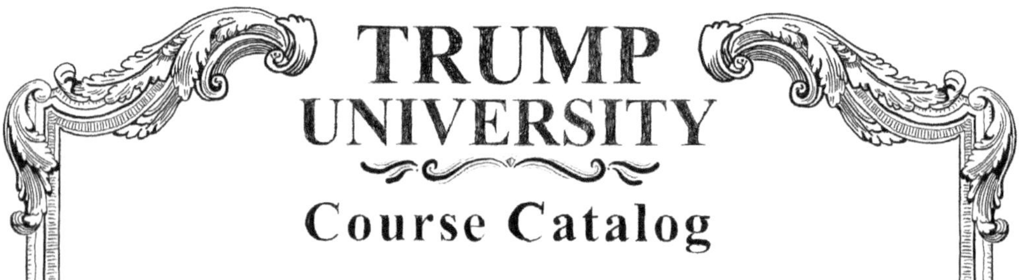

- 101 Ways to Delay Your Trial Until No One Can Even Remember What You Did
- How to Get a Mis-trial
- Never Pay Another Contractor

Crampton

January 23, 2024
Trump's lawyer, Alina Habba, demands a mistrial for a second time in the E. Jean Carroll defamation case over deleted emails from the 1990s. U.S. District Judge Lewis Kaplan denies it.

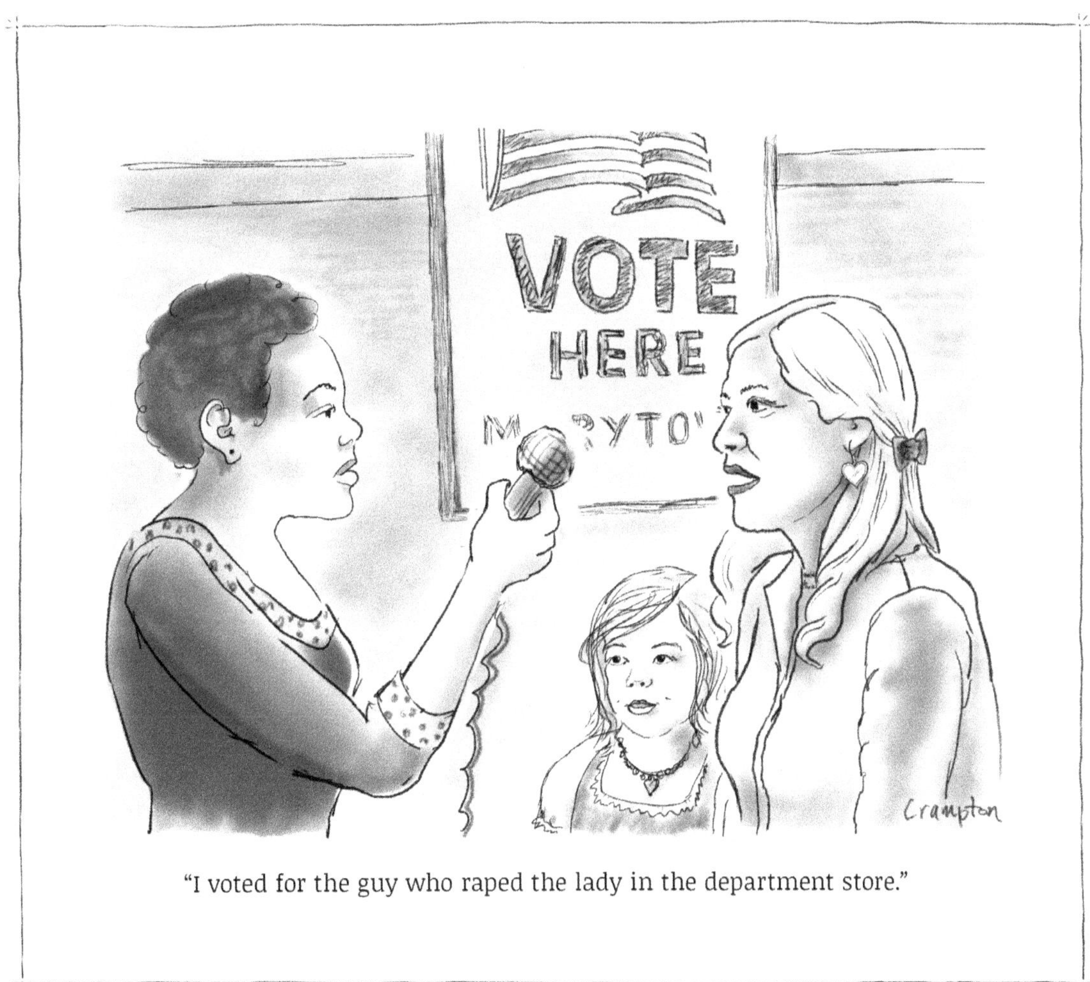

"I voted for the guy who raped the lady in the department store."

January 24, 2024
Many Republicans vote for Trump in the Iowa and New Hampshire primaries, even though he was convicted of rape and defamation in the E. Jean Carroll case. He was fined $5 million. After more defamatory statements, he was convicted again, and fined another $83 million.

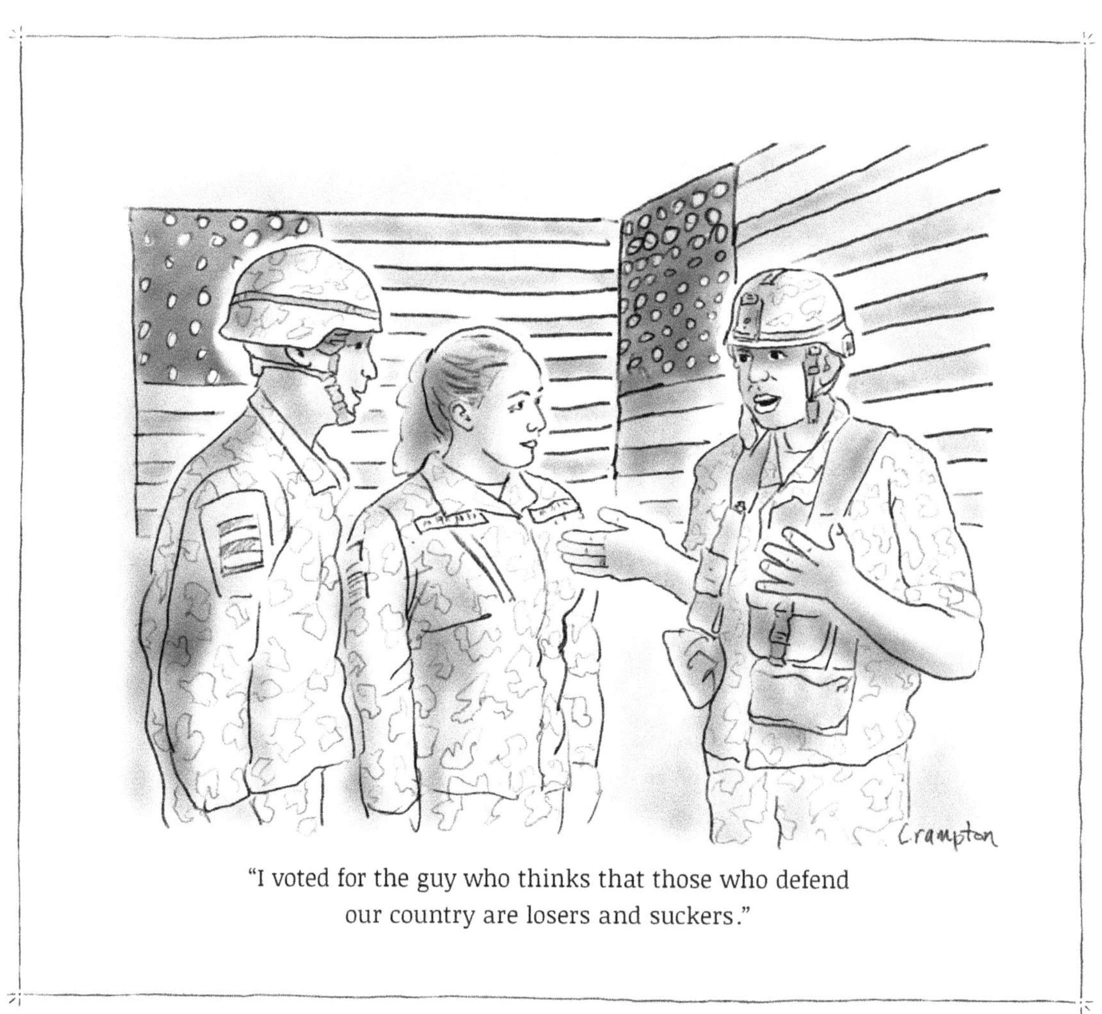

"I voted for the guy who thinks that those who defend our country are losers and suckers."

March 1, 2024
Primaries are held all over the country and people still vote for Trump. Some vote for Nikki Haley.

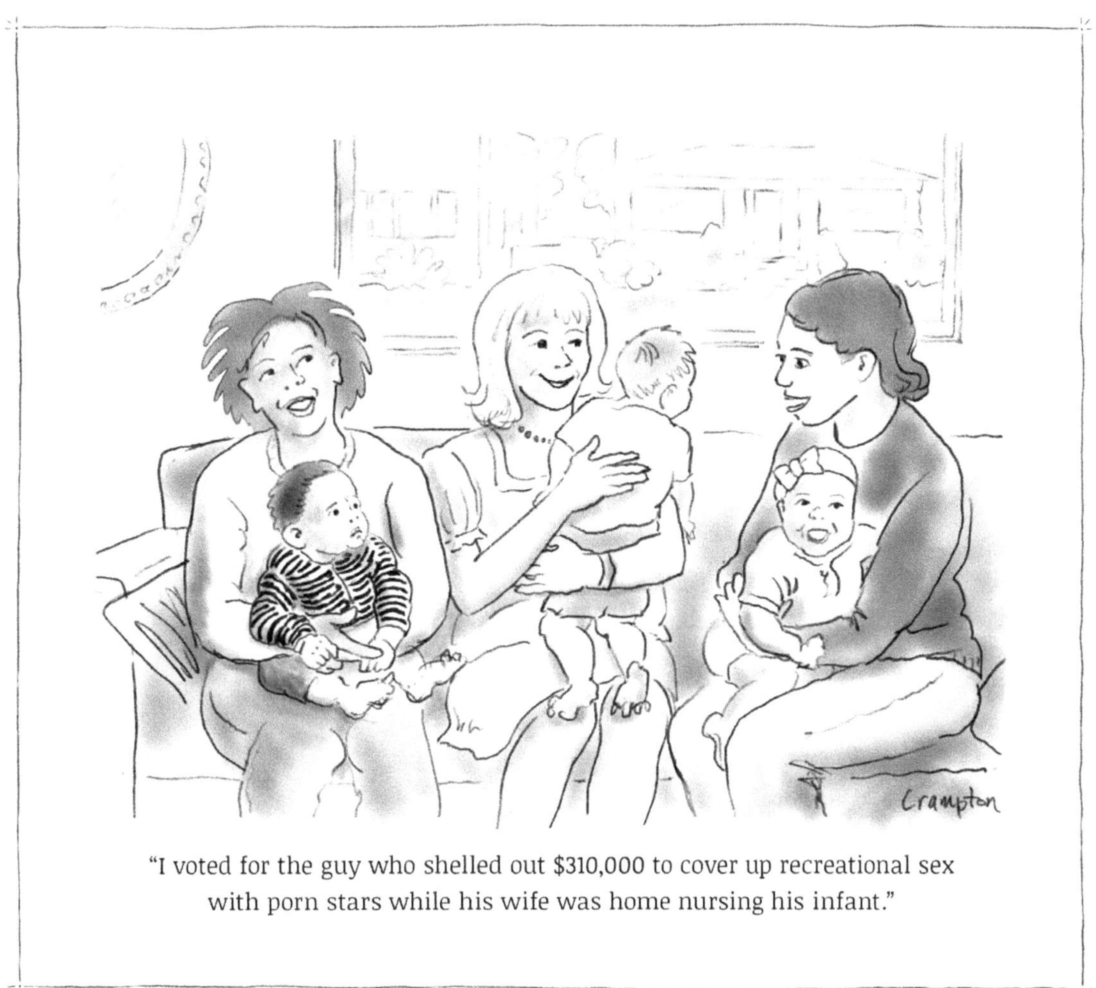

"I voted for the guy who shelled out $310,000 to cover up recreational sex with porn stars while his wife was home nursing his infant."

March 5, 2024
More primaries...Trump's New York election fraud case aka the Stormy Daniels hush money trial looms.

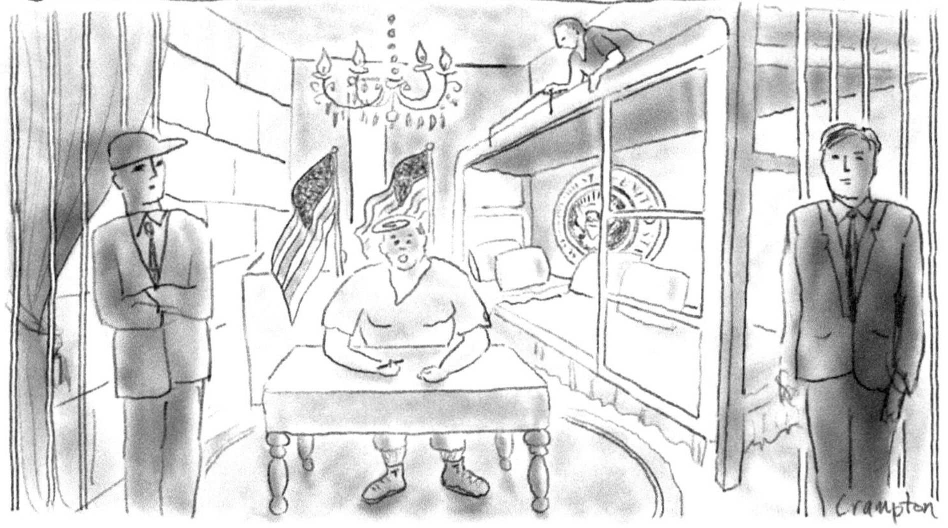

March 5, 2024
News commentators speculate on whether the Secret Service needs to guard Trump when he goes to jail.

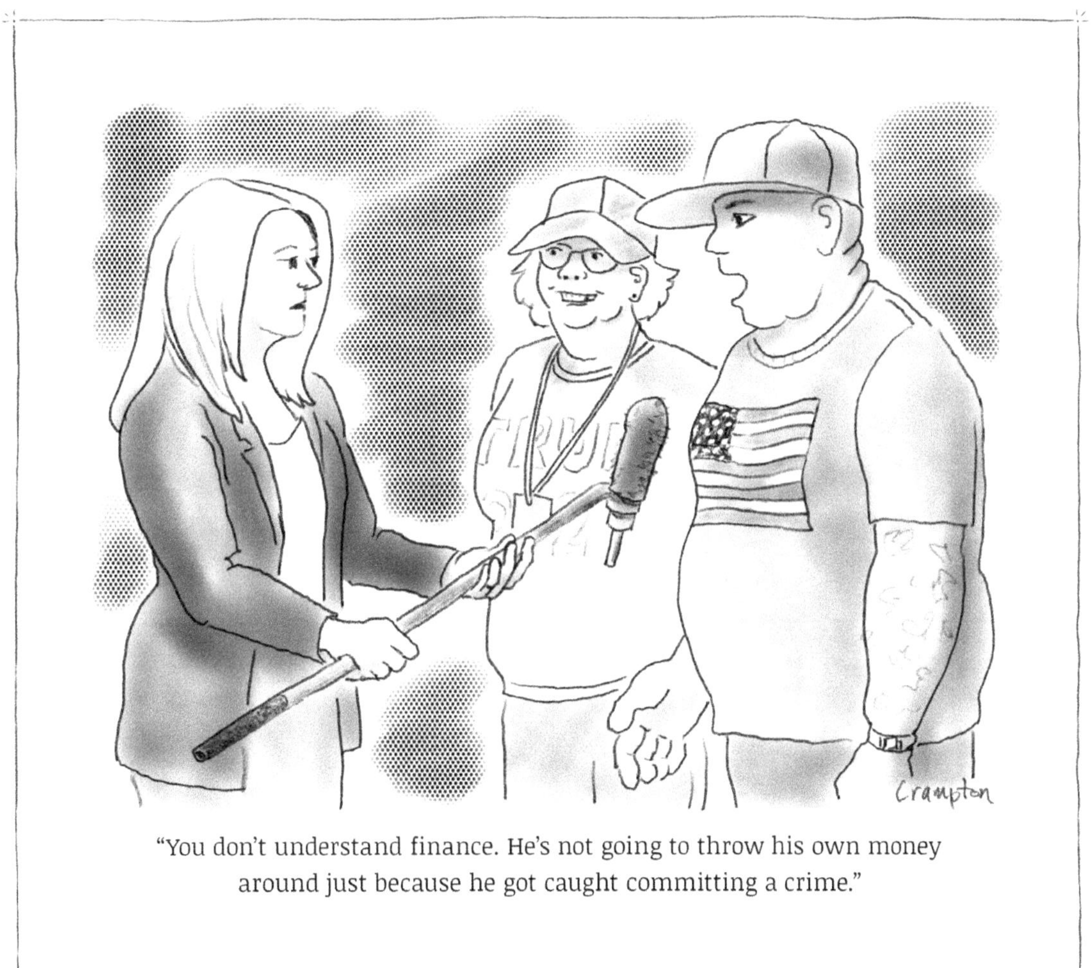

"You don't understand finance. He's not going to throw his own money around just because he got caught committing a crime."

March 21, 2024
Trump supporters' opine about high finance on "Truth Social", after Trump got a bail bondsman for the Fulton County, Georgia trial (The "I just want to find 11,780 votes" trial).

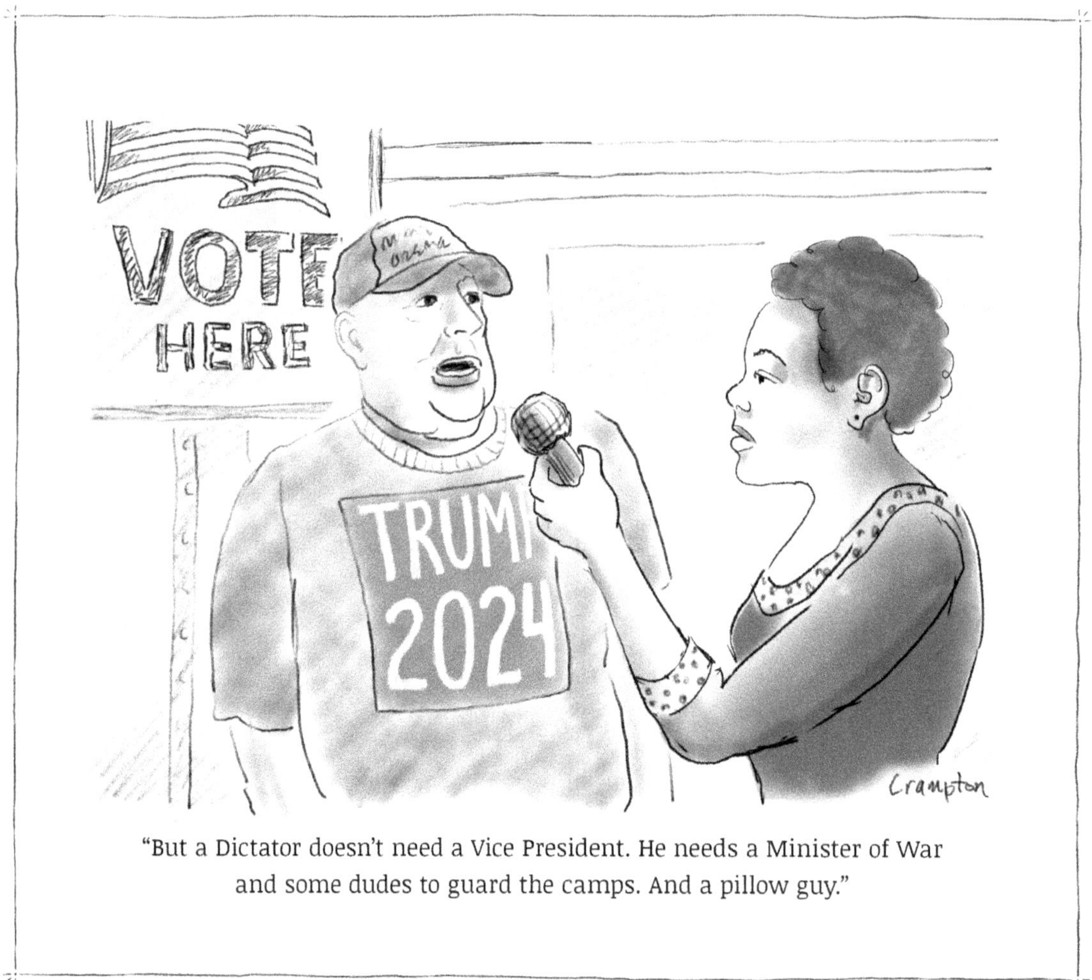

"But a Dictator doesn't need a Vice President. He needs a Minister of War and some dudes to guard the camps. And a pillow guy."

April 4, 2024
Republicans audition for Vice President on TV news shows. Trump says he'll be a "dictator on day one". He quotes Hitler when saying immigrants are "poisoning the blood of our country".

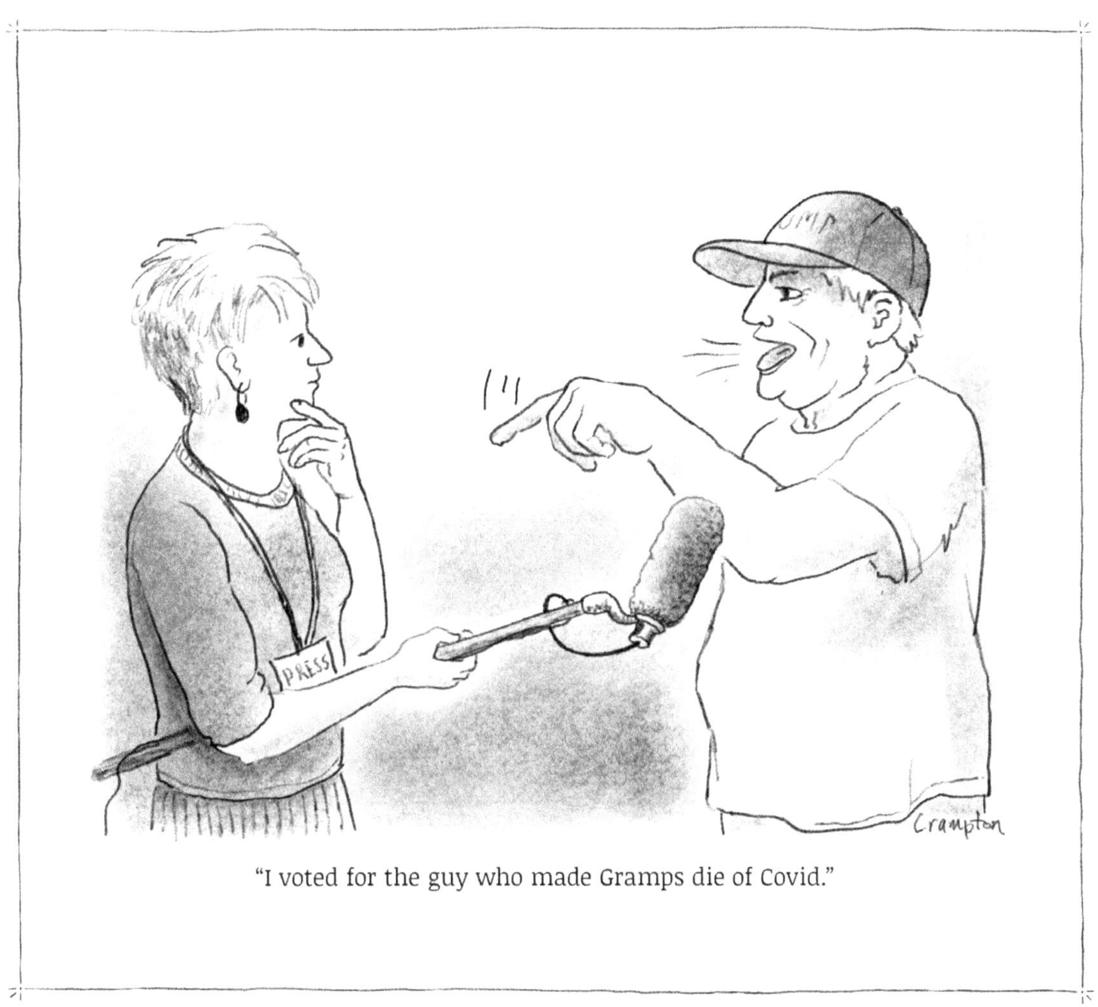

"I voted for the guy who made Gramps die of Covid."

April 16, 2024
More primaries... a "New York Post" article by Philip Bump estimated that Trump's delay in implementing a Covid-19 containment strategy may have caused tens of thousands of unnecessary deaths.

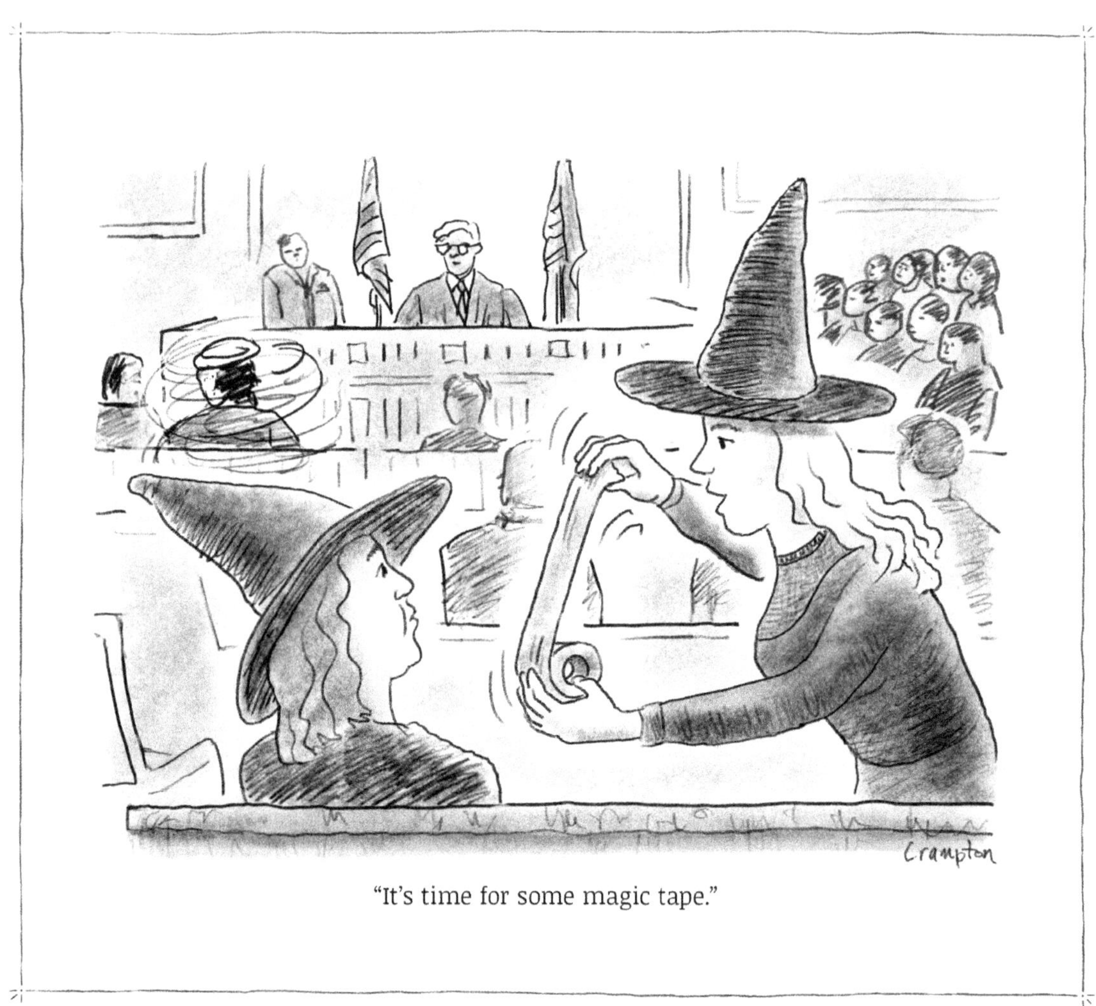

"It's time for some magic tape."

May 6, 2024
Waiting for New York Judge Merchan to impose a Gag Order–because Donald Trump continues to trash witnesses, the Judge, his daughter, Court staff, and President Biden, on "Truth Social" and elsewhere.

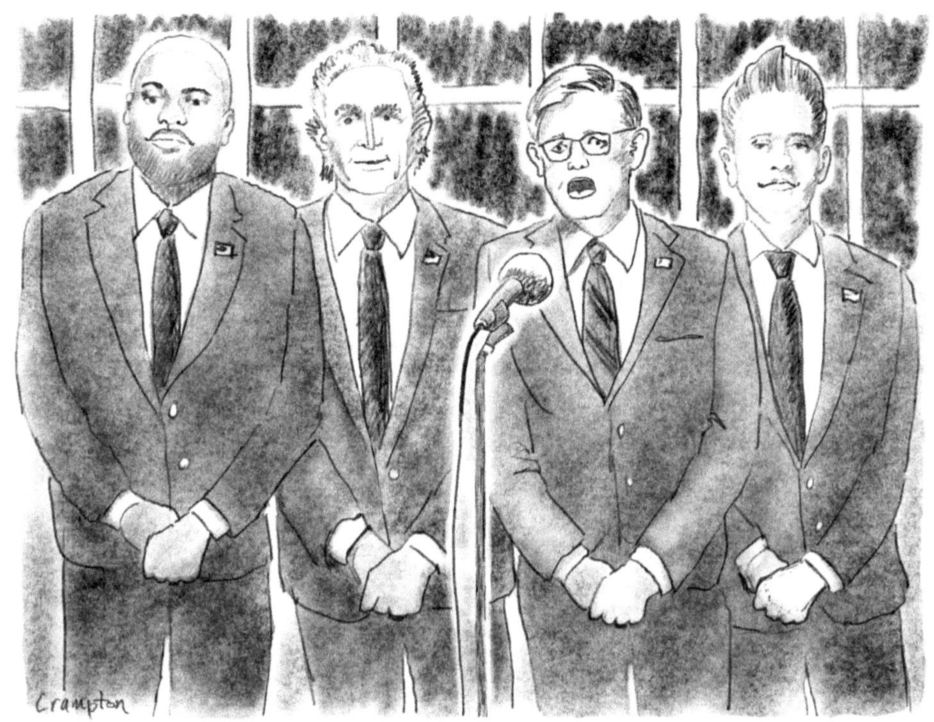

"We Republicans all pay hush money, support election corruption, and aspire to one day bang a porn star."

May 15, 2024
House Speaker Mike Johnson and other Republican leaders show up near the end of the Election Fraud trial to violate the Gag Order* on Trump's behalf. **Also smearing the Court process, the Judge and his daughter.*

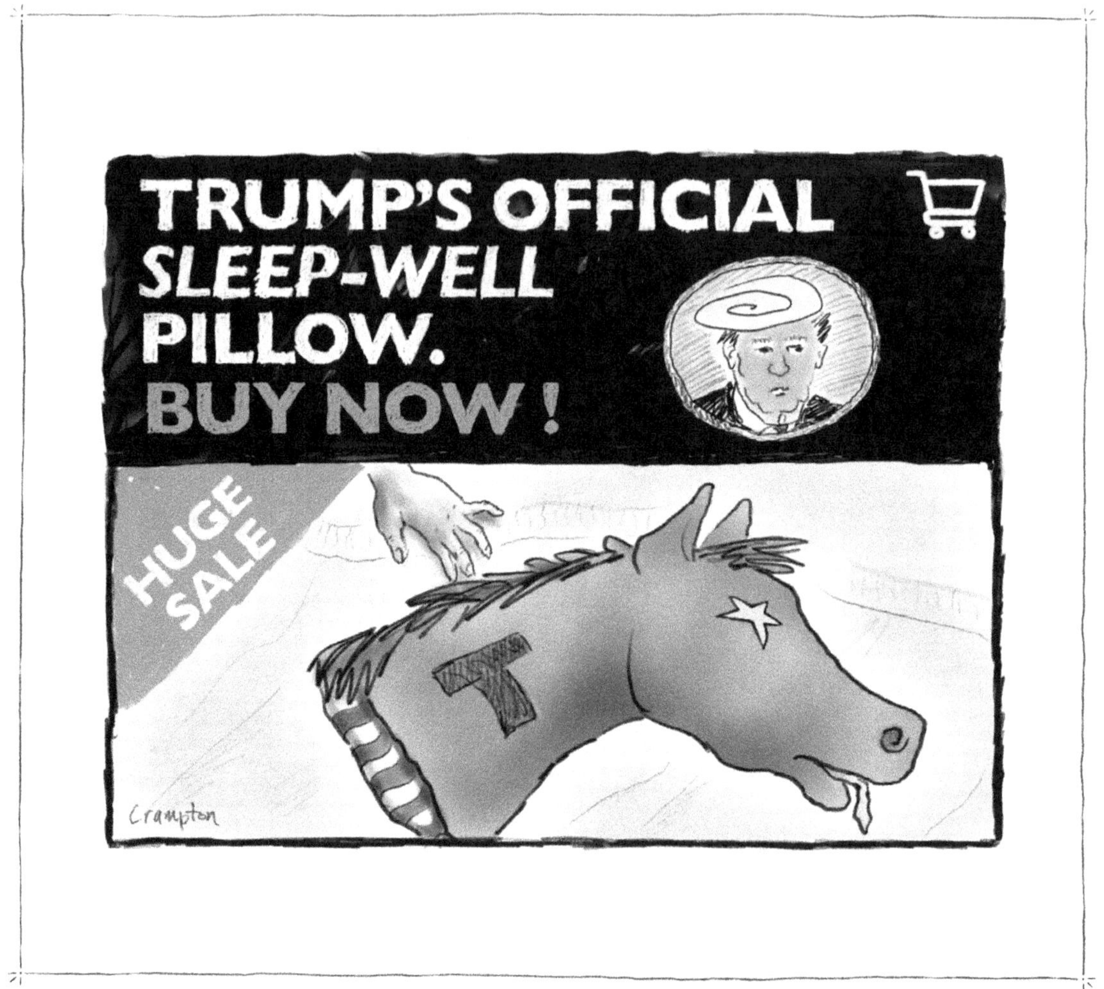

May 21, 2024
Defense witness, Robert Costello, testifies that he told Michael Cohen that he was "loved" by Trump and "had friends in high places." Sounds like a mob threat to me. The campaign sold out of the new Trump gold lamé sneakers. Horse-head pillows are a real thing.

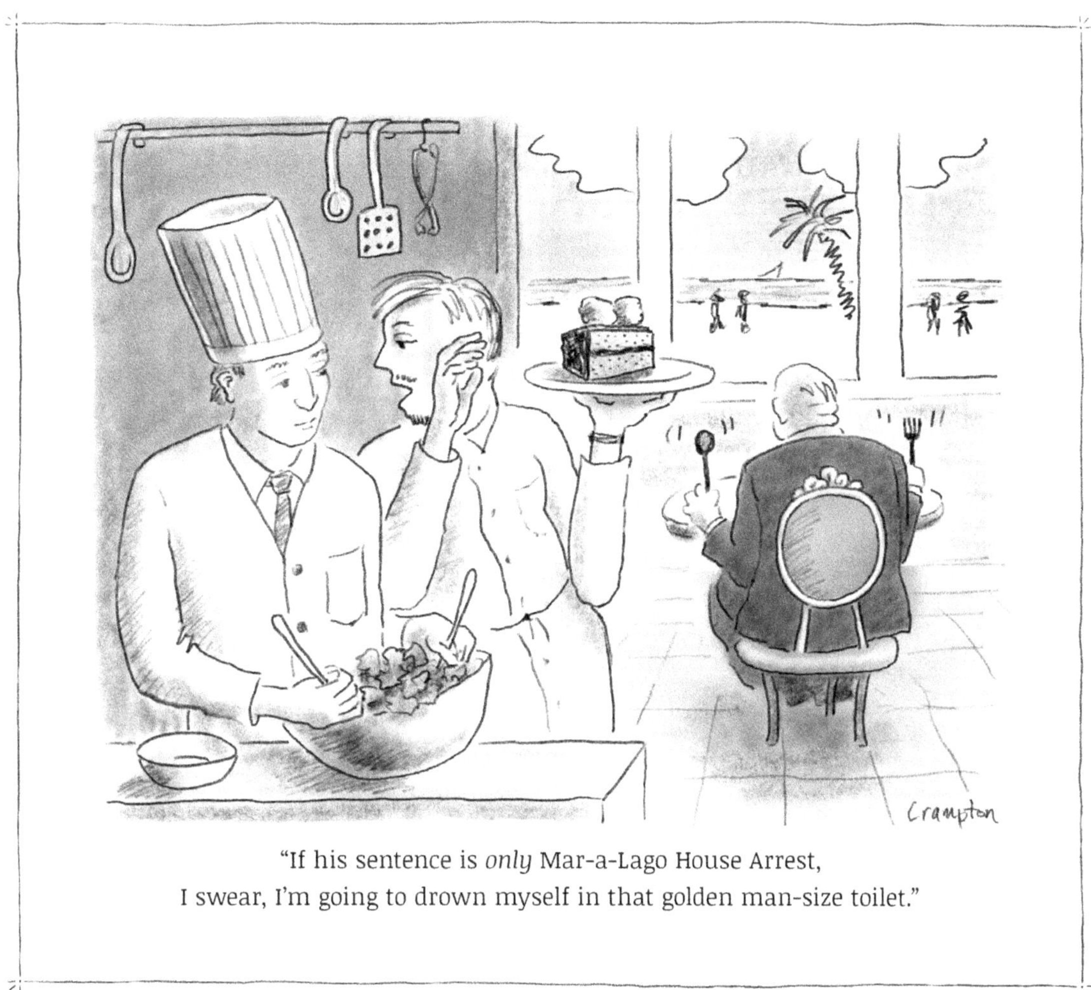

"If his sentence is *only* Mar-a-Lago House Arrest,
I swear, I'm going to drown myself in that golden man-size toilet."

June 5, 2024
Trump is convicted of 34 counts in the New York hush money election fraud trial, but they say he may avoid jail.

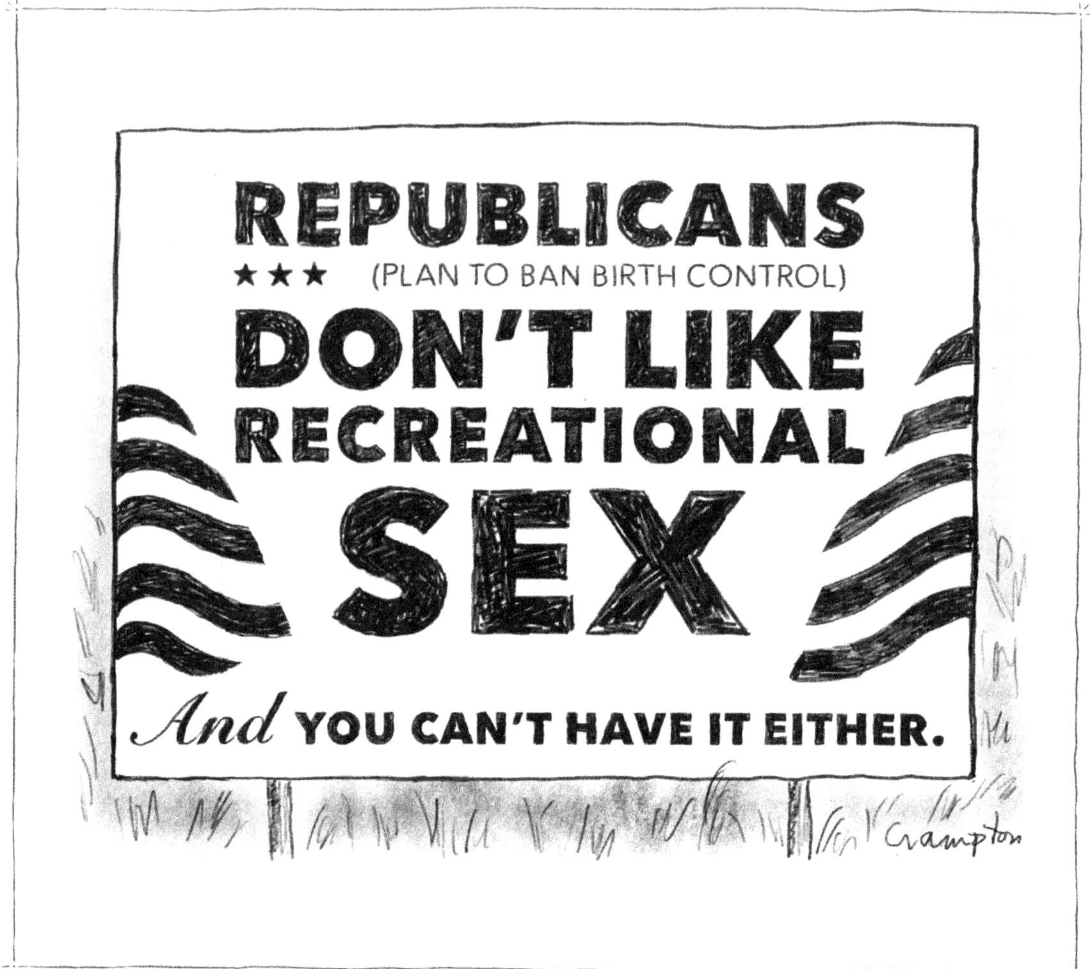

June 19, 2024
Republicans in the Senate refuse to vote on a Bill to protect contraception, saying birth control is not "at risk". But the idea of restricting birth control pops up frequently in statements by Conservatives.

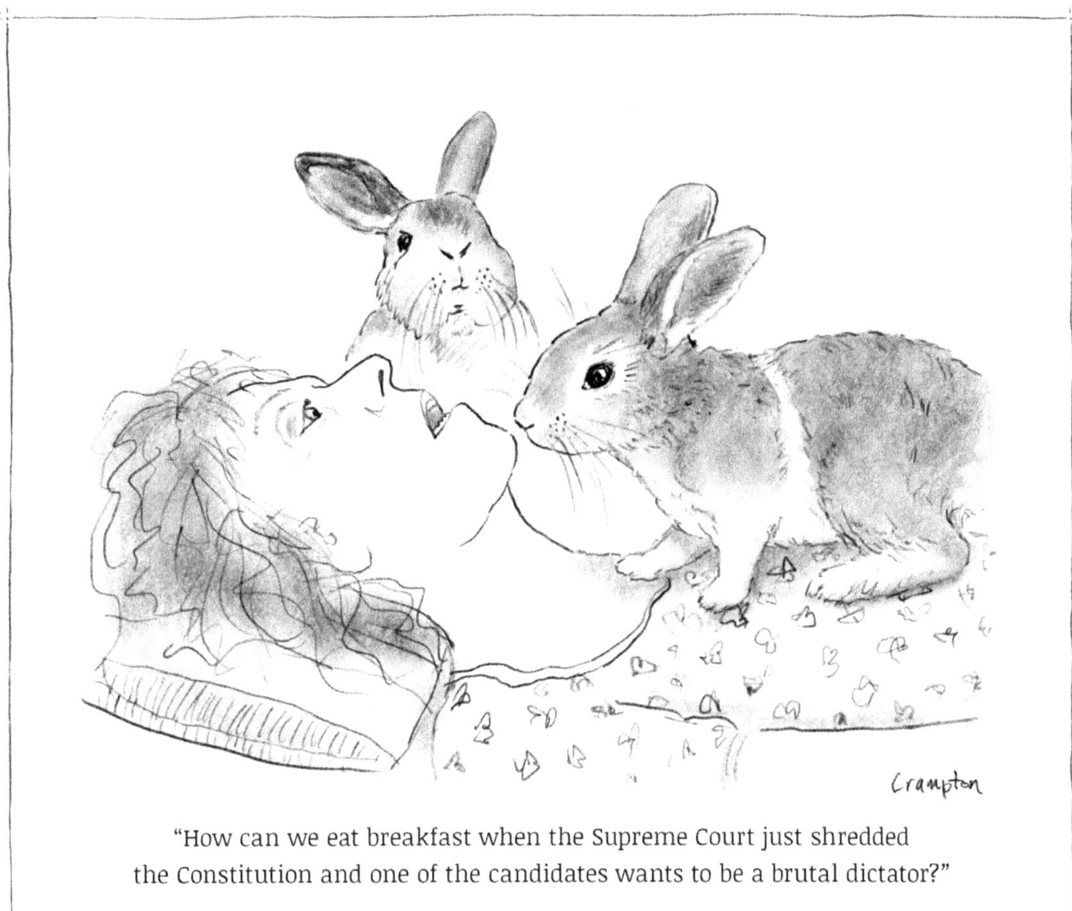

"How can we eat breakfast when the Supreme Court just shredded the Constitution and one of the candidates wants to be a brutal dictator?"

July 10, 2024
The Supreme Court not only hears Trump's case for immunity but grants it, thereby greatly expanding the powers of the Presidency. I feel exhausted and demoralized for two weeks, but it turns out I had Covid.

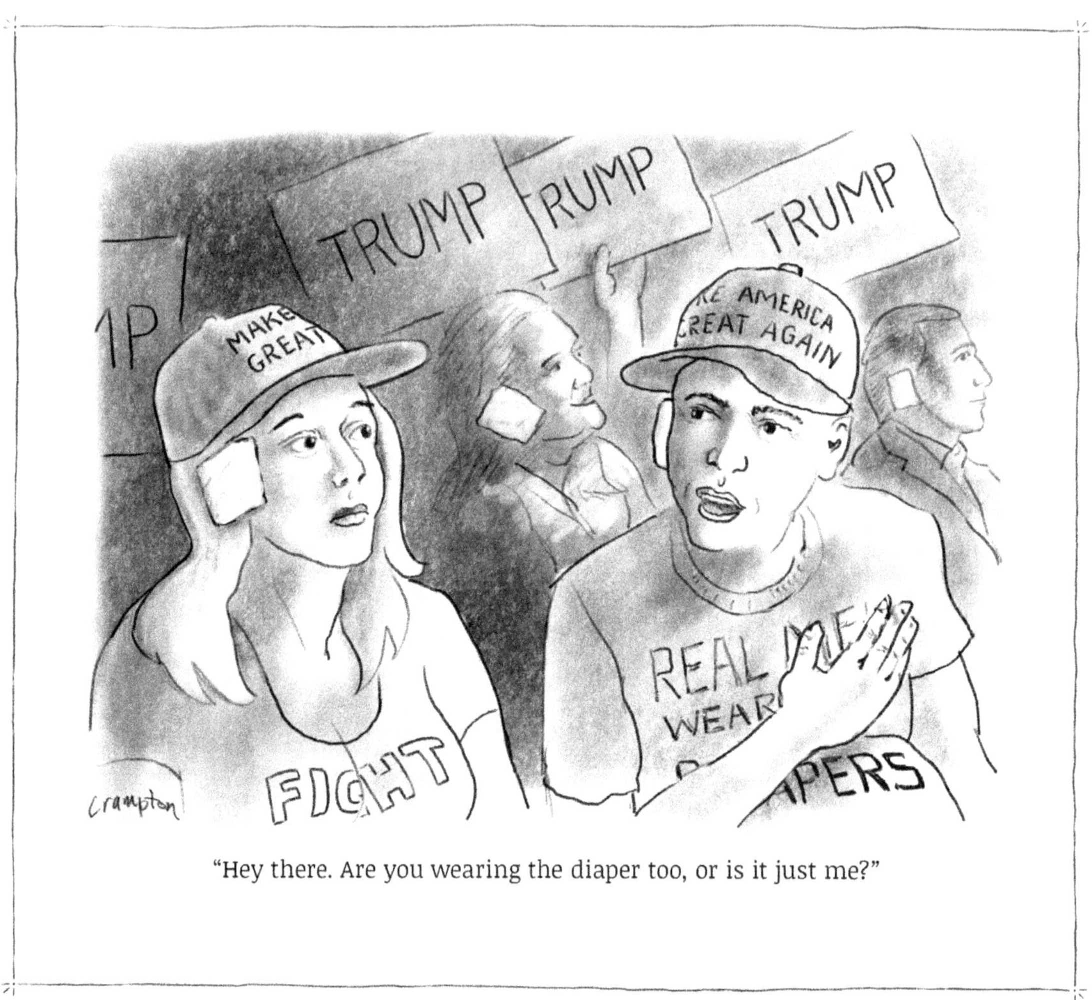

"Hey there. Are you wearing the diaper too, or is it just me?"

July 25, 2024
There was an assassination attempt at a Trump rally. One attendee died and two others were shot. Trump received an ear wound. Instantly, conspiracy theories arose...known as EarGate. At the Republican Convention, Trump wears a large bandage. Delegates wear them too. Some wear t-shirts celebrating Trump's alleged diapers.

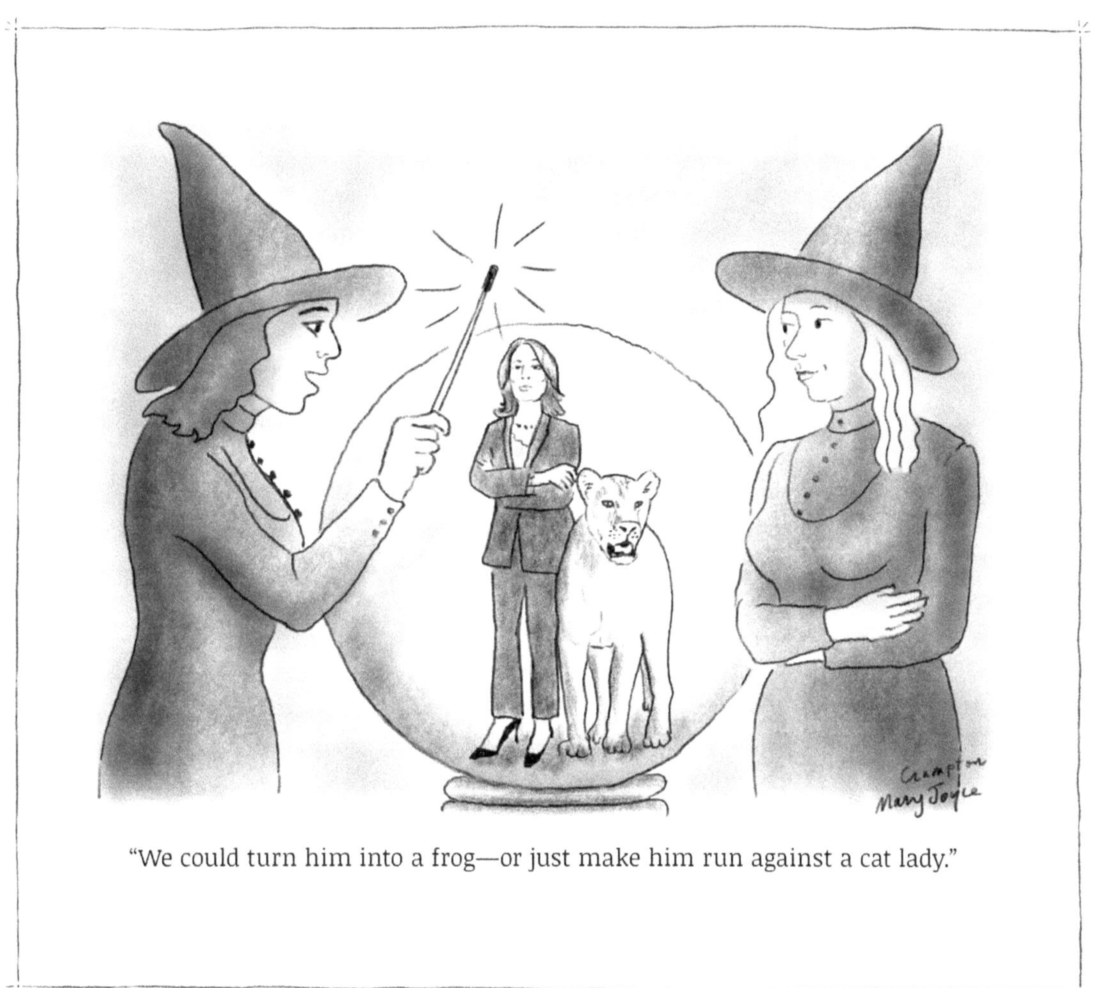

"We could turn him into a frog—or just make him run against a cat lady."

July 27, 2024
Biden gave a terrible Presidential Debate performance. Democrats hounded him to stop running. Then he got Covid. He just announced that he is stepping aside and endorsed Vice President Kamala Harris. Trump's running mate, J.D. Vance, said the country was run by childless cat ladies. *The idea of a lion by Mary Joyce.* ■ *To be continued...*

www.ingramcontent.com/pod-product-compliance
Lightning Source LLC
LaVergne TN
LVHW061246100826
845148LV00008B/1040

9780979308864